Exploring Social Change

Exploring Social Change
Process and Context

Bridgette Wessels

First published 2014 by
PALGRAVE MACMILLAN

Palgrave Macmillan in the UK is an imprint of Macmillan Publishers Limited, registered in England, company number 785998, of Houndmills, Basingstoke, Hampshire RG21 6XS.

Palgrave Macmillan in the US is a division of St Martin's Press LLC, 175 Fifth Avenue, New York, NY 10010.

Palgrave Macmillan is the global academic imprint of the above companies and has companies and representatives throughout the world.

Palgrave® and Macmillan® are registered trademarks in the United States, the United Kingdom, Europe and other countries.

ISBN 978-0-230-36105-8   ISBN 978-1-137-47142-0 (eBook)
DOI 10.1007/978-1-137-47142-0

This book is printed on paper suitable for recycling and made from fully managed and sustained forest sources. Logging, pulping and manufacturing processes are expected to conform to the environmental regulations of the country of origin.

A catalogue record for this book is available from the British Library.

A catalog record for this book is available from the Library of Congress.

For my parents

Contents

x Contents

Figures

Acknowledgments

I have been extremely lucky to experience much support while writing this book. In the first instance, I would like to thank Anna Reeve and Lloyd Langman of Palgrave for respectively commissioning the book and then supporting the work to getting the book published. I would like to thank the Department of Sociological Studies at Sheffield University for providing the intellectual space to develop ideas for this book. Thanks to Helen Rana for her invaluable help in commenting on and proofreading the manuscript. I appreciated the comments of the reviewers because they helped to put the finishing touches to the book. Thanks to Palgrave Macmillan for giving permission to reproduce sections in chapters 6 and 9, which were originally published in my 2010 book: *Understanding the Internet*. Thanks also to SAGE for giving permission to include Figure 9.1 from Harrison, J. and Wessels, B. (2005), 'A New Public Service Communication Environment? Public Service Broadcasting Values in the Reconfiguring Media' in *New Media and Society*, Vol. 7: 6, 834–853.

1

Introduction: Social Change and Its Historical and Contemporary Dynamics

Aim and approach of the book

Most people[1] experience the way social life changes, and they experience change in relation to the times in which they live, the communities in which they live and their relationship with institutions. Social change can be difficult to grasp and make sense of. The playwright Tom Stoppard, for instance, says in *Travesties*:

> In an age when the difference between prince and peasant was thought to be in the stars, MrTzara, art was naturally an affirmation for the one and a consolation to the other; but we live in an age when the social order is seen to be the work of material forces and we have been given an entirely new kind of responsibility, the responsibility of changing society.

The anthropologist David Graeber also shows how difficult it is to grasp social change, and to ask questions about change, he says:

> Normally, when you challenge the conventional wisdom – that the current economic and political system is the only possible one – the first reaction you are likely to get is a demand for a detailed architectural blueprint of how an alternative system would work, down to the nature of its financial instruments, energy supplies, and policies of sewer maintenance. Next, you are likely to be asked for a detailed program of how this system will be brought into existence. Historically, this is ridiculous. When has social

change ever happened according to someone's blueprint? It's not as if a small circle of visionaries in Renaissance Florence conceived of something they called 'capitalism', figured out the details of how the stock exchange and factories would someday work, and then put in place a program to bring their visions into reality. In fact, the idea is so absurd we might well ask ourselves how it ever occurred to us to imagine this is how change happens to begin.

This book aims to address the concept of social change and to explore some particular aspects of contemporary social change. Social change is a key area of research across the social sciences because social change is very much part of social life. The book introduces and places the study of social change within the founding literature of sociology and discusses how key theories of change have evolved through scholarship and in relation to some characteristics of social change itself. From this comprehensive overview of theories of social change, the book develops a conceptual framework that identifies and analyzes key areas of change in contemporary society.

Social change is a central focus of the social sciences, and sociology in particular. This focus on change is rooted in the early development of the discipline, which was formed in response to the social upheaval that resulted from the advent of industrial capitalism in the West. Society continues to change as people make and remake social institutions, which interact with social structures and social values. One main aspect of social science is identifying social change and analyzing its significance for individuals, groups and institutions within society. This requires taking an historical perspective in order to appreciate what is changing, as well as a sociological perspective to understand how this change is occurring. Analysts can only extract the significance of change by understanding the 'what' and the 'how' of change.

Any consideration of the phenomena of change means asking what does 'social change' mean, how can change be recognized and what is the significance of particular changes in social life. On the one hand, change can occur in one or more dimensions, which may, or may not, interact with other dimensions. On the other hand, it can involve radical change and structural changes in *all* dimensions, which fundamentally usher in a new type of society. The interaction and articulation of change within economic, political and cultural spheres generates a social dynamic through which life is experienced, engaged in and embraced or resisted. This dynamic suggests that social science needs to focus on process, which can address how we come to live in the world we live in and how that world changes.

The objectives of the book are to address the following questions:

1. How do we understand social change?
2. What are the key dimensions of change and how do they interact to produce new social conditions, new artifacts and new values and ideologies?

3. What are the main characteristics of social change in contemporary society
   and what are their significance?

The main argument of this book is that social change is multidimensional and
that the articulation of economic, political and cultural factors gives social
change its distinctive characteristic. The need to study change is embedded within the ways social and cultural life changes – which are sometimes
incremental within specific, existing domains of society and, at other times,
broad – and deep changes that create an entirely new type of society. Change
is experienced through social life and across a range of social situations. The
multidimensionality of social change means that people experience change differently and in a variety of ways in relation to their social positions and personal
situations.

The approach this book takes is to explore social change as a process. The
idea and the study of process provide a framework to study what Berger and
Luckmann (1967) call the 'awesome paradox' of the 'two sidedness of the
social world' – the way that society is experienced as a fact-like system that
individuals experience as external to them, yet also something that is made
and remade through their own actions. This paradox requires taking a particular approach to social change – an historical view that addresses the way
in which, over time, actions become institutions and then, in turn, institutions are changed by action; this provides a link between action and structure.
As Abrams (1982) argues, people can only construct worlds on the basis of
what their predecessors constructed for them. The study of process involves
understanding the relationship between personal activity and experience on
the one hand, and social organization on the other, as something that is
continuously constructed in time. To address this question, Abrams supports
Wright Mills's idea that a sociological imagination requires an historical understanding. Wright Mills (1959) argues that a sociological imagination seeks
to understand the relationship between personal troubles and public issues
in social life (also see Chapter 2). The use of a sociological imagination in
addressing various aspects of social life brings together biographical, social
and historical factors to address a particular social issue.

In order to explore social change, it is necessary to analyze institutional
factors and the ways that individuals negotiate change within and across the
dimensions of social life. These include everyday life, relations of production
and modes of labor, consumerism and lifestyles, creative and cultural industries, changes in communication and changing experiences of difference and
diversity in the negotiation of power. Each of these areas highlights a key
aspect of change in contemporary life, as well as a key aspect of the argument
made in the book – that social change needs to be understood in terms of its
process. For example, contemporary change includes the way in which networked individuals manage the fluidity and mobility of their everyday life to
develop meaningful routines; it includes the rise of flexible working practices

that support global informational capitalism; the proliferation of lifestyles within consumerism; globalization of the creative industries in the ongoing commoditization of culture; the rise of interactive, networked communication, which involves the increasing generation of user-generated content; and the difficulties of fostering a genuine cosmopolitan condition in which the notion of 'hospitality' provides a space for difference and diversity to coexist within the social relations of power.

In order to address social change, students and scholars must develop sensitivity towards the areas of change. This sensitivity enables social scientists to identify the particular characteristics of any change, the richness of that change and the dynamics of change. To really understand change, scholars need to be able to understand and describe how change is experienced by the people involved in particular aspects of the change, and how that change affects their respective social worlds. This depth of understanding is important but not sufficient in fully understanding change. It is vital to appreciate that, while institutions play a role in social change, they might also change during the process itself. Their role may vary in particular moments of change, but understanding the institutional factor in change is a key aspect of analyzing change. Once the richness of the change is understood along with the institutional framework of change, then the work of the scholar is to identify the dynamic between agency and institution in a specific historical moment of change.

This book seeks to foster the development of this sensitivity to change so that students and scholars can identify social change as it is occurring around them. Then, from this identification, they can gain awareness of the richness of that change both from the personal experience of those involved in the change and from an institutional perspective. By seeing these aspects of change, scholars can then start to analyze the particular dynamics of that change by addressing the relationship between agency and institutions. In this book, the focus on the process of change and the contexts of change agencies refers to both personal and community activities, while the notion of institutions refers both to social institutions such as the family and to formal institutions such as the state and the media. The structure of the book aims to enable this understanding.

The areas discussed in each chapter combine to create the argument that contemporary social life is characterized by a new materialism within the relations of intermediated and informational life. Individuals in this process of change are situated within the blurring of class formations, as they negotiate the fluid and dynamic development of information capitalism. They use global communication technologies and networks to engage in – or to resist – aspects of change. People who do not have access to these networks are at risk of exclusion across all dimensions – social, political, economic and cultural – which might, in some cases, suppress them down into an underclass. The characteristics of contemporary change point to a world that is ever more informational and mediated, in which the stark reality of generating value within globalization gives this world a new material actuality born out of a more dynamic and mobile economy of things and people and one which is reproducing as well as creating new forms of inequality.

Although social change is an intrinsic part of sociology and the social sciences, it is not often explored as a subject in its own right. This book addresses this gap by focusing on social change by covering the key component areas: historical social change; theorizing social change; the relationship between the economy, the social and the cultural in changing society; and contemporary areas of social change. These topic areas were chosen because they illustrate key issues in the study of social change as well as creating – and comprising – key aspects of contemporary social change. The book does not consider specialist areas such as health, education, environment, religion, citizenship or social policy. To encompass such specialist areas would make the scope of the book to widen, and so, instead, it has selected some aspects of broad social change that illustrate different aspects of the process of social change rather than any specific ethical or policy-related change. However, this review of social change provides a useful contribution to policy, religious and ethical discourse because it provides a theoretical and contextual framework for considering and understanding changing social policies and behaviors.

Outline of the chapters

Chapter 2 outlines Abrams's (1982) assertion that, in order to understand change, there is a need to understand the relationship between personal activity and experience and social organization, as something that is continuously constructed and reconstructed over time. This relates to the 'two siddness of the social world' – the way that society is a fact-like system which individuals experience as being external to them, yet also something that is made and remade through their own actions. It is necessary to take an historical approach to social change to understand how, over time, actions become institutions, and then, in turn, institutions are changed by action. Exploring social change requires an analysis of institutional factors and the ways that individuals negotiate change within and across various dimensions of social life. The concept of process provides a link between action and structure.

Chapter 3 explains that the points and boundaries of change must be identified in order to be explored and understood. Defining historical periods provides a way to characterize specific types of relations of production and consumption; forms of power; individual senses of self and processes of identity; social values and cultural mores; as well as cultural forms and creativity within society. Although exact definitions of historical periods are often debated, they nonetheless act as useful frameworks to aid in identifying change and characterizing the nature of change. The chapter outlines the characteristics of a number of types of historical society, to clarify the ways that society and societal forms change over time. These are feudalism and premodern culture; industrial society and modernity; postindustrial society and late modernity; and information society, late- and postmodernity.

Chapter 4 considers the dimensions of change from the economic, political, social and cultural spheres of life. It does this by considering specific areas of social life over some historical periods to illustrate which dimensions of life have changed and in what ways. The articulation of changes within the economic, political and social spheres is considered in relation to cultural change. One key area discussed is the character of the individual within social relations – which can be traced from a fixed identity within feudal relations, through a class-based identity in industrial capitalism, then a consumer identity within mass consumer society, up to the fragmented, virtual and mediated identities of networked individualism in today's information society. Another key issue is modes of production – which are traced from relations of serfdom within agrarian production, through waged labor within industrial capitalism, flexible labor within a postindustrial service sector economy, up to networked entrepreneurs and casual labor within the contemporary global economy. The chapter reviews the development of consumption and consumer society, from Tudor Elizabethan times, through class-based consumption patterns of industrial society, up to lifestyle consumption practices within globalization. It looks at everyday life, identifying the trend of 'informalization', which stems from popular democratization and increased cultural fragmentation. The role of entertainment is discussed in relation to cultural change. The changing practices of power are also considered and shown to be indicative of social change in terms of legitimizing structures and forms of participation. All these themes form central aspects of social life – and each of their specific characteristics both defines and reflects certain historical periods in society.

After Chapter 4, the book begins to deepen understanding and, to contextualize, the debates from chapters 1 to 3. It moves the study on to consider substantive areas of change from the industrial modern period to the more recent late modern period and contemporary social life. Chapter 5 explores social change by looking at the culture of everyday life, to show how the mundane is created and made meaningful by human agency. It shows how these meanings produce routines that structure the shape of everyday life. One example of this is the way that information and communication technology is used to organize the fluidity of late modern life. Therefore, in order to understand how social change happens in everyday life, it is necessary to analyze how everyday life is normally ordered. This means addressing its structure – the changing routines and institutions – of the everyday and its culture – acquired through the meaningfulness of the everyday. Together, these form the circumstances of daily interaction and process.

Chapter 6 describes how work, and the understanding of work, has changed over historical time. The meaning and characteristics of work provide insights into the way a society is structured and ordered, while the social organization of work creates hierarchies of reward and prestige. This can be expressed in terms of occupational hierarchies, but also in broader social orderings such as class systems. The study of work in certain periods provides insights into the social actors who produce material, social and symbolic goods for society. The character of agency varies, involving diverse skills, gender relations, ethnicity and attitudes to work. It includes a range of people's perceptions to work – from acceptance to resistance and protest over their working conditions. The organization of labor also reveals a political dimension that exists on two axes – the development of trade unions and workers' rights, and the way that the state aligns with economic production.

Chapter 7 explores the historical and contemporary characteristics of consumerism. It outlines the long history of consumerism, from the Court of Elizabeth the First, where consumption was a way for noblemen to catch the Queen's attention and set themselves apart from their peers, through the industrial revolution, which created the capacity to produce surplus goods and thereby triggered changes in patterns of consumption, to the rise of mass consumerism from the 1950s until the current day, with consumers drawn from most echelons of society. The major role that marketing and the rise of the middle classes have played in the development of consumerism is discussed. The focus on fashion and consumer goods for the home is shown to be significant in sociological analysis because they are important in the spheres of the economy and everyday life that have both been affected by women's increased access to income. Furthermore, consumerism has become a core ethic of modern society, in which the ideals of Romanticism are played out in contemporary forms of hedonism, travel and self-development, through which people construct particular lifestyles from a range of consumer goods that they believe express particular aspirations or ideological convictions.

Chapter 8 explores the development of the creative and cultural industries in relation to changing ideas about creativity and culture, as well as changing notions of producers and audiences. The changes described in the aforementioned text regarding chapters 5, 6 and 7 are all aspects of what some commentators call 'the cultural turn': changes in everyday life, in production and consumption that began in the 1960s and placed the concept of 'culture' more centrally within social life. These changes were, to some extent, a consequence of the emergence of mass culture industries, including the mass media industries that developed during the mid- to late industrial period. Many commentators argue that the creative and cultural industries have undergone major transformations since the early 1980s, moving closer to the center of the global economy, with changing modes of ownership and organization and the formation of powerful alliances, partnerships and joint ventures. Some creative companies are vast global businesses, which work in many domains, such as film, publishing, television and music. Cultural products are increasingly circulating across national borders, and images, sounds and narratives are being borrowed and adapted from other places to attract audiences to particular cultural texts. In late modernity information, brands and an emphasis on creativity is important in the speed of innovation in the creative industries. Many of the contradictions of late modern life are played out in the institutions of the creative sector and by the audiences of their products.

Chapter 9 explores communication and the media as a defining feature of modern and late modern life. In contemporary everyday life, audience participation can be understood through the role the media play and by the audiences' own experiences, which, in part, shape their understanding of the world. Mediation and mediated discourse are both distinct features of contemporary technologically advanced societies. These processes form part of the communicative and interpretive practices of individuals and groups that are differently positioned – socially, culturally and in their relations to media institutions. The media context constitutes a mediapolis through which questions of public culture and personal interest are articulated and mediated. In modernity, the media play a key role in shaping the public sphere. This chapter considers how the character of people's engagement has been approached differently over time. Early media studies posited that audiences are passive, with the media maintaining a dominant ideological power. Later theorists addressed the way in which media messages are encoded by texts' producers and then decoded by audiences, with a hegemonic view of culture. Contradictions within this approach led researchers to undertake audience studies, finding that the interpretive practices of actors are important in the way that various media intersect with, and structure, everyday life and public life. The chapter discusses how the rise of new media – which is characterized by digitization, convergence, interactivity and the rise of networks – is reshaping the communications environment. The cultural contexts of new media diverge from traditional media, by allowing users to participate more interactively in media forms, and to generate the content themselves. However, they are still part of the media environment's culture of global capitalism, which continues to reproduce dominant mainstream media concentration and to generate new media nodes.

Chapter 10 considers social and cultural difference in terms of diversity and the negotiation of power. Globalization and heightened levels of geographical mobility are producing societies that are more diverse and the experience of diversity varies for different people, depending on their own situations and identities. To move beyond a consideration of racism, sexism and homophobia, some progressive commentators seek to change the discourse around difference while ensuring that society is more open to diversity. Although multiculturalism aims to encourage diversity within a framework of tolerance, it actually essentializes difference and therefore has an adverse effect. The shortcomings of these types of discourse, aligned with ongoing social change, are producing contemporary debates around cosmopolitanism. To assess the dynamics of difference, diversity and power, the processes through which these phenomena materialize and are negotiated must be understood. As this book's central thesis is that the social change is both material and ideational, it is clear that any contemporary analysis of power must be rooted in the relations of a diverse society, which are lived and experienced within certain modalities. This chapter considers two cases of negotiating power and difference – the lives of women in one Latin American country and the issue of diversity within European Union enlargement. These examples materialize in the modalities of power in contemporary society, including racial and gender struggles, which also involve spatial power within the mobilities of a diverse society. These modalities have their own processes and interrelate to form new conditions of oppression, while also providing spaces for agency in which inherited prejudices and forms of domination can be resisted and new opportunities created.

The book concludes with Chapter 11, which argues that the study of process can make human experience and agency understood in relation to the formation and reformation of social institutions that frame social values and structures of action. This involves understanding change in sociocultural terms in which production, discourse and agency interact to produce the distinctive characteristics of change. It shows how a focus on process can enable scholars to understand the relationship between agency and institutions in creating social change, and the changes that have shaped – and continue to shape – contemporary society.

2

Exploring Social Change

Introduction

This chapter sets the scene for identifying and analyzing change. The character of change is often untidy, messy and imperfectly grasped, and it may involve continuity as well as transformation. On the one hand, social change can be incremental, with change occurring only in some domains of social and cultural life but not in others. On the other hand, social change can be transformational in *all* dimensions of social life, producing change that is revolutionary and which ushers in a new type of society, such as the transition from an agrarian feudal system to an industrial capitalist society. This chapter argues that, in order to address either kind of social change, sociological analysis needs to situate people within changing social relationships. Addressing change through its shifting social relations and through people's experience of it requires a focus on process, which takes account of both structure and agency[1]. The articulation of change within and between economic, political and cultural spheres generates a social dynamic through which people experience and engage with change in their own specific social contexts. This dynamic leads to an approach that studies change in all its richness, asking how the world we live in has come about, and how does our social world change (Abrams, 1982).

The chapter first considers an overall framework for addressing social change as a process through time and then discusses the key questions in exploring social change. It then addresses the relationship between action and institutions through time in terms of grand social transformations. This is followed by a consideration of how change is experienced in intersubjective and subjective terms. This is followed by outline of an approach to social change that does not fully address both structure and agency, namely convergence theory. The chapter then considers the issue of the relationship between structure and agency in order to consider both broader social change and personal senses of change. This is then followed by a discussion about understanding change through the relationship between social and natural order in contemporary experience. Recent social change in terms of the development of an information society is then explored before discussing a study of social change in two cities in the North of England. This empirical study serves to show how scholars seek to understand senses of change and how change might be framed.

Studying social change

To study social change involves scholars having to identify change, which requires considering what constitute the points of change and what the boundaries of change are. Thus, historians construct historical periods and sociologists identify characteristics typical of particular historical moments. To really grasp a sense of change means understanding the dynamics of people's actions and interpretations, the social contexts of change and the social relations in which change is occurring. Abrams (1982) argues that social science does not always capture change in a rich and analytical way. Rather, he contends that in some cases different aspects of social life are captured, analyzed and abstracted from their contexts within and over time. This can be seen in ahistorical research that captures a 'snapshot' of a social phenomenon without reference to the dynamics of process in time. This type of approach tends to produce a mechanistic review of areas such as class, work, gender, ethnicity and globalization, which theoretically extract the phenomenon under focus out of its lived actualities. The focus on time is brought into research through the discipline of history in addressing historical and social change. Historians identify distinct periods through empirical methods to create a rich understanding of particular temporal periods. History, however, is less concerned with theorizing the mechanisms and dynamics of social change, such as class conflict, cultural reproduction and structural differentiation. To counter some aspects of sociology that produce ahistorical analyses, sociologists such as Elias (1978), Shills (1975), Bourdieu (1973, 1977) and Wright Mills (1959) address the importance of time in their studies.

When studying change, it is important to consider the ways in which social and cultural life changes at the institutional, as well as at the individual, level. Change, whether revolutionary or incremental, is experienced at all levels of social life, and is addressed at these levels across a range of social situations and by various social actors. The multidimensionality of social change and the way in which change progresses through society means that people experience change in varying ways, depending on where they are positioned within society. Given the dynamism of this field, the study of change must address the 'puzzle of human agency', because social agents firstly create change through their own actions, and then encounter that change in their lived realities (Abrams, 1982, p.x).

Key questions in exploring social change

A key sociologist in the study of social change is Abrams. Writing in the 1970s and early 1980s, he brought the concept of social change to the forefront of scholarly debate. In his book, *Historical Sociology*, he asked three questions about the study of change:

1. How do we understand social change?
2. How do we as active agents make a world of objects, which then become subjects, making us their objects?
3. How do actors perceive their world as one which they construct but one that also constrains them?

(Abrams, 1982, p.2)

Abrams suggests that addressing change requires understanding the 'two sid-edness of the social world' (Abrams, 1982, p.2) – the way that society is a fact-like system that individuals experience as being external to them, yet also something that is made and remade through their own actions. People perceive their world not only as one that they construct but also as one that constrains them. Abrams (1982) argues that society is experienced as an objective system, as something external to the individual, which is often understood as being 'given' or 'coercive', even though individuals had made that society and continually remake society through their imagination, communication and actions. Thus, Berger and Luckmann (1967) point out an 'awesome paradox' – that it is possible for human activity to produce a world of things that then binds them into certain conventions, situations and structures. Given the way that human activity produces a world of fact-like systems which human agents then change through their activities to create new externalities, change involves reviewing processes over time. Therefore, an historical approach is needed to understand change and the social phenomena within that change, because 'in time actions become institutions and institutions are in turn changed by action' (Abrams, 1982, p.2).

Abrams suggests that the 'idea of process and the study of process' offer a way to address the 'awesome paradox' of how actors act in relation to given situations and frameworks of society that are historically formed and presented to them. This means understanding 'the relationship of personal activity and experience on the one hand and social organization on the other as something that is continuously constructed in time' (Abrams, 1982, p.16). Furthermore, he asserts that actors can only construct new worlds on the basis of what their predecessors have constructed before them. To understand this point, it is vital to grasp the meaning of actions in relation to institutional conventions, in order to understand the dynamics of change. Abrams posits that the focal concern of social analysis should be 'the continuous process of construction', since 'the fact that social action is something we choose to do and something we have to do is inseparably bound up with the further fact that whatever reality society has is an historical reality, a reality in time' (Abrams, 1982, p.16).

The dynamics of change: The relationship between action and institutions through time

What Abrams (1982) means by the 'two sidedness of society' is the ways in which actions become institutions over time, and institutions are in turn changed by actions. He provides examples of this, including the way in which taking and selling prisoners becomes slavery; how offering one's services to a soldier in return for his protection becomes feudalism; and how organizing the control of an enlarged labor force on the basis of standardized rules becomes bureaucracy. As slavery, feudalism and bureaucracy become fixed and external settings, they become sites of struggles for prosperity, survival and freedom. By substituting cash payments for labor services, for instance, a lord and peasant jointly embark on the dismantling of the feudal order that their great-grandparents had constructed (Abrams, 1982, p.16).

This example about the demise of feudalism illustrates how the social world is historical and how process provides the link between action and structuring dimensions. The study of process provides a sociological approach to scrutinizing change, because what people choose to do and what they are obliged to do are both shaped by their historically given possibilities. However, this does not mean that history is a force in its own right – any more than society is – but rather that 'history has no direction of its own accord, for it is shaped by the will of men [sic] and the choices they make. Yet with every second that passes, men are making their choices by their behaviour' (Mousnier, 1973, p.145). This refers to the decisions that are made within a framework of choices, for example whether people throw a bomb or join a peace march and whether they protest about inequality or thrive on it – each decision shapes emerging contexts of social life (Abrams, 1982). These decisions are largely a matter of what previous experience has made possible for people, and what is meaningful for them.

Abrams (1982) argues that people can only construct worlds on the basis and within the framework of what their predecessors have already constructed for them. They do, however, actively interpret sets of conditions that they may seek to change. On that basis, and within that framework, the context of human activity may reproduce existing institutional arrangements or it may challenge and dismantle those institutions. The shaping of action by structure, and the transforming of structure by action, both occur as processes in time. It is therefore by bringing senses of historical time and sociology together that it becomes possible to find answers about why the world is as it is, and why people make their own particular choices (Abrams, 1982).

The relationship between action and institutions in the context of grand transformations

The idea of process is central to sociological thought and research. Sociology as a distinct of body of thought was itself formed at a time of historical change – during the industrial revolution – and it was shaped by the experiences of that time. The social upheaval created through the industrial revolution and the political revolutions in Europe left a sense of chaos – as Lamartine wrote: 'the world has jumbled its catalogue' (cit., Burrow, 1966, p.94). Faced with intellectual and social anarchy, the founding theorists of sociology sought to find an understanding of the processes of social change that would explain how society could be ordered in the new form it was taking. They specifically looked at the changes involved in industrialization, at capitalist economic development and spatially at the rise of urbanism. Marx (1818–1883), Weber (1864–1920) and Durkheim (1858–1917) made industrialization the organizing principle of their work, and from their analysis of industrialization they sought to understand social process more generally. Their contemporaries Comte (1789–1857), Spencer (1820–1903) and Hobhouse (1864–1929) also addressed these issues. All these theorists were aware of living in a dramatically changing world in which the relationship between the changes people wanted and the changes that actually occurred were mysterious, frustrating and obscure (Abrams, 1982, p.4). The issues they identified include the following:

- Why did the pursuit of wealth seem to generate poverty on an unprecedented scale?
- Why did the principles of liberty and equality appear to go hand in hand with monstrous new forms of oppression?
- Were the changes that industrialization was bringing to social relationships a matter of chance, choice or necessity?
- How far was industrialization an unavoidable destiny?
- Which of its characteristics could be altered by human action, and how?

(Abrams, 1982, p.4)

These questions show how their approaches to change not only sought to understand change but also took a critical stance to change. Due to the revolutionary change of that period, these theorists focused on what can be termed 'grand transformations', with each viewing a particular aspect of that change from a distinctive perspective. For example, Durkheim (1984) developed a methodology for analyzing social change in relation to the development of organic solidarity in complex industrial societies. Marx (1976) produced a structural materialist approach to historical change by exploring the laws of a capitalist economic system on the one hand, and class struggle on the other.

Weber (1922) focused on the process of rationalization in industrial society and on how a bureaucratic and rational world produced disenchantment. Velben (1899) addressed the emergence of a leisured class in the developing consumer society and the controlling functions of the business process.

Each theorist focused on specific aspects of social change. Weber considered the tendency to create bureaucracy and the ways in which the 'iron cage' of bureaucracy is experienced by members of society. The study of bureaucratization comprised an examination of the relationship between individuals and institutions, and of the possible ways of living in an industrial society. Weber's (1922) approach scrutinized the relationship between agency and structure by addressing the meaning of action as well as institutional structures, as did Marx. However, Marx (1976) emphasized the formation of classes and the structuring of class conflict within the capitalist relations of production in an industrial society. He described how capitalism alienated workers from their work, and from each other. His focus was a way of identifying how people could act within their social settings, and to what effect. Durkheim (1893) took another view of the process of industrialization, exploring how the division of labor, differentiation and lack of social cohesion was producing a new facet of society – 'anomie', which meant feelings of isolation and meaninglessness individuals were experiencing. At the center of all these sociological explorations is the question that frames the analyses of change critically:

● To what extent does the world have to be the way it is?

To address this question, Abrams (1982) supports Wright Mills's idea that sociological imagination requires an historical understanding. As Chapter 1 noted, Wright Mills (1959) argues that a sociological imagination would reveal the relationship between personal troubles and public issues, bringing together biographical, social and historical factors to address a particular social issue. Abrams (1982) stresses the importance of taking an historical approach to social change, emphasizing the significance of the relationship between personal experience and institutional structures and frameworks, specifically in relation to change. He stresses the sense of social change as a process through time, giving an historical sensibility to framing the change under review. If change is understood as a process through time, it encompasses the way that dynamics of social change can be articulated through cultural, political, economic and spatial dimensions of society.

The relationship between action and institutions: Intersubjectivity and experiencing social change

This focus on grand transformations is complemented by studies that concentrate on the subjective and intersubjective experiences of change in everyday life and in terms of cultural sensibility. These studies center on the way human agency creates social worlds and how social worlds are organized from agency. These studies take a different approach to those described in the previous section. They focus on meaningful social action, viewing action as the driver and shaper of change, instead of understanding structures in a more abstract way as being located outside of human agency. These approaches to the analysis of social life relate to the way Weber recognized that social action has meaning for social actors. Schutz (1962, 1971) developed a philosophical underpinning of human agency for the social sciences – phenomenology – building on Weber's idea that human action is meaningful and exploring this through theoretically prioritizing agency. Weber (1922) argued that meaning is attached to action; however, the way in which meaning is attached to action remains problematic in his work. By making human agency and experience a theoretical priority, Schutz's (1962) point of departure was the individual's own definition of the situation. In defining their situation, the individual draws on a common stock of knowledge, made up of social conceptions that relate to types of things that are material or symbolic. It is through these 'typifications' that individuals develop routines and definitions of situations within their own social worlds. Symbolic Interactionism (SI) was developed from these approaches and philosophy to consider how meaningful social action is, and the symbols it creates generates social life as something that is emergent (Herman-Kinney Reynolds, 2003). Within SI, there are two main schools of thought that take slightly different approaches to how social reality is structured through meaning. One approach is Structural Symbolic Interactionism, which addresses social structure directly by seeing how structure emerges out of social action. A variant within this is approach views social structure as something that is achieved through negotiated social action (Stryker, 1980; Burke, Owens, Serpe and Thoits, 2003). The other approach was influenced more heavily by Blumer, which sees social reality as something that is constantly constructed through action and communication rather than through social structures however defined (Atkinson and Housley, 2003; Martin and Dennis, 2010). Within SI, generally social change is understood as change emerging from action and agency rather than a process between action and institutions.

To summarize, giving attention to the meaningfulness of social life is part of a broader trend within a sociological tradition that addresses agency and symbolic meaning within the social world. The general framework of this approach is 'Symbolic Interactionism', which was developed at the University of Chicago, primarily by Blumer (1969), based on the work of Mead in the 1920s. SI has three main premises:

• Human beings act towards things on the basis of the meanings that things have for them.

- The meanings of things arise out of the social interaction one has with one's fellows.
- The meanings of things are handled in and modified through an interpretive process used by the person in dealing with things they encounter.

These basic premises encouraged research that focused on the social worlds of various groups in society. This research resulted in studies that were varied, and included explorations of the lives of groups who were considered to be outside mainstream society. These included the lives of Italian migrants in a slum area (Whyte, 1943) and research into how individuals learned to become marihuana users (Becker, 1953). SI studies looked at some institutional aspects of life, such as the experience of being a patient in an asylum (Goffman, 1961) and police work (Manning, 1977). It was also used in race and ethnicity studies (Park, 1950) and in terms of the spatial aspects of social life, in urban ecology research (Park, 1952)[2]. However, SI did not prioritize the relationship between agency and institutions as part of the dynamics of social change.

Goffman (1959) developed SI further through his work on dramaturgy. In his seminal work *The Presentation of Self in Everyday Life*, Goffman (1959) explores the way in which individuals present themselves and their activities to others in everyday life. This emphasized how individuals seek to construct and manage the impressions others form of them, which is aptly called 'impression management'. What all these SI studies showed is the way that people make sense of their situations and, through symbolism, create meanings for their social life and society. Although they did not take a long perspective in terms of chronological time, to varying degrees they addressed the ways in which people interpret and understand their own historical reality. This was clearly shown in the study of Willie, an American car mechanic, who could see how his work might become redundant as car production grew more standardized. Willie understood that such standardization would mean that his personal mechanical knowledge was no longer needed to carry out car repairs (Harper, 2002).

These types of approaches focus on social action and human agency. Generally, they see structural properties as routines, repertoires and rituals that are created through agency and so define situations. However, it is difficult to understand change in broad historical terms using these approaches because they often need to be contextualized within a particular historical period. For instance, changes in children's rights can be explored through examining the practice of social work or reviewing court cases. Furthermore, although the focus of these studies was often on process, through which meanings emerged, they might not easily be periodized historically. This may therefore overlook some of the institutional dynamics of a particular period, which might frame the context of the action and, thus, the action itself.

Convergence theory and social change

A different general approach to social change from those which view change as either revolutionary or incremental is one based on the premise that change is evolutionary. In the context of social change, this approach reduces change to 'laws of tendency' within an evolutionary path (Buckle, 1857, cited in Abrams, 1982). From this perspective, laws of evolution underpin and govern the process of historical change. This means that a society has tendencies that predispose it to move in a certain direction, through particular stages of development and in relation to specific laws of development. Therefore, individuals and groups align their behavior to the direction of change, and the change itself. According to this evolutionary approach, change is generated within social systems and human agency is insignificant because systems behave according to the laws of evolution. Therefore, the meanings and actions of individuals and groups – agency – simply cease to be interesting or important. A significant example of this approach is 'convergence thesis', which is rooted in functionalist sociology in the United States. Briefly, convergence theory argues that the functional requirements of a society mean that systems need to be stabilized to produce equilibrium, and that the needs of these systems inevitably push society into one organizational form – so there is an evolutionary path on which systems converge (Abrams, 1982).

Parsons took an evolutionary perspective in his book *Societies: Evolutionary and Comparative Perspectives* (1966). In this book, he posits that there is one overarching 'directional development' from a single Western origin leading to an international system of modern industrialism. He argues that this process would result in modernity, which, at the time of his writing, had become fully achieved in the United States. In *The System of Modern Societies* (1971), Parsons writes that the logic of development is rooted in the functional necessities of the modernizing social system. In analytical terms, his general thesis is that there is a functional relationship between problems and solutions through which social systems evolve towards ever higher levels of organization. For instance, Parsons (1949) addresses the transformation of family relationships during and after the industrial revolution. He presents the separation of home and work and the structural isolation of the conjugal family unit as a change demanded by the requirements of the modernizing occupational system, which family members had to adapt to.

The convergence theory is also linked to debates about postindustrialization. Convergence is explored in terms of asking if there is an industrial destiny that all preindustrial or industrializing nations will eventually reach, raising the question whether any such postindustrial destiny can be discerned in the changes occurring within industrial society. Followers of the convergence theory assert that there is a predefined outcome, whereas opponents argue that this is a simplistic and reductionist argument of social change. Some of these arguments are presented in terms of change from a postindustrial society to an information society – although definitions and understandings of these concepts are highly debated. It is important to keep a clear distinction between legitimate justifiable analysis of a tendency towards, for example, a postindustrial society, and the presumption of a teleology that simply sees postindustrial society as already existing in industrial society (Abrams, 1982).

Structure and agency: Relating broader social change to personal senses of change

Giddens (1979) sought to theorize the relationship between structure and agency through his structuration thesis, but his analysis of the relative influence of structure or action within the dynamics of change is inconclusive. According to structuration theory, social relations are seen as being structured in time and space as the outcome of the 'duality of structure'. This means that the regular actions of knowledgeable and reflexive actors establish patterns of interactions that become standardized practices in organizations. Over time, the habitual use of such practices becomes institutionalized and forms the structural properties of organizations. These institutional properties (structure) are then drawn on by humans in their ongoing interactions (agency), which, in turn, reinforces the existing institutional properties they are drawing on (Giddens, 1979). According to this approach, neither structure nor agency should be accorded primacy in sociological explanations. Thus, Giddens (1979) argues for a concept of a 'duality of structure' in which:

- Structure is both the medium and the outcome of the conduct it recursively organizes.
- Structure is defined as 'rules and resources', which do not exist outside of actions but which continuously impact on their production and reproduction.
- Analogies with physical structures, of the sort used by functionalism, are regarded as wholly illegitimate. In Giddens' formulation, 'structure' is both enabling and constraining.

However, reformulations of relations between structure and agency (including Giddens')[3] have not put an end to debates about the appropriate conceptualization of relations between the two – or indeed about the prior or interrelated question of how 'agency' and 'structure' should be defined in the first place. Thus, Layder (1981), for example, considers that Giddens' conception of 'structure' deprives the concept of any 'autonomous properties or pre-given facticity'. Commentators such as Rawls (1989) have also detected a persistent bias towards agency in Giddens' reasoning (see also Bryant and Jary, 1991). Giddens himself presents the structuration theory as an 'ontology' to aid analysis and as an orientation in social research, rather than a finished theory.

Applying structuration theory to concrete historical cases is, therefore, only of limited value, particularly since it is difficult to understand the dynamics of change without an understanding of the precise nature of their action and structure, especially if actions are seen as capabilities rather than intentional acts. Thus, as Archer states:

> ...the theory of structuration remains incomplete because it provides an insufficient account of mechanisms of stable replication versus the genesis of new social forms.
>
> (Archer, 1992, p.131)

Thus, although Giddens seeks to address both structure and agency, it is difficult to see how structuration theory can fully address social change.

Social and natural order: The state and mobility in contemporary experience

Urry (2000) argues that modern society is based on industries that enable and utilize new forms of energy and resulting patterns of social life. He asserts that this observation creates an analysis based on the shift from a traditional to a modern society, as occurred in the North Atlantic rim countries between 1700 and 1900. The dichotomy between tradition and modernity has been variously described; for example, Maine (1861) identifies a shift from status-based positions to contract-based relations. Toennies (1957) sees a change from a *gemeinschaft* sensibility rooted in close-knit communities to associations based on exchange, creating a sense of *gesellschaft*[4]. Spencer (1873) points to another aspect of modernity, the move from a militant to an industrial society. Foucault (1964) distinguishes between the classical and bourgeois ages in his historical analysis of mental illness. However, Urry (2000) points out that an overarching characteristic of these writings is that they view social order as being different and separate from natural order, which is something both he and Scott Lash address through their focus on the ordering of industrial and postindustrial societies, as well as the spatiality of the way this order materializes in global flows of capital.

Lash and Urry (1987) examine the ordering of industrial society, a system that both uses natural resources and seeks to control nature. They argue that, during the Western industrial period (1900–1970s in Europe and North America), capitalism was 'organized' – whereby most economic and social problems and risks were largely framed in the context of individual nation states (with some alliances such as Western and Eastern blocs during the Cold War), which were seen as sovereign and based on social governmentality. Within this framework, it is generally understood that the role of the state within each country was to solve its own problems as they emerged in industrial society independently. In this context, issues within each nation state are addressed by national policies. This is clearly seen in the development of a Keynesian-based 'welfare state', which posited the idea that the risks of an organized capitalist economy could be managed through economic policy and that perceived social problems could be addressed through progressive social policy. This perspective is tightly aligned with the concept of national citizenship, whereby individual citizens have both rights from, and responsibilities to, the state. These rights and responsibilities are administered through institutions of the nation-state (Roche, 1992).

From the discussion above, it becomes noticeable that the concept and the role of the state is an important factor in social life and in social change. Defining the state is complex, and there are many different theories of the state, but Weber provides a useful starting point. He argues that the state is a necessary political organization that operates through centralized government, which maintains a monopoly of the legislative use of force within a certain territory (Owen and Strong, 2004). From this point of view, there are certain categories of state institutions such as administrative bureaucracies, legal systems and military and religious organizations. Weber denotes the state as part of the rational organization of industrial society, in which agency is channeled into bureaucracy and thus shapes institutional forms of administration. However, theorists from a more Marxist tradition view the state as ruling class instrument for dominating society. From this perspective, the state comprises an elite group whose members have the same background as the capitalist class (Miliband, 1983). Still within the critical viewpoint, Gramsci (1971) describes the state as having the ideological function of supporting the hegemonic position of the ruling class. His approach posits that state power and ideological domination is realized through the institutions of civil society, which include churches, schools and the media. According to these critical approaches, the state as a ruling class form of elite has the agency to manage and control the working classes, exercising this control through ideological as well as civil and civic institutions.

There are other, more pluralistic accounts of the state that allow for more negotiations between groups in society. Dahl (1973) theorizes that the state is not strongly determined by class or elite influence, but rather acts as an institutional space for debate and challenge between different interest groups in society. Dahl (1973) concedes that there is, however, inequality that may affect the capacity of some groups to lobby and act within this pluralistic arena. Duncan (1989) shows that Habermas also addresses the complexity of the state within modern society. He asserts that state has a role in structuring the economy, which it does through regulation (to various degrees), and, by influence, as a large producer and consumer within the economy. It also manages the economy through redistributive strategies enacted through various types of welfare policies. Given this complexity, Duncan (1989) notes Habermas' point that the state cannot be simply seen as protecting and promoting a dominant, elite economic class.

The ambiguity about the way the state works is also evident in the work of the neo-Marxist Poulantzas (1973). He argues that the state did not always act on behalf of a ruling elite, even though officials may wish to do so. This is because the state must support its own long-term interests, which, in some contexts, might favor the needs of the working class. Given this situation, Poulantzas (1973) promoted the idea that the state is relatively autonomous. Skocpol, Evans and Rueschemeyer (1985) provide a 'new institutionalist' approach to develop this point further, arguing that the state and its officials can pursue their own interests independently. These interests may conflict with certain groups in society, but, given the dependence of many groups in civil society on the state, the state has the power to impose its decisions or strongly influence the acceptance of its decisions.

Thus, the state has been theorized in a range of ways, ranging from a dominant position to that of engaging in society in a more pluralistic way. The role of the state has changed throughout historical time and is shaped by specific ideologies, economic conditions and political power. That role continues to be negotiated in late modern culture, in the organization of advanced capitalism and through globalization.

Lash and Urry (1987) propose that the organization of capitalism changed after the 1970s, when the mode of industrial society became disorganized. This was because of the changing flows of capital, labor, commodities and information across time and space, via global networks. The organized model of capitalism based on factory time was no longer able to respond to changing markets quickly enough, and could not innovate fast enough to remain competitive in the new global market. Given these changes, Urry (2000) questions the prevailing focus on nation-states, suggesting instead that societies are embedded within a system of 'nation-states-societies', with reference to Mann's description of the contemporary world as a global society (Wiles Lectures, Queen's University, Belfast, 23–26 May 2000). This global society is not a unitary culture or an ideological community or state, but a single power network (Urry, 2000) whose 'interconnections [are] open to different types of threats, it transports many people, materials and messages within it, and it also has repercussions for the environment' (Lash and Urry, 1993, p.11).

There are two main responses to this proposition: global enthusiasts and global skeptics. The global enthusiasts believe that globalization is ushering in a global age of cosmopolitan 'borderlessness', which, they argue, will offer new opportunities to overcome the restrictions that nation-states held over the freedom of corporations and individuals (Urry, 2000). Global skeptics, on the other hand, see the global world as a new medievalism (Cerny, 1997), which is characterized by a lack of clear territorial boundaries and which comprise a contemporary manifestation of empires with centers and peripheries constituted from many networks of competing institutions with overlapping jurisdictions and identities.

The state is a central institution in society, and its role has been differently conceived during various historical periods and within different ideologies. In the context of contemporary globalization, Cerny (1997) asserts that nation-states are being reconstituted as competition states run by powerful commercial companies, which have a global reach and which reconfigure economies and cultures in their own interests, reducing intranational military threats. Lash (1999) discusses how the global information culture and circulation of objects are reconstituting social relations, suggesting that social relations are made and remade through machines, technologies, objects, texts, images and physical environments. Human experience is created through the interconnections between humans and material objects, including signs, machines, texts, physical environments, animals, plants and waste products. According to this view, human agency does not have any ontological priority and culture is generated through another rationality that combines human and nonhuman systems.

Both Lash (1999) and Urry (2000) propose human-system hybrids in which human agency is distributed and does not have any ontological priority – it is just another thing that flows across networks (Wessels, 2012). Urry (2000) focuses on 'diverse mobilities' such as the intersection of sensuous relations of humans with diverse objects; the time and space quality of relations that stretch across societal borders; and the complex and unpredictable intersections of many 'regions, networks and flows'. In fact, the writings of Urry and Lash provide another way to consider agency within the 'two sidedness of society' in the process of change, showing that agency in contemporary society is now seen to be distributed across hybrid systems. This analysis is useful because it provides insights into the character of contemporary society; however, it does not fully address some of the cultural or structural aspects of change. Commentators such as Robins and Webster (1999) take a more modernist approach to social and technological change, stating that the way technologies are organized in capitalism is realized through human values within, as well as, the social relations of production.

The following sections of this chapter discuss two studies that bring together a sociological and historical analysis as they review change through agency and institutions.

Framing contemporary society in historical terms: Information society

Robins and Webster (1999) address the development of the information society historically by addressing the cultural meaningfulness of technology within social change. They take a long historical view of change to consider the relation between science, technology and industrialization on the one hand, and ways of life, culture and subjectivity on the other. This approach is taken from Jennings (1985) who comes from the same British intellectual tradition as Williams, Thompson and Inglis, being located in a broad 'culture and society' tradition. This tradition is rooted in the Romantic Movement, which was concerned with the historical relationship between culture (in its multiple senses) and the processes of industrialization. This view addresses the degradation of nature in both human and physical terms by the machinery of commerce and industrialism, as well as the underlying capitalist relations of power and its forms of oppression.

Robins and Webster (1999) follow on from Marx, Durkheim and Weber, who took as their starting point transformations from a feudal agrarian society to an industrial capitalist society. Although none of these writers take a technological determinist perspective[5], they recognize that the development of industrial society involved a period of 'accelerated and unprecedented technological change' (Robins and Webster, 1999, p.3). The first industrial revolution (approx. 1775–1840) utilized technologies such as the steam engine, the spinning jenny and Cort's metallurgy process, as well as a more general adoption of machines that replaced hand tools. The second industrial revolution (approx. 1840–1920) involved technologies such as electricity, the internal combustion engine, science-based chemicals, efficient steel casting and the early communications technologies of telegraph and telephone. The significant factor was not the technology in itself, but rather how these new technologies were used to affect the relations of production.

The way these technologies were used transformed the processes of production and distribution, generated new products and moved wealth to countries whose elites could exploit the potential these technologies offered. Castells (1996) argues that part of this process was tied to imperialist ambitions and inter-imperialist conflicts as well as rapid urbanization, new class formations and new forms of inequality. These technologies on their own could not generate change; rather, it was a configuration of social, political and economic factors that enabled the technologies to be exploited. Castells (1996) also states that the process of technological innovation is embedded in particular institutional and commercial environments, in which there are the required skills to define and solve technical problems and the economic ability to judge the cost-benefits of different technical applications scenarios. This environment includes users and producers who build knowledge and experience cumulatively through learning by doing and learning by using. Castells (1996) argues that this interactivity of actors, institutions and skill-sets of a milieu of innovation is as relevant to the 'digital revolution' as it was to the industrial revolution.

In a similar vein, Robins and Webster (1999) argue that the history of technological change needs to move beyond the characteristics of technology itself to address the characteristics of 'technoculture', which refers to the way technology is embedded within ways of life. They take a critical perspective, not just to the technologies but also to the values that inform the design and use of those technologies. The main focus of their argument is the way in which capitalism is both the driver and shaper of a new technology agenda, which, in contemporary society, is digital technology. They posit that the capitalist agenda and its values shape digital technology as the dominant technological network that extends and infiltrates market conditions into many areas of social life, human expression and culture.

What Robins and Webster (1999) offer is a longer-term historical view of technological and social change. Rather than looking at the history of digital technology in terms of its technical development or economic analysis, they take a rounder view to include the meaning of these changes in cultural terms. They see developments as forming part of a long revolution of capitalist development, starting from the Enclosures Acts of Parliament (1750–1850)[6] up to current developments in the digitally networked global society. They adopt a Luddite frame of reference in assessing the sociocultural dynamics of digital technology (Wessels, 2010). The ethos of Luddism offers a perspective that reflects on the impact of technological developments on broader ways of life. Robins and Webster (1999) argue that Luddism is more than a movement against technology *per se*, in that it is a protest against wider changes to existing ways of life through new social mobilizations of *laissez-faire* capitalism. The relevance of Luddism, for Robins and Webster (1999), is that they believe 'the global network society' to be the logical extension of the Enclosures Movement, in which capitalist relations are being reconfigured, but nonetheless remain capitalist and market oriented. Therefore, although there are changes in working practices, in education and in the spatiality and design of urban spaces, there is continuity whereby the dynamics of social life are still embedded within the social relations of capitalism.

A study of social change that addresses structure, agency, place and history

Taylor, Evans and Fraser (1996) address some of the details of social change alluded to in the sections above. Their book, *A Tale of Two Cities* (1996), is based on a comparative study of Manchester and Sheffield in the United Kingdom, which explores global change, local feeling and everyday life in the North of England. The underlying conviction of their study is that it is still sensible, even in globalizing times, to recognize local cultural differences between cities (especially in an old country like England) and to treat them as having a sociological significance and continuing cultural provenance and impact. They argue that, although people may increasingly relate to a global marketplace and mediascape, they nonetheless still hold down jobs (or not), own and rent housing (or not) in specific cities, which they have to negotiate and interpret as places of sociability and pleasure or, perhaps, of solitude and fear. The way in which people understand, interpret and manage their everyday lives is a recursive practical achievement, which the authors believe involves the development of practical local knowledge.

Taylor et al. (1996) offer an analysis of these industrial cities as an exercise in comparative sociology that does not just identify their shared and common structural features, but also seeks to understand the cultural differences between them. They seriously consider the idea of unevenness and differences between cities in industrial capitalist societies, arguing that these are linked, in particular, to local forms of industrial organization. These local forms of organization are made up of many dimensions, such as the gendered character of the production process in the cities of Manchester and Sheffield, as well as the history of immigration into these two cities within local political and social history.

One aspect of their research was the importance of introducing 'real' voices into the field of urban studies – the Northern voices in this study give expression to local (as well as national and global) fears and hopes. The authors hear these voices through a realist framework – that is to say, in terms of what they recognize are the mundane and routinized patterns in which people make use of their cities, whether they live in the inner city, old terraced streets, the inner suburbs or what Northerners call 'nice areas' of the outer suburbs. They allow local voices to lead them in different directions, to cover issues regarding many areas of social life, such as gender and race; homelessness and poverty; shopping and consumerism; sexuality; transport; ageing (including memory and nostalgia); and being a young person in the process of becoming a 'Mancunian' or 'Sheffielder' in the deindustrialization period that occurred in both cities in the 1990s.

People's own interpretations and perspectives are understood in that historical moment of social change, as the study addresses structure and agency in the process of change. To do this, it draws on the work of Williams' *Long Revolution* (1965), in which Williams first posed his notion of 'structures of feeling'. Williams uses this term to mean that the routine and taken-for-granted 'social practices' give a particular social formation its distinctive characteristics. Social practices are part of a complex organized whole ensemble of social relations, which have a powerful influence in shaping an individual's beliefs and behavior. However, although he found these influences to be strong, he concluded that they did not determine human behavior and thought. Taylor et al. (1996) note Williams' point that 'in any individual social formation there would be unexpected as well as expected correspondence' (Taylor et al., 1996, p.5). Williams (1965) emphasizes that the analysis of culture should be aware of 'the nature of the organization which is the complex of these relationships' (Williams, 1965, p.61). Hall sums this up as follows:

> The purpose of analysis [must be] to show how the interactions between all these practices and patterns are lived and experienced as a whole, in any particular period. This is its 'structure of feeling'.
>
> (Hall, 1981, p.22)

Taylor et al.'s (1996) study is also undertaken within the framework of critical sociology, building on Wright Mills's (1959) call to focus on public issues and private troubles. Taylor et al. (1996) do this in the context of two 'dirty old towns' in the North of England at the end of the 20th century. They observe how Sheffield and Manchester are differently positioned as they move into a postindustrial context and that their 'local structures of feeling' inform their respective processes of transcending their long historical past. The study addresses each of Abrams's (1982) questions about social change. In response to the question of how we understand social change, Taylor et al. follow Abrams (1982) in suggesting that sociological explanation is necessarily historical, so they examine the change from industrialism to deindustrialization. To answer Abrams's question about how people make a world of objects, which then makes them subjects of these objects, Taylor et al. (1996) look at social practices, feelings and institutions in the configuration of the two distinctive cities. Finally, in relation to the question of how actors perceive their world as one that they construct but one that also constrains them, Taylor et al. (1996) argue that this can be done through understanding people's structures of meaning.

Senses of change and framing change

In order to identify and analyze social change, we need to understand the way in which subjective feelings of change and structural change relate to each other. This point leads straight to the central theme of social change, which is exploring the significance of agency in generating change and the significance of the processes that foster structural change. One of the enduring concerns about change is the way in which structure and agency interact and the respective influence each has on the other. However, there has been relatively little emphasis on systematically addressing change through the ways in which social life is meaningful to various actors in society. Although attention has been paid in anthropological terms to the meanings of change, and sociological commentators have addressed the role of culture in change, there has been little analysis of the sociocultural dynamics of change. By addressing the sociocultural dynamics of change, it is possible to start identifying and understanding the process of change – the way in which the dimensions of change become enacted and interact with one another to produce specific changes at particular historical moments.

Many aspects of sociocultural phenomenon are articulated and materialized through social institutions. One way that social analysts can progress their studies of change (without diminishing the agency–structure debate, which is revisited later) is by considering the way that institutions change and the processes through which they change. Institutions are a key aspect of society and social life, covering a wide range of areas including family, education, the media, legal systems, welfare systems and nation-states, world regions and global political arrangements. Institutions hold within them, mediate and make visible social values and the ways in which the economic, political and cultural dimensions of societies are organized and structured. Institutions represent both human agency and the way in which agency becomes structured within specific ways of organizing society. Very often change is experienced and articulated in relation to institutions, whether they are being questioned, resisted or affirmed. However, the question of how one can recognize institutional change and understand the social dynamics that lead to such change remains.

The focus on institutional change and the process of social change is embedded within an approach that seeks to understand change in terms of its sociocultural dynamics. This approach includes the consideration of broader structural change because the context of economics, politics and social organization is meaningful both within their respective life-worlds and structures and within broader social life, where these types of changes materialize and become interpreted. In order to understand these dynamics, there needs to be a framework of analysis that captures the richness of change, the dimensions of change, the way these dimensions interact and their interdependencies. This book proposes a framework of analysis that is based on a sociocultural dynamic made up of the social relations of production, the discourses within societies and the characteristics of participation within social life.

The idea of a sociocultural dynamic in social change acts as an organizing principle for understanding social change and situates change within three main areas along with the relations between these areas. The first area is concerned with how goods and services are produced by people around the world – the relations of production at local, regional, national and global levels. This involves asking who is producing what, where and how, what resources they are using and what the power relations exist within the social organization of production. The second area considers the ways in which the economic, political and cultural dimensions of social life are narrated and interpreted – how change is made sense of, by both those experiencing the change and by those observing and commentating on the change. These types of perceptions are articulated in the discourses of particular societies, and these

discourses are open to analysis. The third area addresses the forms of participation in society and the characteristics of participation – the way that humans
engage with each other individually, with each other through the social institutions they develop and how they engage with the structural arrangements
of economic systems, political systems, regimes of welfare and cultural life
in general. The forms and characteristics of participation create a culture of
participation, which often materializes in a continuum between inclusion and
exclusion. Participation is experienced, as well as structured, in different ways
for different people. The shaping of participation involves senses of identity
and the recognition and validation of identity by those with power to define
which sectors of society will be included or excluded, and to what degree.
Participation also involves considering which resources people need to be able
to participate, and whether these resources are economic, political, social or
cultural.

Conclusion

A dynamic sociocultural approach to change facilitates an appreciation of the
complexity of change while, at the same time, providing a framework with
which to analyze change. The three main areas of production, narratives and
participation are populated with various groups, perspectives and institutions
involving social change. The way these areas link together show the many
ways in which individuals, institutions and structures can come together to
form specific configurations in the various transformational spaces and times
of social change. These three aspects of a sociocultural dynamic of change are
drawn into a broader environment in which production, narratives and participation are generally organized. This broader environment involves many
of our defining institutions, which organize modern and late modern societies, including developed and developing nations and world regions. Those
involved in the relations of production, in the formation of narratives and
as participants, move between these spaces, and the meanings and knowledge gained through these interactions shape change. Transformative change,
however, only occurs when there is a level of interdependence between all
three areas and when all interactions are symbolically framed in the process
of change. This means that change has to be recognized, made sense of and
legitimized.

To this end, the study of process, following Abrams (1982), involves understanding the relationship of personal activity and experience on the one hand,
and social organization on the other, as something that is continuously constructed in time. This relates to the 'two sidedness of the social world' – the
way that society is experienced as an objective system that individuals experience as external to them, while also being something that is made and
remade through their actions. This paradox requires a particular approach

to social change, an historical approach that addresses the way in which, over time, actions become institutions and in turn institutions are changed by action – this sense of process provides a link between action and structure. An examination of social change requires addressing institutional factors and understanding how individuals negotiate change within and across the dimensions of social life.

3

Key Periods of Change

Introduction

In order to understand and explore change, it is necessary to identify the points and boundaries of change. This involves defining historical periods as a way of characterizing specific modes of relations of production and consumption, forms of power, senses of individual selves and processes of identity, social values and cultural mores, as well as cultural forms and creativity within society. Although exact definitions of historical periods are often debated, they nonetheless act as sensitizing frameworks to aid in identifying change and characterizing the nature of change.

To clarify this approach to the way that society and societal forms change, this chapter outlines the characteristics of the following well-known types of historical society:

- Feudalism and premodern culture
- Industrial society and modernity
- Postindustrial society and late modernity
- Information society, late- and postmodernity

To identify the characteristics of social change as understood as a process through time, this chapter first covers earlier periods of social life. The focus on feudal society and early modern society serves to show how social change involves several dimensions of change, and how some of those changes were precursors to further social change in the late industrial, postindustrial and information society. Since the main focus of this book is on more recent social change in shaping the characteristics of contemporary society, more attention is paid to developments in later historical periods. The chapter first considers feudalism and pre-modern culture, and then discusses industrial society and modernity. It moves on to explore postindustrial society and late modernity, and this is followed by addressing information society and late- and postmodernity.

Feudalism and premodern culture

To explore the way that various dimensions of social life interact in social change, this section will draw on the work of Roche (2010). Roche (2010) provides a good overview of the dynamics of social change in the feudal period by addressing the economic, political and social aspects of social life that hold within the dynamics of change. His work follows on from Bloch (1989) and, to some extent, engages with Bloch's thesis. Bloch worked within the Annales Tradition in addressing the characteristics of feudal society. The Annales School is a historiographic approach that incorporates social science into the analysis of long-term social history. Although Bloch does not take an explicitly Marxist approach to the social relations of feudal society, he nonetheless emphasizes the economic and social relations of feudal society. He discusses feudal ties among the subject position of the peasantry, a class of specialized warriors and other emerging groups in feudalism. Although Bloch addresses other dimensions of feudal society, the strength of his analysis lies in his focus on feudal relations.

Roche (2010) also writes that in Europe during the early medieval period a localized feudal agrarian economy developed, which was based on an unequal social contract between peasants and landowners. Peasant serfs were given access to land to grow food to feed their families and support their wider community. In return for this access to land, they had to produce a surplus of food to pay for protection by warrior elites and the nobility. This system expanded across Europe throughout the medieval period with the process of forest clearing. However, and relevant to the central argument of this book, Roche (2010) focuses firmly on the conditions that produced change in feudal society. He identifies how certain trading networks, innovative technologies, state building and religious and cultural change formed a dynamic that loosened feudal ties and created mercantilism, which is a precursor to early industrial society.

Roche (2010) places feudal developments in broader global trade routes, arguing that expansion was not just reliant on European resourcefulness, but also resulted from new agricultural technology being imported from the Middle East and beyond, which increased the productivity of both land and labor. These included windmills and watermills, heavy turn ploughs and breeds of heavy horses to pull them, together with horseshoes and collar harnesses to make the system work. Roche (2010) points out that feudalism was a politico-military-based system as well as an economic system. He states that this can be seen in the new social contracts between peasant farmers and the local warrior nobility which meant that the noblemen provided military protection for farmers in return for tithes, taxes and military service from the peasantry. The dynamics of this relationship between elites and farmers generated new power balances and social contracts between empowered local nobilities and centralizing authorities, with state builders such as claimants to kingship[1].

A significant period of social change was the 15th–16th centuries in Europe – a period of major transition towards modernity. Roche (2010) argues that this was particularly the case in the dimension of European culture. At this time in Europe, three cultural revolutions occurred, which all had a significant impact on the development of modernity. The first was the innovation of the printing press and development of printing, which transformed the continent's communications and cultural transmission system. Second was the long process, often referred to as 'the Renaissance', in which art and humanistic culture reached new heights. The third significant change occurred in the early decades of the 16th century – the origins and the first manifestations of the Protestant Reformation (Roche, 2010).

European culture and society in this period was a key aspect in the development of modernity. However, it is important to recognize that these changes did not occur solely within Europe, since much of the basis for change was externally induced and consequently paved the way for further development of European societies in the 16th century and beyond. These developments included long-distance oceanic trade routes for spices and silks to India, Indonesia, Japan and China, the appropriation of South American gold and silver, the European colonization of the Americas and the transatlantic slave trade (Roche, 2010). These developments created the conditions for a postfeudal and a postcity-state world. The world that emerged from these economic, political and cultural changes was one of large-scale, centrally organized, commercially adventurous and competitive nation-states (Roche, 2010). This was evident particularly in England, the Netherlands, France and Spain, each of them developing finance-accumulating capital cities and city networks.

To summarize, Roche (2010) writes that the 'long 15th century', interpreted in terms of its cultural revolutions as well as its political, economic and politico-military revolutions, and including transoceanic colonialism, began a historical process of modernization in Europe. This process also evolved through the development of nationalism, nation-state differences and war-making. Roche (2010) details how these dimensions interacted in specific ways to produce transformative change. He also shows how feudal society started to develop into distinct nation-states, and how its culture changed to form early modern culture.

Industrial society and modernity

In broad terms, the Industrial Revolution was a period in the late 18th and early 19th centuries when major changes in agriculture, manufacturing, production and transportation had a profound effect on socioeconomic and cultural conditions, first felt in Britain. The changes subsequently spread throughout Europe, North America and, eventually, worldwide. The transition from an agricultural-labor-based economy towards machine-based manufacturing began in England during the 1700s[2]. It started with the mechanization of the textile industries, the development of iron-making techniques and the increased use of refined coal. These technologies improved levels of production, which, when combined with the introduction of canals, better roads and railways, provided an efficient distribution network for goods and created an expansion in trade. Further developments such as the introduction of steam power fuelled by coal, the wider utilization of waterwheels and powered machinery (mainly in textile manufacturing) led to even greater increases in production capacity. The development of all-metal machine tools in the first two decades of the 19th century facilitated the manufacture of more production machines to enable manufacturing in other industries. The onset of the Industrial Revolution and industrial capitalism (as well as industrialization organized in collectivist systems within communist states) marked a major turning point in human society, which eventually influenced almost every aspect of daily life in some way. This can therefore be seen as a period of revolutionary change.

Another aspect of industrialization was the presence of an entrepreneurial class, which believed in progress, technology and hard work. This class is often linked to Protestantism and the Protestant work ethic (c.f Weber, 1930). In England, the entrepreneurial class also developed from the dissenting Protestant sects, such as Quakers, Presbyterians and Baptists, which had flourished during the English Civil War (Hobsbawn, 1971). Other factors that supported entrepreneurial activity included a renewed confidence in the rule of law following the establishment of the prototype of British constitutional monarchy in the Glorious Revolution of 1688. A stable financial market also emerged, based on the national debt being managed by the Bank of England, which contributed to the capacity for, and interest in, private financial investment in industrial ventures.

The role of dissenters was varied, but they each contributed to the dynamics of industrialization (Hobsbawn, 1971). Religious dissenters had been barred or discouraged from almost all public offices, as well as excluded from being educated at Oxford and Cambridge, England's only universities at the time (although dissenters were free to study at any of Scotland's four universities), due to the Test Acts[3]. However, with the repeal of these acts, dissenters could become active in banking, manufacturing and education, which resulted in an opportunity to participate in social life. For instance, the Unitarians were particularly involved in education and they ran Dissenting Academies. In contrast to the universities of Oxford and Cambridge and schools such as Eton and Harrow, these academies focused on mathematics and the sciences, areas of scholarship that were vital to the development of manufacturing technologies. While members of these sects were excluded from certain circles of the government, they were nonetheless considered fellow Protestants by many in the middle class, such as traditional financiers or other businessmen. Given this relative tolerance and the supply of capital, the natural outlet for the more enterprising members of these sects was to seek new opportunities in the technologies being created in the wake of the 17th-century scientific revolution.

Industrialization is a broad and multifaceted process that involves the following key characteristics:

- A complex division of labor
- An occupational-based stratification system
- Rationalized procedures for achieving social integration

These attributes are the basic structural characteristics of industrial society, which leads to the three types of social structural change:

- In the division of labor
- In the nature and sources of inequality
- In the ways that societies are integrated or held together

This outline of characteristics demonstrates how complex and multidimensional the changes in industrial society were. When taken together, these types of structural change can be said to constitute an overall process of 'structural differentiation' – a process in which different tasks or functions are increasingly separated out from one another and attached to specific social positions or roles.

Two approaches towards analyzing such changes are the 'contrasts type' or 'theories of tendencies' (Abrams, 1982). Each account offers a contrast between industrial society as a general type and preindustrial society as an alternative general type. Abrams (1982) points out that the 'contrasts of type' approach involves developing models that identify what are deemed to be the essential characteristics of industrial society and then contrasting those with the essential characteristics of the preindustrial model. In many cases, these contrasts of type are based on a single main trait. For example, Toennies (1957) describes industrial society as a type of social system organized in terms of the impersonal links of 'association' (*gesellschaft*), and contrasts this to preindustrial society, which was a system organized in terms of the closer, tighter links of 'community' (*gemeinschaft*). Maine (1861) distinguishes between the present and past by substituting 'contract' for 'status' as the basis of social action in industrial society. These types of approaches identify the defining features of different types of historical society.

Theories of tendencies takes a slightly different focus, looking at how the present is constructed out of the past by addressing the historical interaction of social action and social structure that produces tendencies towards substituting the industrial type for the preindustrial. In some cases, the tendency is treated as strong, and almost unavoidable; in others, it is much weaker, more variable and much more actively constructed by the immediate activity of individuals.

Contrasts of type can be reductionist, and they tend not to fully address wider contextual considerations of social change. Theories of tendencies are often located within evolutionary theories of change (e.g. Parsons, 1966), which, as discussed earlier, tend not to emphasize the role of human agency in change.

Abrams (1982) elucidates the richness and complexity of change in industrial society, asserting that in preindustrial society the whole life was encompassed within a relatively limited array of social roles. Social positions were fixed and tightly linked to roles, such as being a peasant, a lord, a merchant or a monarch, a child, a man or a woman, a believer or a heretic. These basic social positions governed and restrained every other action or possibility in life: peasants served their lords and the whole process of production was contained within that relationship; the social standing of an individual's family determined their occupation and marriage opportunities; children were reared within the family and perpetuated its status by taking on the economic functions and social position of their parents. However, the range of occupations increased enormously during industrialization, and the strong connection between family background and occupational task was broken. The work of production, government, administration and education became divided into distinct tasks performed by people specifically recruited for that purpose. Abrams (1982) argues that life became more fragmented from the individual's point of view. For example, being a child in a family was different from being a pupil in a school, and the child's occupational destiny was no longer necessarily the same as that of their parents. Other examples include the way that being a wife ceased to provide a status that determined the whole of a woman's working life and the way that family life became separated from work life. Thus, people's roles and status positions became less rigid, more fluid and differentiated.

Part of the change to industrialized society involves the development of early modernity to modernity. Giddens (1990) states that 'modernity' is a shorthand term for modern society, or industrial civilization, which has three main characteristics. First, 'modernity' refers to a set of attitudes that consider it possible for the world to be transformed by human intervention. Second, it comprises a set of economic institutions that relate to industrial production and a market economy. Third, it involves a range of political institutions that support the nation-state and mass democracy. Giddens argues that modernity is vastly more dynamic than any previous type of social order, largely as a result of these characteristics (Giddens, 1990, p.94). This changing social order, in philosophical terms, creates a general loss of certainty (Delanty, 2007). This is reflected in culture, with Baudelaire (1964) defining modernity as the fleeting, ephemeral experience of life in an urban metropolis, asserting that art must capture that experience. Modernity includes the development of an intellectual culture that relates to secularization and postindustrial life (Toulmin, 1992).

More specifically, Williams (1958) traces the meaning of 'culture' historically in relation to ways of life. In addressing the ethos of Industrial England (circa 1776–1890), he identifies five key words that have a particular resonance for the period: industry, democracy, class, art and culture. One example that embodies a changing understanding of culture in the transition from traditional to modern culture is the way in which the meaning of 'art' changed – from its original sense of a human attribute or skill to that of a particular group of skills of the imaginative or creative arts. The meaning of the 'artist' also changed during this period – from a broadly skilled person as artisan to someone with selected skills of the creative arts. Art was thus understood to be a special kind of truth – an imaginative truth, and the artist to be as a special person – someone artistic – the aesthete. Literature, music, painting, sculpture and drama were grouped together as 'the arts' and distinguished from other general human skills. Thus, a separation emerged between artist and artisan and between artist and craftsperson.

During this time, the word 'culture' also changed. Before industrialization, culture meant 'tending to natural growth', which led to a related idea of the process of human training. However, Williams (1958) shows how this notion of culture as human training changed again in the 19th century, moving from culture being 'of' something to culture being a 'thing in itself'. This covered four key aspects:

- A general state or habit of mind
- The general state of intellectual development in a society as a whole
- The general body of the arts
- A whole way of life – material, intellectual and spiritual

(Williams, 1958, p.xvi)

Williams traces the changing meaning of art and culture in relation to changes in economic, political and social life. By doing so, he shows how the meaning and status of 'knowledge' and how people are considered 'knowledgeable' are contingent upon historical circumstances and ongoing engagements with understanding life and its meaning. The changes to the meanings of the words 'art' and 'culture' relate to broader changes in the mode and relations of production, as well as changes to frameworks of participation. He posits that changes to notions of industry were linked to industrialization but went beyond that, to indicate new kinds of personal and social relationships. He argues that the emergence of this new sense of culture was a response not just to industrialization but also to the new social and political developments of democracy. A third influence was the new emphasis on personal and private experience, which also affected the meaning and practice of art. Together, a particular mode of production, a framework for participation and the individual's interaction and sensibility to material and ideational life-worlds constitute a culture – a culture through which the world is known and is made knowable.

Through industrialization, people became exposed to different ways of life. Abrams (1982) argues that social change from the industrial period onwards created a world that was more diverse and differentiated, citing Spencer, who calls it a world of 'complex heterogeneity'. This complex heterogeneity continued into the 20th century, as some nation-states became deindustrialized and developed into postindustrial societies.

Postindustrial society and late modernity

A postindustrial society is defined as a society in which a transition has occurred from a manufacturing-based economy to a service-based economy, a diffusion of national and global capital and mass privatization. The prerequisites for this economic shift are the processes of industrialization and liberalization. This economic transition spurs a restructuring in society as a whole.

Bell is a key figure in the debates surrounding the development of postindustrial society. In his 1973 work, *The Coming of Post-Industrial Society*, he describes the Soviet Union (USSR) and the United States as the only two industrialized nations. The dichotomy between the two was their opposing capitalist and collectivist mindsets. Although he is criticized by labor-process theorists (see below), he predicted many attributes of the postindustrial capitalist society, such as the global circulation of capital, the imbalance of international trade and the decline of the manufacturing sector in the United States domestic economy. Bell's (1973) perspective emphasizes that the changes to postindustrial society are not just structural and economic but also experienced by changing social values and norms, with rationality and efficiency becoming the paramount values within postindustrial society. Bell (1973) uses the notion of an axial principle[4] to define the character of society, which acts as an energizing principle for all the other dimensions of society. In postindustrial society, Bell argues, the axial principle is 'theoretical knowledge', which becomes increasingly important in the economy, along with a corresponding rise in professional, scientific and technical groups in society.

Ritzer (1993) notes that the economy has moved from one based on the production of goods to one based on the provision of services. One sees, for instance, that manufacturing declines and the selling of entertainment experiences and offering advice on investments increases. There are certain sectors that predominant, which include health, education, research and government services. Another factor in the transition is that the predominance of manual labor declines (e.g. factory assembly line workers) and one sees a rise in professional (such as lawyers) and technical work (such as computer programmers). In particular, one sees is the rise of scientists (e.g. engineers with specialist knowledge, such as genetics, electrics or data analytics) as an important group in the economy. These changes are based on a shift from the importance of practical know-how to importance of theoretical knowledge in a postindustrial society. Theoretical knowledge is seen as the basic source of innovation (e.g. the knowledge created by those scientists involved in the Human Genome

Project is leading to new ways of treating many diseases). These types of developments in knowledge also produce a need for other innovations, such as dealing with the ethical questions raised by advances in cloning technology.

These developments place the emphasis on theoretical rather than empirical knowledge, and on the codification of knowledge. The exponential growth of theoretical and codified knowledge, in all its varieties, is central to the emergence of the postindustrial society. In postindustrial society, there is a strong focus on needing to assess the impacts of the new technologies and, where necessary, to exercise control over them. There is a belief – and indeed – hope that society can monitor machines like nuclear power plants and to improve them so that accidents like those at Chernobyl or Fukushima can be prevented in the future. The goal is to have a safer and more secure technological world. To handle such assessment and control and, more generally, the sheer complexity of postindustrial society, new intellectual technologies and methodologies are developed and implemented. These include cybernetics, game theory and information theory. The above developments mean that a new relationship is forged in the postindustrial society between scientists and the technologies they create, as well as the systematic technological growth that lies at the base of postindustrial society. This leads to the need for more universities and university-based students to create increased technological knowledge and innovation. In fact, university is crucial for the postindustrial society, producing experts who can create, guide and control the new and dramatically changing technologies.

Ritzer (1993) argues that this focus on theoretical knowledge and services also feeds into a culture that aligns itself with the creative industries. He suggests that adults with a tertiary education are in the best position to thrive in an increasingly technological society. This relates to another change in society, whereby education now focuses on producing people who seek to develop their creativity and self-expression. The drive for tertiary education, both in terms of improving employability and in terms of self-development, has resulted in the development and expansion of the tertiary education sector, with more providers offering a wider variety of formats and course designs. This results in a blurring of credit and noncredit workforce offerings across the tertiary landscape and is more often based within countries who have – or who are committed to attaining – future high engagement in the information economy (Kasworm, 2007).

Kasworm (2007) argues that the development and variety of tertiary offers and the uptake of these offers is found in countries with higher levels of education, which support and attract a greater involvement of adults in postsecondary and continuing education activities. Kasworm cites the examples of Australia, Canada, the United Kingdom, the United States, Norway, Sweden and Israel, each of which has 30% or more adult students within their total tertiary enrolments (Kasworm, 1993). Kasworm continues by writing that another, equally important trend is that of adult participation in job-related continuing education and training. For example, in the OECD countries of Denmark, Finland, Sweden and the United States, research found that more than 35% of their population aged 25–64 years had participated in some type of nonformal job-related continuing education and training in the previous 12 months (Organization for Economic Co-operation and Development, 2007, p.348).

Another trend is in the broader realm of adult learner participation. In 2004–2005, 52% of the United States's adults participated in formal courses and training programs offered by a private business, company, hospital or tertiary institution (O'Donnell, 2006). Kasworm (2007) points out that there is also a significant but often undocumented involvement of educated professionals who participate in additional, self-directed learning through providers including professional organizations, tertiary continuing education providers, private providers and a number of self-managed learning groups. Those adults participating in continuing professional development are working towards varied professional qualifications in subject areas such as medicine, engineering, education, business and technologies. Kasworm (2007) argues that, by drawing on various sources, it is possible to speculate that between 70% and 80% of these professionals are engaged in continuing education each year, with many professional groups in the United States and Canada mandating involvement in continuing professional development to maintain best practice in their employment.

These trends give some indication of the rise of continuing education in its many different forms. This engagement with education is creating an environment in which individuals are reflexive and creative in late modern culture, thereby gaining the ability to contribute to the creative industries. Another aspect of late modern society is the doctrine of speed, mobility and malleability, which is well suited to the rapid innovation cycles of the dynamic creative industries. This combination of good technical skills, creativity as defined in late modern terms and a general sensitivity to managing rapid and fluid change provides an ideal environment for creative types. Creative professionals' skills suit the tertiary and quaternary sectors, which provide services focusing on finance, education, communication, management, training, engineering and aesthetic design. The development of creative industries in postindustrialist society is reflected by the economic history of postindustrial societies, where there is a move from economic activities in the primary and secondary sector to creative activities in the tertiary and quaternary sectors.

Bell (1973) discusses some characteristics of change in postindustrial society, which are outlined above. However, he is criticized for not addressing some of the continuities from industrial society, such as the conflict between management and labor and the persistence of gender inequalities (McLoughlin, 1999). Furthermore, Lyon (1988) argues that Bell's approach does not fully account for how class-based distinctions are influential in shaping society. Touraine (1971) raises the issue of class dynamics and reasserts the question of class conflict by arguing that there is a major cleavage between a technocratic class and disparate social groupings whose lifestyles and livelihoods are governed by technology. The dominant class of technocrats holds power through its knowledge and its control of information, and the rise of social forecasters forms a new stratum that wields power through their knowledge and planning capacity. Perkin (1990) suggests that certified expertise is the 'organizing principle of post-war society', in which the 'expert' has displaced once-dominant groups with an ethos of service, certification and efficiency. Gouldner (1979) goes further, identifying a new class 'composed of intellectuals and technical intelligentsia'. This new class is divided in various ways, with some members taking technocratic and conformist positions and others – humanist intellectuals – taking a critical and emancipatory stance.

This distinction helps to identify which people have the knowledge and power to shape social and economic developments. It may also indicate which groups are in subordinate positions and how this is materializing in working conditions and in class- or status-based social formations. The development of techno-elites or technocrats (Robins and Webster, 1999) is a significant factor because such individuals and groups have powerful leverage over social, economic and political affairs. These elites are empowered by their communication skills, analytical abilities, foresight and capability to formulate strategic policies; and their skills are often obtained through privileged education, shared clubs, boardrooms and access to Information and Communication Technologies (ICT) (Robins and Webster, 1999). The rise of theoretical knowledge, the reconfiguration of class positions and new sources of power give some indication of social change in the postindustrial society, raising the following question: what are the specific aspects and necessary prerequisites of an information society (Webster, 1995)?

Information society, late- and postmodernity

In relation to the information society, the question is whether information and its circulation via ICT or digital technology is a central dynamic in changing social relations and society, and whether information is therefore an axial principle. Lyon (1988) criticizes Bell, asserting that his analysis underestimates the resilience of some existing patterns of social relations and the extent to which new conflicts and struggles could arise in the information society, because it does not address the social relations aspect of this development. Lyon claims that, in order to understand postindustrial society and information society, analysts should seek to identify who holds the theoretical knowledge, which groups carry out the practical tasks determined by theoreticians and what the structures are for doing so. If information and its use through ICT is a key dynamic in socioeconomic relations, then researchers need to analyze how it is changing the social relations of production and consumption in society.

Technological innovation is often cited as defining the information society, because developments in ICT-based information management and communications have led to the pervasive implementation of ICT throughout social life. Within this technological determinist perspective, a convergence argument about the networking of computers is compared to the provision of electricity in the industrial age, in that the 'information grid' is considered analogous to the electrical supply (Webster, 1995). The development of technology is seen as an evolutionary process in which Integrated Services Digital Networks (ISDNs) and Digital Broadband technology provide the basis of an information society. Once these information networks are established, they become the highways of the information age in the same way that roads, railways and canals were the highways of the industrial era; thus, 'computer technology is to the information age what mechanization was to the industrial revolution' (Naisbitt, 1984, p.28). This determinist approach towards technology simplifies the process of change and posits that society becomes an information society when there is a critical level of technology take-up (Webster, 1995). This is a reductionist approach because it does not consider the complexity of social change or the fact that technological change also requires institutional change.

Freeman (1992a, 1994) counters this technological determinist view, arguing that it is the way technology is embedded within innovation cycles that gives it meaning in socioeconomic change[5]. Researchers at the Science Policy Research Unit (SPRU), based at the United Kingdom's University of Sussex, take a neo-Schumpeterian approach to sociotechnical change. Their approach combines Schumpeter's theory of innovation with Kondratieff's theme of 'long waves' of economic development, to explain how ICT represents the establishment of a new epoch. This perspective avoids a reductionist technological determinism by analyzing change through techno-economic paradigms (Freeman, 1992b, 1994). Freeman (in Mansell and Steinmuller, 2000) argues that an information-based economy is set to mature early in the 21st century and supports Piore and Sabel's (1984) argument that much of this economy will be characterized by flexible specialization, in which small production units respond rapidly to niche markets with customized products or services being produced by adaptable, multiskilled workers.

This type of production is related to the idea of a network – both the network as an organizational form (Castells, 2001) – and a networked society (Castells, 1996). Information society production and consumption is facilitated by network s based on ICT (Castells, 2001). Castells (1996) argues that the rise of networks based on ICT, which link people, institutions and countries, characterize contemporary society. The purpose of these networks is for information to flow in what he defines as an 'informationalized society' – one in which 'information generation, processing, and transmission become the fundamental sources of power and productivity' (Castells, 1996, p.21). The significance of this for Castells is that it is 'the new information technology paradigm [which] provides the material basis for the network's pervasive expansion throughout the entire social structure' (Castells, 1996, p.469). Thus, the network provides the infrastructure of society. However, this raises questions regarding the character of the networks' social relations, the role of institutions and information as a commodity within them.

Fuchs (2008) addresses this issue, arguing dialectically between the dynamics of old and new social relations. He defines a networked society as one that comprises transnational network capital or transnational informational capitalism, proposing that networked ICT provides the technological infrastructure that facilitates a global network of capitalism. However, he does not abstract this out of social relations, because networked capitalism involves regimes of accumulation, regulation and discipline. These economic, institutional and cultural factors make use of ICT to coordinate global production, distribution and consumption, and they require new strategies for executing corporate and political power and domination. Some of these strategies involve restructuring the organization of capital. This includes the rise of dynamic nodes of production that can be formed and reformed within a more fluid economic, political and cultural global marketplace.

However, this capitalism retains many of its traditional features, the principal one being that it is based on structural inequalities. There are central hubs such as global cities and technopoles[6] that have the power and resources to centralize the production, control and flows of their economic, political and cultural capital (Fuchs, 2008), in contrast to the industrial era's nation-state centers. Therefore, networks are used in economic activity, while society is still characterized by the social relations of capitalism. Both Marxist perspectives and postindustrial approaches suggest that there have been many changes in the patterns of production and consumption. Some scholars seek to measure this change based on categories of economic activity and occupation, which are considered next, before returning to the issue of social relations and restructured capitalism.

Machlup (1962) seeks to assess the size and growth of the information industries by establishing measures of the information society in economic terms. He identifies five broad industry groups: education; communication media (radio, TV, advertising); information machines (computer equipment, musical instruments); information services (law, insurance, medicine); and other information activities (research and development, nonprofit activities). He argues that, as early as 1958, 29% of the United States' Gross National Product (GNP) came from the knowledge industries. This led management commentators such as Drucker (1969) to argue that knowledge was the foundation of the economy, with a shift from an economy of goods to an economy of knowledge, with its organization being the prime creator of wealth (Porat, 1977). However, as Webster (1995) states, there is a methodological problem of categorization here because work-related outputs are divided between informational and noninformational domains, whereas the division between 'thinking' and 'doing' is ambiguous. For example, it is difficult to identify the division between 'thinking' and 'doing' in operating the computerized line management functions that are an integral element of the production process. The second complication is that the aggregated data homogenize a vast range of economic activities, although, as Webster (1995) argues, informational activities vary qualitatively: for example, four million sales of The Sun newspaper cannot be equated with, or considered more informational than the 200,000 circulation of the Financial Times, even though the sales are doubtless of more economic value. On top of the ambiguities of measuring information work, there is also the issue of identifying 'at what point on the economic graph does one enter an information society?' (Webster, 1995, p.56).

Another theoretical approach focuses on occupational profiles within a society, contending that it becomes an 'information society' when the majority of occupations are based on informational work (Webster, 1995). This argument asserts that the 'information society' has arrived when clerks, teachers, lawyers and entertainers outnumber coalminers, steelworkers, dockworkers and builders, and it is frequently combined with economic measures (Porat, 1977; Stonier, 1983). This recognition of the changing distribution of occupations is a central aspect of sociological approaches, which contend that there is a postindustrial society, and which have informed debates regarding the information society.

Bell (1973) suggests that a postindustrial society comprises a 'white collar society', in which there is a rise of service-related work, including informational work, with a corresponding decline of industrial labor. There is continuity in some of these positions in terms of exploring an information society. These include positing that changes in occupational structures results in changes in the social realm, such as the end of class-based political conflict, the development of a more communal consciousness and increased equality between the sexes. Many of the discussions regarding information society fuse with those of the emergence of a postindustrial society, but neither approach adequately identifies a new society that is either an information society or a postindustrial society (Webster, 1995).

The drive towards networked communication and the networked organization of economic production has a spatial dimension to it, which, when taken with other dimensions of change, starts to allude to the richness needed to define the information society. The logic of networks is that they connect locations globally, overriding the industrial organization of space and time, thereby introducing the capacity to alter the organization of capitalism or nation-states.

Goddard (1992) shows how four interrelated elements in the transition to an informational economy are related spatially via networks:

1. Information is a 'key strategic resource' on which the world economy is dependent.

2. Computer and communication technologies provide the infrastructure that enables information to be processed and distributed.
3. There is a rapid growth of the 'tradable information sector' seen in the expansion of new media and online bases of information, as well as in the reorganization of the world's financial system with the development of high finance trading.
4. The growing 'informatization' of the economy is, with supporting policy and infrastructures, facilitating the integration of national and regional economies.

(cited by Webster, 1995, p.18)

Therefore, Goddard (1992) argues from a geographical perspective that these trends when taken together emphasize the centrality of information networks linking together locations within and between towns, regions, nations, continents and the world. This partly addresses Webster's (1995) point that networks have played a role in social life in both traditional and industrial societies, which means considering how new ICT-based networks are significant in forming an information society. In a geographical sense, one can see changes that interact with the economy, which impact on national and regional society. Part of the social dimension of this trend is the cultural characteristics of the various flows of information and the way these interact with contemporary culture. Castells (2001) notes in his analysis of the Internet in economic and business terms that the networking logic of the Internet has spatial consequences. He suggests that the digitally networked organization of business is creating mega-cities and digital regions as global nodes and generating migration from rural areas to these global nodes. Sassen (2002) picks up on some of these spatial globalizing trends and analyzes them in terms of the growth of global cities, and in the relationship between citizens and nation-states. She notes that, in institutional terms, the idea of citizenship being tightly related to nation-states is being unsettled through globalization and this rise of the global city.

Sassen (2002) addresses the conditions of migration and the agency of migration in terms of power dynamics within global cities, stating that the negotiation of power by citizens, states and global corporations is the context in which 'aliens' or migrants seek to construct their own social and economic lives. She argues that this context provides opportunities to consider how membership of contemporary society is both localized and transnational. This requires a radical approach to understanding the way membership is negotiated between institutions such as the state and people living in cities – whether they are citizens of the nation in which the city is located, or migrants. Thus, as with the other characteristics of the information age, the relation between agency and institutions is based on the logic of networks and it is one that requires a reconsideration of the relationship between institutions and agency.

Sassen's (2002) analysis of globalization and migration alludes to another issue in late modernity, which is the way that power can be negotiated in contemporary society. A distinctive feature of power is that of 'discourse' and how discourse shapes particular power relations. Foucault views discourse as systems of thoughts, which are compiled from ideas, attitudes, beliefs and practices that combine systematically to construct subjects, objects and worlds. The role of discourse, for Foucault, is in the wider social processes that give legitimacy to social order and authority to existing power relations. Foucault (1977, 1980) argues that power and knowledge are interrelated, and, therefore, human relationships are struggles in the negotiation of power. The way that discourse works and operates power is through the rules of exclusion (1977, 1980). The dynamics of inclusion and exclusion in the way migrants negotiate the city is therefore, in Foucauldian terms, shaped through discourse.

The circulation of discourse is a key feature of late modern society. Discourse permeates every aspect of social life, and one way it is circulated is through the media. An important element of contemporary culture is the pervasiveness of the media circulating a large amount of information in daily life, spanning the public and private spheres. In Westernized countries, there is a high penetration of television, radio and new media. In such contemporary society, social experience is mediated (Smith, 1988) by actors adapting, rejecting, interpreting and using media in different ways (Harrison and Wessels, 2005; Silverstone, 2005a). The web-enabled mobile phone, for instance, is a central communication medium for organizing everyday personal and work life as well as circulating information and news (Haddon, 2004, 2008). One of the main developments of 21st-century society is social media, such as Facebook and Twitter. These digitally enabled services facilitate what Castells (2009) calls 'mass self-communication', whereby individuals within mass society communicate directly with each other at scale via social media. The content of these media is generated and shared across social media networks by the users themselves (Bontcheva, Gorrell and Wessels, 2013). Commercial companies and public sector organizations also use social media for marketing and raising awareness of their companies and products (OECD, 2013a). A further development of social media is what the OECD calls the 'app economy', where mobile applications (or 'apps') are increasingly used for business-to-customer communication and to encourage two-way dialogue with customers and organizations (OECD, 2013b). Social media is thus highly integrated into people's personal lives. All mass media, including social media, has an extensive reach, which informs – but does not necessarily determine – the style and aesthetics of individuals, homes and lifestyles within their symbolic and cultural lives (Webster, 1995). The intrusion of information in these realms is accomplished through the international advertising businesses, publishing empires, the fashion industry and global agencies of media production.

With regard to this trend, some commentators argue that the culture of an information society can be understood as being postmodern. Information society and its culture can be seen in the 'explosion of signification' in contemporary society. Baudrillard (1994) argues that the 'death of the sign' has occurred in media-saturated societies through the circulation of more and more information, which has less and less meaning. Previously, clothes used to signify status, a political statement or a political philosophy, and television news reflected world events. However, the way in which the reach of media has expanded and has reworked symbols means that signs no longer signify such an established symbolic order or social meaning – thereby potentially emptying meaning from representation. Many people in the Western world, therefore, experience social life as hyperreality, as spectacle and artificiality, which Poster (1990) defines as a new 'mode of information'[7]. Although there is a proliferation of media-generated images, it is the way in which these are interpreted and adapted in social life that grounds them and gives them significance within social formations. Hence, they have become just one aspect of the ways in which life becomes meaningful to individuals – they are part of culture, rather than a determination of culture.

To be more specific and with respect to the difficulties of observing and understanding social and technological change, Mansell and Steinmuller (2000) assert that it is difficult to assess change in an information society because the transformations occurring in the use of the ICT infrastructure are so pervasive. Their research on developments towards an information society in Europe finds that the use of new ICT and services is influencing not only the costs of inputs and the nature of economic outputs but also the way in which work is organized and skills are articulated. For instance, if researchers want to assess the potential effects of a specific feature of information society developments, such as the growth in e-commerce, it is necessary for them to take into account the possible implications that e-commerce will have on existing ways of doing business, the organization of work and the use of leisure time. They see an associating structural transformation of the labor force with the spread of ICT infrastructure, which leads to a growth in the service economy, along with a growing need for technological advances to improve service activity and productivity. These service outputs are extremely malleable and can change rapidly, including altering the way that labor is organized, through innovations such as call centers, user-support hotlines and direct marketing automation.

In their research, Mansell and Steinmuller (2000) argue that changes in the economy cannot be attributed exclusively to the development of ICT and the diffusion of new services. The increasing levels of education and the expansion of specialized labor make it possible to engage in a growing variety of activities that are connected with, or ancillary to, the production of goods and services. They posit that the development of an information society is extremely difficult to predict, pointing out that any new development has to be carved out from incumbent legacies and must embrace insurgent strategies – not only for economic competitiveness and improving political engagement but also to facilitate a virtual community strategy to underpin an ICT-literate society. Mansell and Steinmuller (2000) assert that these aspects of change involve the mobilization of society across all dimensions and require an expansion of the vision of information society by dynamic players and emergent communities. This observation suggests that any analysis of the information society must include broader social and economic issues as they interact with cultural and political dynamics.

The discussion so far shows how patterns of production, distribution and consumption are changing and the fact that ICT forms part of those changes. They are configured around a rethinking of the use of information in economic and cultural life, in which the features of social relations based on capitalism are retained. A key feature of these trends is the development of a data economy, with one emerging trend being the development of a movement advocating open access to data (Wessels, Finn, Smallwood and Wyatt, 2014). The amount of data being collected from a variety of social and digital media provides huge potential for both the public and private sector. This data is being described as the 'new oil' (Sveinsdottir, Wessels, Smallwood and Linde, 2013) because of its value to the knowledge economy, demonstrating the real economic value that data created through the Internet and Web-enabled financial and commercial transactions. Thus, information and data start to become significant resources in terms of capital accumulation.

To trace some of these trends spanning both continuity and change, Fuchs (2008) argues that a society based on informational capitalism is a class society, because capital accumulation achieved through knowledge is a stratifying, class-forming process. He notes the current ambiguities of change by pointing out that knowledge labor is simultaneously a nonclass and a class, based on the argument that economic class is a relational economic category. He defines knowledge labor in a similar fashion to the postindustrial trends discussed above – as labor that produces information, communication, social relationships and ICT. According to this definition, knowledge labor is not a separate class, but an economic production process constituting a vertical sector of the economy. This quaternary sector produces knowledge and so, in these terms, knowledge labor is a nonclass.

The crux of Fuchs' argument is that, by viewing knowledge as a broad social category instead of a narrow sector-specific economic category, it becomes evident that it lies at the heart of class formation in informational capitalism. Knowledge forms part of the commons of society; it is a social product that is produced and consumed by all and includes educational knowledge, entertainment knowledge, practical knowledge, technological knowledge and public infrastructures (for instance, institutions in the areas of health, education, medical services, social services, culture, media and politics). There is, therefore, a blurring of clear, observable class distinctions because most people contribute to the production and reproduction of the commons while global capital exploits surplus value. Therefore, although there is some evidence of changing occupational categories and cultural change, broadly speaking the social relations of capitalist society are being reproduced in new forms. These theorizations give some indication of the complexity of researching and understanding social change.

Conclusion

This chapter shows that social change is complex and multidimensional. It describes the key characteristics of four main types of society – feudalism, industrial society, postindustrial society and information society. The way in which transitions between these types of society occur is through the inter-action of economic, political and cultural dimensions of social life. Social relations within society change over historical time as the means of produc-tion change, as trade routes and international relations change and as the status of individuals change; their capacity for agency changes through polit-ical processes and the way that social life is organized in the development of institutional frameworks. In many ways, it shows how social change is cultural, because the economic, political and social spheres are made mean-ingful through culture – and cultural change is the process where change is negotiated.

Thus, it is evident that culture has changed from being embedded in ways of life in premodern times through being abstracted as a domain within industrial society, to being circulated globally – with cultural representations losing their meanings once they are taken out of their contextual frameworks. Therefore, each key period of change has its own social and cultural framework through which social life is experienced. In exploring some aspects of change through time, the process in which agency and institutions interact to give change its dynamism becomes clear. Change occurs through structural transformation – seen mainly in economic terms – but also in terms of agency, in the ways that people negotiate their new realities. Both combine to create institutional change.

4

Exploring the Dimensions
of Change

Introduction

The discussion about social change so far has raised the point that there are different dimensions of change. The way these dimensions configure to catalyze change while simultaneously changing themselves is an important characteristic of change. An aspect of these dimensions is the way each might relate to the other and articulate change through their relationship; this characteristic emphasizes the external relations between dimensions. Another related aspect is the way these dimensions may change internally during periods of social change and have their own internal dynamic, for example the way the experience of work and its institutional framework changes in different historical periods. This chapter covers several main areas of social life as dimensions of change, considering each dimension in terms of its own internal characteristics as well as its relation to broader social, economic, political and cultural dimensions of social change. The preliminary exploration of these dimensions also starts to indicate the way that relationships between agency and institutional frameworks change over time.

The areas covered in this chapter are as follows: first, the character of the individual as it materializes through specific social relations; second, the way modes of production are changing within the current global information economy; third, the dynamics consumption; fourth, changes sense of everyday life; fifth, culture – specifically in terms of entertainment; and sixth, this chapter considers the changing practice of power that is indicative of social change, in terms of legitimating structures and forms of participation.

The character of the individual within social relations

In modern and late modern discourse the use of the word 'individual' is taken for granted, however, the idea of human beings as being autonomous, self-defining units only emerged during industrialization and through the culture of Romanticism.

Marx (1976) understood the rise of the individual in terms of the need for men and women to be free to sell their labor in the capitalist system. He noted that the way these individuals organized themselves and gained a sense of identity was through the structuring of society, which, in a capitalist society, is class based. Durkheim (1984) spoke about the rise of the individual and the sacredness of the individual, viewing the emergence of the individual in terms of a move from mechanical solidarity to the organic solidarity of a complex industrial society. He explained that, in the differentiation of industrial society, the individual gains a distinctive character and position through their work. He or she needs to be socialized into the social and cultural norms of society based on the fact that the moral order of society rests with the sacredness of the individual.

Weber (1922) addressed the idea of the individual through the lens of status, class and power, which nonetheless sees the individual as a core unit of analysis in industrial society. Weber (1922, 1949) particularly noted that human action is meaningful and that humans attach meaning to their actions. He recognized that the ordering of industrial society creates bureaucracies that, while managing society, also produce an 'iron cage' in which individuals have little freedom. This lack of freedom is part of a greater societal ambience, one of disenchantment. He asserted that the rise of rational society organized along bureaucratic rules left many people without any imaginative or spiritual compass.

The way in which individuality was encountered in the industrial society was also based on class, status, power and gender. Individuality was experienced within gender relations at the same time that these positions were shaped by perceptions of gender, largely understood in patriarchal terms (Richardson and Robinson, 2008). These relations have changed over time and have been challenged by various women's movements. The suffragette movement fought to secure political rights for women, and this was followed by women activists fighting for women's access to education, health care and other social benefits. For instance, Eleanor Rathbone campaigned for improved welfare for women and Maria Stopes sought to increase women's control of their sexuality. Developments in feminism in the 1960s and 1970s resulted to a certain degree of greater equality with men and increased individual freedoms for women (Richardson and Robinson, 2008).

One element of the industrial process in the West was the legacies of colonialism and imperialism (Bhambra, 2007). This relationship involved identities that were based on a sense of the 'other'. Here, the sense of the individual was interlaced with perceptions of 'race', ethnicity and the idea of a 'native'. The way in which an individual was categorized during colonialism reflected characteristics of wider social relations based on the prominence of the Global North vis-à-vis their exploitation of the Global South. The status of the individual in the context of one aspect of this relationship, slavery, was one in which the individual had no freedom and could be bought and sold as a commodity. The colonial and imperial relationship that defined race and ethnicity in this case cut across the meaning of the individual. Following social reformers' efforts that led to the abolition of slavery, these socially bound racial and ethnic identities were challenged by the civil rights movement in the United States in the 1960s. In Europe, during the 1970s, ethnic protests triggered state-supported policies to promote multiculturalism. In contemporary society, these types of discourses have developed further, with a general recognition of the advantages of society being diverse. Thus, changes in understanding the significance of an individual emerge in terms of the way that individuals are valued in society and in the establishment of the rights of the individual[1].

The sense of an individual who is located in a diverse society was reinforced in the transition to a postindustrial society, with globalization and the postimperial world. The notion of individuality was further influenced during this period by the rise of the consumer society. Consumer culture as a mass phenomenon is rooted in the Romantic movement of early to mid-industrial society. The Romantic ethic heightened senses of individuality since it involved a quest to achieve one's full potential as an individual (Campbell, 1987). Consumerism taps into this ethic because the way that individual fulfillment and achievement are realized is through the constant quest for new experiences. In later industrial society and the information society, this quest continues to be achieved via consumerism (Wessels, 2012).

The dynamics of these various trends and dimensions, from early industrial society onwards, has resulted in a particular form of highly individualized and individuated society. Giddens (1991) describes how the individual in late modernity is reflexive because the social relations and structures of individualism are less fixed and much more open to interpretation. The individual in late modernity has to construct his or her individuality through the process of creating identity. Beck (1992) provides important insights into the social relations of individualism in contemporary society[2], outlining the current paradox in individualism. This is one in which individuals are forced – or feel they choose – a life course that is liberated from personal and traditional obligations – and yet that very liberalized push to individualism can only be achieved through increased institutionalization of the individual. By freeing the individual from traditional ties and by loosening institutions such as marriage, the individual is dependent on market mechanisms and its supporting institutions such as education, welfare policies and personalized support services such as counselling. The individual in his or her individuated condition instead has to engage with the mechanics of the market, education and other support institutions, and consumer culture, in order to construct their own individuality.

To summarize, the experience of the individual is located in the social relations of any particular historical period. The notion of the individual has changed from something that was prescribed in feudal social relations to the concept of a reflexive individual who has to determine his or her own individuality in late modernity. The actions of individuals are framed by institutional structures and discourses. However, there is a dynamic relationship between agency and institutions that provides the contexts of types of individuality. Each type and experience of individuality is also negotiated through agency in relation to the institutional frameworks of the same period. Some of the influences shaping the general context of the relation between society and the individual are situated within the social and cultural aspects of production, which provide the economic and material actualities of social life.

Modes of production

The way we produce goods and services is socially organized. The characteristics of this social organization are often called 'modes of production', a term which originates in the work of Marx (1976). Marx considered that a mode of production has two main components – productive forces and the relations of production. Productive forces refer to the power of human labor and the available knowledge in relation to the type and level of technology in the means of production. This could include, for example, tools, equipment, buildings, technologies, materials and land. The relations of production refer to both social and technical relations, including the property, power and control relations governing society's productive assets, which are often codified in law; cooperative work relations and forms of association; relations between people and the objects of their work; and the relations between social classes.

Marx (1976) took an historical materialist approach to analyze the way in which humans socially produce the goods and services they need and desire. Although this approach, if taken in its absolute form, can be seen to be reductionist and determinist, it does show how production is historically shaped and produced. For instance, primitive communism was organized along traditional tribal structures, being typified by shared values and consumption of the entire social product. As no permanent surplus product was produced, there was no possibility of a ruling class coming into existence. The Asiatic mode of production was an early form of class society, where a semi-theocratic aristocracy extracted social surplus through violence from preslave and prefeudal communities in China, India and the Euphrates and Nile river valleys. The antique mode of production was different to this Asiatic mode in the sense that property was considered to be the direct possession of individual humans and the ruling class believed itself to be descendants of gods, or sought other justifications for its ruling status. Ancient Greek and Roman societies were the most typical examples of this mode.

Feudalism was discussed in the previous chapter, and, to recap, the primary form of property in that system was the possession of land worked by serfs in contract relations with the nobility. Early capitalism saw the development of wage labor in which the bourgeoisie extracted surplus from the proletariat. The key forces of production in that structure included the overall system of modern production with its supporting structures of bureaucracy, the modern state and, above all, finance capital.

The capitalist system was adaptable and flexible, and, in late modern society, it developed into various forms – such as monopoly capitalism or state or corporate capitalism (Sciulli, 2002). This latter form was widespread across nation-states and in the global process of capital accumulation. In 21st-century contemporary society, this form predominates in a modern mixed economy, which is largely based on oligarchical multinational corporations with a highly socialized and globalized system of production. The failed centrally planned economic systems of the earlier communist bloc nation states were not genuinely egalitarian but were, in fact, state-induced industrialized economies based on another form of exploitation. Marx and Engels (1974) thought that state capitalism would emerge as the final form of capitalism before the contradictions would reach a point where capitalism could no longer sustain itself and socialism would emerge as its successor. It is, however, important to understand the details of the social organization of production in order to appreciate that production – and the work that produces goods and services – are not necessarily determined by the forces of production or the relations in which that work is embedded.

The organization of capitalist production has changed from an industrial society to a postindustrial service economy and information society (McLoughlin, 1999). The general context is the move from Fordist to post-Fordist modes of production, which are reshaping both work and social and cultural life, including, for instance, the readjustment of women's roles in the workplace and their related roles in everyday life. Fordism refers to the use of the assembly lines, standardization and mass markets based on class that primarily characterized production and consumption between the 1940s and 1960s (McLoughlin, 1999). However, this production model was undermined by national economic recessions within the manufacturing and industrial sectors and the emergence of globalization in the mid-1970s. Post-Fordism signifies a change to more flexible production for niche markets based on diverse consumer typologies and preferences. Production is now often based on 'just-in-time' processes, which are, in part, enabled through ICT on a global scale. This has meant a rise in white-collar and service sector jobs in which there is a feminization of the workforce (McLoughlin, 1999). Shifts to post-Fordism have created new dynamics of social inclusion and exclusion, which interact with aspects of the digital divide such as needing the relevant skills to work in the new economy (Wessels, 2013). Post-Fordism is closely interrelated with the consumer society and the development of mass consumption, trends which form part of the globalization of the economy, in which the production and consumption of goods is organized on a global scale.

A significant aspect of the global economy is e-business, which is 'any business activity whose performance of the key operations of management, finance, innovation, production, distribution, sales, employee relations and customer relations takes place predominantly by/on the Internet or other networks of computer networks, regardless of the kind of connection between the virtual and physical dimensions of the firm' (Castells, 2001, p.66). Castells argues that: 'by using the Internet as a fundamental medium of communication and information processing, business adopts the network as its organizational form' (Castells, 2001). He defines the network enterprise as a 'lean agency of economic activity, built around specific business projects, which is enacted by networks of various composition and origin: the network is the enterprise' (Castells, 2001, p.67). The capitalist firm continues to be the unit of accumulation of capital, property rights and strategic management, but networks perform their business practice. Networks are flexible and adaptable and can therefore meet the requirements of continuous innovation and the rapidly changing demands of the global economy. The role of the Internet in these kinds of network enterprises is that it enables 'scalability, interactivity and management of flexibility, branding and customization in a networked business world' (Castells, 2001).

The way in which the network materializes in practice is varied and is open to debate; however, the notion of virtual working can act as a sensitizing concept for discussing any possible changes in the character of work. Jackson (1999) identifies the key themes in the literature on virtual working as follows:

- The collapse of hierarchy and an erosion of boundaries, both within and between companies
- A concentration on 'information processing', in which teams and individuals, using ICT, create and manipulate information-based 'virtual' products
- The use of networked ICT to empower consumers, providing new ways of interacting with businesses and greater access to information about their products
- A movement away from employment relations, towards more arm's-length, contractual relationships with workers
- Transient, project-based work systems, involving networks of coworkers, suppliers and associated companies
- Flexibility in time and space, with interactions mediated by cyberspace
- Reduced use of 'centers', buildings and offices
- A sense of disembodiment, with imagery emphasizing a lack of physicality and corporeality

- An emphasis on continuous innovation and learning, and a capacity to rapidly reinvent business models

(Jackson, 1999, p.13)

These trends embody many of the characteristics of the social relations of production in the information society: an emphasis on the circulation and use of information, networking, the renegotiation of time and space, senses of the virtual and the real, ongoing learning throughout the life course and a shorter value chain between consumers and producers. The hallmarks of late capitalism are consumerism and financialization, a process whereby 'making money' is seen as key. Both of these practices are a means to sustain the flow and accumulation of capital (Castells, 2001).

This section has shown how modes of production have changed over time and how that change is realized through the way economic activity is organized in society. The development of capitalist relations, from feudal agrarian times was developed through trade and markets. Early capitalism developed industrial techniques and technologies, which led to the rise of an urban working class. Capitalism is flexible, and institutions, capital infrastructures including digital technologies and globalization have all shaped a networked capitalism that has speeded up innovation to meet the rapid changes of a global economy. Workers with the knowledge skills can adapt, shape and, to some extent, resist these changes by developing portfolio careers and finding ways to manage contract-based work, whereas those who cannot compete in such a mobile and contractual market become increasingly excluded from the flexible labor market. The demise of union power in this context means that workers have less institutional support to manage labor relations, so their agency rests in their own ability to navigate the labor market.

Patterns of consumption

Although consumption takes place in all human cultures, it has only existed on a mass scale in the 20th and 21st centuries, as a foundational rather than epiphenomenal characteristic of advanced economies (McCracken, 1988). It is only in the context of subsistence production that one finds what can be termed 'subsistence consumption'. This is where everything that is produced is consumed, so there is no surplus – either in terms of products or services. In this context, items such as food and clothes may appear plain and functional to Western consumers, who are used to abundance and choice. Such minimalist societies only exist in extreme conditions, such as in areas of severe poverty in the Global South.

In any society whose social relations of production create surplus, the way that surplus is distributed is contentious (McCracken, 1988). The distribution of surplus in capitalist economies usually follows class and status demarcations. The upper, upper-middle and middle classes benefit more from the allocation of consumer resource and power than those who occupy working class or underclass positions. This fits the Marxist thesis, whereby the allocation of resource is based on class, defined through the economics of the social relations of production. In a society based on inequality, there are people who are redundant in the 'reserve army of labour', whose consumerism is at the level of subsistence, as they struggle to afford basic necessities. However, the development of a consumer society has also created what Bauman (2007) terms the 'new poor'. Bauman (2007) raises the issue that, in consumer society, poverty cannot only be understood from the more traditional point of view of being excluded from productive labor, by being unemployed. Bauman asks what poverty means in a consumer society, viewing it as being seen as 'flawed consumers', who are the new 'reserve army of labour'. He argues that this leaves the new poor 'without a social function that has far reaching consequences for the social standing of the poor and their chances of improvement' (Bauman, 2007, p.4). However, the production of surplus and proliferation of consumer goods and services provides an accessible market for consumerist pleasure for the affluent groups in society.

In both cases, whether individuals can participate in consumer society or are excluded from it, consumerism touches on senses of alienation (Lefebvre, 1984, 1991; Pilgram and Steinert, 2007). If relations between people are commoditized and people feel estranged from each other and from their work, then consumerism feeds that alienation, whether individuals are incorporated in an ongoing consumer logic or are excluded from it through their lack of resources (Steinert and Pilgram, 2007). The discussion of consumerism so far sees consumer society as one based on production – where production creates surplus, which drives and shapes consumer markets. Alienation feeds into the cycles of production and consumption, and these dynamics work through a society creating inequalities that are material and symbolic, being expressed though status positions of varying sorts.

It is important to keep the production aspect of consumerism in mind. However, the pervasiveness of consumerism across all groups in market-based societies raises questions about the relation between production and consumption. Campbell (1987) argues that the industrial revolution necessarily entailed a simultaneous revolution in production *and* consumption: just as making money came to be seen as an end in itself, so the consumption of goods came to be seen as an end in itself, and both of these represented a new convention. In traditional society, particular patterns of 'proper' consumption could be learned, but in modern society a general orientation to consuming is acquired. Campbell (1987) contends that, just as the Protestant work ethic provided the spirit of production, Romanticism, with its cult of the expressive individual, was central in providing the spirit of consumerism. In this way, just as the working classes were fundamental to the development of production, the readers of novels – to take just one example – were fundamental to the development of consumption.

Rather than seeing production as driving the dynamics of consumerism, consumerism is thus seen as both driving and shaping production. Commentators such as McKendrick, Brewer and Plumb (1982) maintain that, because so many people have access to the 'ever growing consumerist fruit of the productivist tree' (McKendrick et al., 1982), it is time to turn Marx on his head and argue that consumption, rather than production, is the central motor of contemporary 21st-century society. Corrigan (1997) points out that competition among and between status groups is a key driver of consumer society. He draws on Weber's (1990, [1948]) assertion that status groups are organized around modes of consumption, stating that this competition between status groups is now more important than a class struggle organized around the modes of production.

Consumerism has a long history. McCracken (1988) argues that the court of Queen Elizabeth the First fostered consumption among noblemen as a way of catching her attention and gaining attention through the types of goods they consumed. The Industrial Revolution, which created the capacity to produce surplus goods, triggered changes in patterns of consumption. Developments in marketing and the rise of the middle classes also played a role in the development of consumerism. The dynamics of changes around consumption relate to the fact that having socially 'correct' goods confers social status, which are increasingly signified and understood through marketing and advertising.

The rise of mass consumerism in the United Kingdom is generally acknowledged to have occurred in the period after the Second World War, from the 1950s[3] and extending into the rest of the 20th and early 21st centuries, when the working classes employed in the growth sectors were also propelled into the class of consumers. Women with their own incomes shaped female consumerism of products such as clothes, curtains, linens, pottery, cutlery, furniture and fashion accessories. The focus on consumer goods for the home and in fashion is significant in sociological analysis because they are important in the spheres of the economy and everyday life (Corrigan, 1997). These items developed huge markets, and the interpretation and agency of women in creating their home and personal surroundings is part of the process between the economy and everyday life that propels change. Furthermore, consumerism has become an ethic of the modern society in which the ideals of Romanticism are played out in contemporary forms of hedonism, travel, lifestyles and self-development. This has resulted in the development of lifestyles in which people construct their own identities from a range of consumer goods that are meant to express particular aspirations and ideological codes of living (Chaney, 1996).

The further strengthening of consumerism is integral to the global economy. One distinctive development in contemporary society is the rise of an e-economy through which consumerism is enabled via the Internet on a global scale (Wessels, 2010). There is continuity in some aspects of consumerism such as shopping, which has partly moved to online research and ordering systems.

What has changed is the way that cultural content and information is shared and developed by consumers themselves. Within a culture of popular democratization, social media enables nonprofessionals to create cultural content for other people to consume. This activity and its agency through individuals is an example of 'prosumerism', whereby production and consumption are more tightly linked by consumers' other role as producers (Wessels, 2012). The circulation of more goods and services globally raises concerns about environmental degradation (Beck, 1992; Lash, Szerszynski and Wynne, 1996). Lash and Wynne (1992) in the introduction to Beck's 1992 work point out that a global economy with high levels of consumerism will have environmental consequences. The individualization process within the development of a consumer society combines to form a cultural fabric that exploits environmental resources through cultural industries such as tourism, food and consumer experiences (Beck, 1992; Lash et al., 1996).

Although consumerism can be considered pervasive in contemporary developed society, this is not to say that people are just naively incorporated into a consumer ethic. Consumerism is debated across and between social groups – both what is deemed to be appropriate consumerism and the social relations of production. There are numerous interest groups and social movements as well as anticapitalist activists who question the consumer practices of the Western world. These critiques are often based on the fact that Western consumption depends on the exploitation of poorly paid Global South labor (Pahl, 1988). Another key critique of contemporary consumption is rooted in the environmental movement, which emphasizes how consumption exploits the world's natural resources and asserts that its global production infrastructure is creating environmental degradation (Lash et al., 1996). Therefore, as shown throughout this book, the sociocultural fabric enables critique and change. The rise of the environmental movement is a good example of this process, as it is producing a cultural ethos of green initiatives, lifestyles and alternative forms of production and consumption. These dynamics are all dimensions in the shaping of contemporary lifestyles and politics.

To summarize in general terms, as Campbell (1987) argues, contemporary consumerism is a type of duty – an obligation to engage in 'want satisfaction' as an 'end in itself'. This reveals an ethic underlying consumption just as for Weber there is an ethic underlying production. Likewise, if production can be linked to the Protestant work ethic, then consumption can be linked to the Romantic ethic. Consumerism has changed from elite and mass consumerism through to a consumerism that materializes itself in contemporary society in the form of lifestyles. Lifestyles articulate the relations of production and consumption in everyday life and they express agency in terms of consumer choices, whereby individuals express identity and status association. Lifestyles are also linked to the rise and significance of the creative and cultural industries in contemporary society.

Everyday life and cultural change

One way to understand everyday life is to consider the social and cultural forms through which everyday life is shaped and which, in turn, give shape and meaning to the everyday. These forms are located in, and in many ways structure, the situations of daily interaction in meaningful ways. The framework of social and cultural forms is applicable in the context of everyday life in that 'social and cultural forms which make sense of everyday life do so practically for their inhabitants and as representations to be observed, enjoyed, and interpreted as cultural performances' (Chaney, 2002, p.3). Generally speaking, the social sciences and humanities started to address everyday life as a distinct category in its own right when it became identified as a site for political and social engagement in the 1960s. Radical and countercultural movements during the 1960s not only affected university life but they were also located and played out within society more broadly. At that time, some genres of mass entertainment began questioning established conventions, social and gender orders. From these activities, the notion of everyday life became a focus for social theory as well as a theme of cultural representation (Crook, 1998). Crook suggests that since the early identification of the importance of everyday life for social thought, it has remained a significant domain when analyzing the cultural changes of late modernity.

Silverstone (1994, 2005a, 2006) asserts that technologies including ICT and media are located and given meaning through the dynamics of the everyday. According to the idea of a 'communicative turn' (Silverstone, 2005b) within late modernity, such new forms of communication are embedded within the social relations of everyday life. However, this includes not just the take-up and use of these technologies but also the way in which they become vehicles for forming meaning that shapes contemporary culture and the way it is experienced. These technologies are both a communicative medium and a source of representation and cultural content. Silverstone (1994) calls this their 'double articulation', whereby they comprise both a media artifact and a sphere of the production and interpretation of cultural content. The dynamics of the everyday can be both progressive and reactive, with some forms of communication being adopted within new ways of everyday life while everyday life proves resistant to some of the opportunities, or threats, that these new technologies may bring.

Within contemporary change and everyday life there is a rise of what can be termed 'popular democratization', in which populism is dominant in public discourse but which may not entail any substantial popular emancipation and, in which, there is a pervasive sense of cultural fragmentation (Chaney, 2002). Chaney does not use the term 'fragmentation' to imply that culture is becoming less important, but to suggest that the authority of a dominant culture is increasingly contested from a variety of perspectives (Chaney, 2002). Together, these processes are seen as part of a wider process of 'informalization' in which there is a blurring of many of the authority structures dominant in earlier phases of modernity. This undermining of a dominant culture has made 'the everyday' a focus for cultural criticism, and it has become a source of both cultural production and representation in cultural discourse (Chaney, 2002). None of this, however, means that everyday life has grown more 'transparent' or has ceased to be the context for social action (Silverstone, 1994, 2005a).

The concerns of everyday life in the second half of the 20th century and in the early 21st century have been, and continue to be, articulated and thus constituted through what Dorothy Smith (1988) calls the 'materiality of consciousness'. She suggests that consciousness is realized through artifacts, technologies and symbolic forms, which provide the means for overlapping physical and virtual environments, asserting that 'the simple social acts of tuning in, ringing up, and logging on can therefore have complex meanings for subjects' (Smith, 1988, p.86). This refers to the way these practices constantly overlay and interlace both the situated and the mediated worlds of late modernity (Moores, 2000, p.9).

The use of digital technology in everyday life is part of a broader change in institutional frameworks since it features in the disembedding of time and space within late modernity (Giddens, 1984). The development of mobility in everyday life (Urry, 2000) has also contributed to the way the everyday acts as a framework in which social identities are established and re-established. The different ways in which individuals play with and display their identities is a characteristic feature of the taken-for-grantedness of everyday life, which is not only accomplished at the local level but also draws on individuals' respective interaction with the creative and cultural industries. If everyday life appears to be local, then the borders of locality have been diffused or extended by engagements with cultural industries that have global reach (Kellner, 1995).

People achieve cultural change as they engage with the world around them, which is manifested through ordinary and extraordinary experiences and ordered through routines (Chaney, 2002). Cultural change is evident not only in the changing character of routines but also in the ways these routines (whether changing or static) are talked about and mediated in public discourse within modes of performance, including the 'factual', the 'fictional' and the 'staged' (Chaney, 2002). The alteration of routines is a significant part of change, seen for example in the concept of 'disruptive technologies', in which the use of technologies break established routines as part of the social constitution of change.

The dynamic character of cultural change means that any analysis of change must address both the substantive aspects of change, for instance, lifestyles and levels of engagement in types of entertainment, the forms and content of that change (Chaney, 2002). Forms includes structures of change framed by members of a community or culture, their sense of identity and selves, their characteristic discourses, representations and artifacts as well as their actions,

habits and accomplishments (Chaney, 2002). These aspects are interwoven
in the culture of everyday life, and can be seen in the relationship between
everyday life and personal settings, the way the self is dramatized in everyday
life, and the dynamic of authority and expertise in everyday life. The distinctive feature of change in everyday life in late modernity is its informalization,
whereby individuals, groups and communities actively create the routines and
meaning of their own daily lives. Some of that agency interacts with, and is
a response to, broader institutional change such as disenchantment and the
fragmentation of cultural authority.

Culture and entertainment

There has also been an expansion in the means of entertainment for most people in the Global North through, for example, the development of television as
a mass cultural form, the transformation of popular music using new means of
recording and distribution, the development of web-based cultures and a proliferation of types of performance (Chaney, 2002). There is debate about the
meaning of 'mass culture' and its dynamics. However, Strinati (1995) provides
a useful definition that frames the many aspect of this debate. He defines mass
culture as 'popular culture which is produced by mass production industrial
techniques and is marketed for a mass public of consumers' (Strinati, 1995,
p.10). Strinati refers to cultural products and forms including mass television,
Hollywood films, popular music and other forms of mass-produced entertainment. In many ways, mass culture is now more personalized, in that cultural
content can be distributed and accessed using digital technologies that allow
consumers to shape not only what content they want to receive but also how
and when they want to access it. Nonetheless, the culture of modern and late
modern life – as both content and practice – is often produced and shared
using the technologies and industries of mass communication, including the
pervasive use of digital technology.

Part of the development of mass culture was the expansion of leisure time
during the postwar period of the 1950s, 1960s and 1970s (Critcher, Bramham
and Tomlinson, 1995). This expansion led to the incorporation of entertainment into daily, weekly and yearly routines. For example, in the West, cinema
became a weekly cultural event for many people during the 1950s, annual
holidays increasingly became part of normal expectations and popular music
framed young people's lives. Although leisure time is still an important feature in social life, the development of flexible work patterns, contract-based
employment and new forms of parenting practices, the assumption of additional leisure time cannot be adopted without further consideration. On the
one hand, negotiations over the control of time and space have changed the
structure and rhythms of daily time and place, and, on the other hand, they
introduced a new range of consumer goods and services for the management

of time and location in everyday life. However, cultural and recreational activities are still a significant feature of social life and time is allocated into weekly routines for entertainment (Roberts, 2006).

The way entertainment and culture are embedded within social life show how mass and new media are appropriated in the ways people carve out time for their specific cultural interests. These interests include entertainment such as film, music and television or other leisure activities such as visiting museums, galleries and attending cultural events. Although there is debate about the level of agency people use to engage in culture, it is evident that cultural products, forms and genres are selected by individuals, groups and subcultures in the formation of their specific tastes and shared cultural understandings. Chaney argues that by people: 'adopting, using, rejecting – that is selecting amongst the performances, services and artefacts of mass culture industries – practical understandings are institutionalized' (Chaney, 2002, p.53). What this points to is that culture, entertainment and the media do not necessarily determine people's core expectations but they are nonetheless a key resource in the embodiment or materialization of cultural expectations and mores. Given this, it is therefore more useful to think of the 'products' of mass cultural industries as being environments rather than texts, performances or services (Chaney, 2002). This is because, when these products are used and brought together within cultural frameworks, they help to shape and constitute the everyday world through various types of entertainment and cultural interests. In a similar vein, Silverstone (2005b, 2006) suggests that the media are best understood as an environment that is made up of different platforms, channels and audience participation. The media environment is intimately linked with everyday life and its elements are mutually constitutive of the mediated and situated life, which are characteristic of late modern everyday life. However, as Silverstone (2005b) shows, this does not mean that media and its cultural content are straightforwardly adopted by consumers. Rather, he argues that it is the process by which both the forms of media and its content are interpreted and embedded in social life that locates a particular media and its content within broader a media environment and broader cultural frameworks.

The expansion in telecommunications through mobile phones and the development of digital networks has enabled people to create new spaces and sites for engaging in communicative and media practices. This means that traditional spaces for communication, entertainment and cultural performances such as theater, cinema, television, radio and phone are no longer the only places for communicative cultural activities (Wessels, 2010). These spaces are still key sites but have been expanded within environments in distinctive ways, such as digital video installations in built environments, social networking sites and social media and user-produced content on blogs, wiki-based media and media-sharing channels such as YouTube. The development of mobile media means that individuals can stay connected while on the move, becoming – in effect – the 'primary unit of connectivity' (Wellman and Haythornthwaite,

2002). This has resulted in individuals having to learn how to manage a network of people and places in different contexts, through the form of networked individualism (Wellman and Haythornthwaite, 2002). Most late modern Western citizens are networked individuals who are connected via digital technologies. Each individual has to manage the local and the global, work and domestic life, as well as their entertainment, communication and cultural activities through digital and social media.

The key change in the way entertainment is consumed and located in the 21st century is the heightened flexibility and selectivity of how people engage in culture. During the modern period, entertainment is differentiated with different forms and genres having established and clear practices of engagement. Thus, institutionally, entertainment was not only identified as having a distinctive culture (often in terms of 'high' versus 'popular' culture), but it also regulated through critics and experts to maintain certain levels of taste. In the late modern period, those institutional structures have been undermined to some degree, boundaries between high and popular entertainment have become blurred and now individuals can also act as content producers and share that content among networked audiences.

The modern sense of an audience has been undermined by networked individuals who can access entertainment in various places while they are mobile and in connection with other individuals who are often remotely located. In terms of engaging in entertainment, agency is distributed and selective across networks of consumer-producers. In institutional terms, the cultural and creative industries have harnessed the flexibility of digital technology to engage with audiences in new ways. There are still established ways to engage – through galleries, cinema, concerts and theater – and they still have authority in terms of cultural value. However, these forms of entertainment now coexist with more flexible, networked and interactive audiences, which are made up of self-selecting and highly interpretive individuals who can play with the genres of entertainment in a more ironic way. At times, there is agency in subverting cultural authority and, in other contexts, the power of traditionally produced entertainment to seduce audiences remains.

Practices of power

The way in which power materializes, is structured and practiced is located within the social relations of a particular historical society (Westwood, 2002)[4].

Marx (1976) explored the practice and structure of power in the development of capitalism. He recognized that ideology is a powerful dynamic in society, but that there is also space for collective action by class-based organizations. He saw the way that individuals undertaking class-based action held within themselves the power to act in a revolutionary way, based on one hand upon the power of the bourgeoisie who acted in line with their own interests and, on the other hand, upon revolutionary power among the growing proletariat once it had become a class in itself. Although Marxist approaches address coercion, particularly by the state, they recognize the difficulty of maintaining power through this means. There is, however, a more subtle form of power that emerges out of 'the necessities of life, the organization of capitalist production, the power of poverty and the power of ideas and representations expressed in the language of ideologies' (Westwood, 2002, p.130). This observation, and especially its reference to ideology, is a key aspect in understanding power as it is historically constituted and contextualized.

Gramsci (1971) identified the importance of the ideological sphere in shaping political action, deeming senses of culture as 'lived practices' (Westwood, 2002, p.13). He recognized the way that power elites within the ruling classes could create consensus among people by manipulating ideology in hegemonic terms. Hegemony refers to the ways in which ideas can become embedded within culture to shape particular viewpoints and understanding. In the 1960s and 1970s, Hall and members of the Centre for Contemporary Cultural Studies, based at the United Kingdom's University of Birmingham, developed this notion of hegemony. The center's work addressed popular culture and the media and the way ideology was, and is, negotiated in late modern consumer society. Hall and others explored the role of the media in relation to capitalist consumer society and its 'seductions'. This was balanced with understandings of the way in which diverse groups with different social identities engaged and negotiated with the products, services and sensibilities of consumer society.

Further developments following on from Gramsci's work are found in the analysis of power dynamics between civil society and the state. Research in this area focuses on the Global South rather than the Global North, with particular attention being paid to Latin America, for example, especially after the 1980s when democracy emerged in that world region (Radcliffe and Westwood, 1995). The development of social movements as a form of power in these contexts highlights civil society as a space for action. Further areas of study have included comparative studies, such as Skocpol's (1979) comparative analysis of the characteristics of revolutionary change in France, Russia and China. Her focus is on the importance of the state in terms of its organizational responsibility for managing a police service, military capability and economic development.

Weber's (1922) analysis of power involves distinguishing legal-rational power from traditional and charismatic forms of authority in relation to the presence or absence of the state. Traditional and charismatic forms of power are found in premodern societies and in various sects in modern society. In these contexts, power is practiced through charismatic leaders and through the hierarchies of traditional small-scale societies. Legal-rational power, however, is related to the historical development of state-governed nation-states. He asserted that the practice of power in modern states was based on the development and entrenchment of rationalization and bureaucratic procedures that spread into and across all domains of social life and which were distinctive from any charismatic power exercised by a particular individual. This exercise of power was not generated through capitalism *per se* but rather through modern forms of governmentality and modern management of populations.

Although industrial society was organized in bureaucratic ways, modernity was also characterized by a more fluid and nebulous ambience – Berman (1982) deemed it a time when 'all that is solid melts into air'. This sense of movement and the intensity of modern life were observed by Simmel (1950), who understood the significance of money in modern life. Simmel argued that commodification created a separation between objective and subjective senses of self, experience and society. This separation was created by the power of money in the form of commodity exchanges, which were embedded within every aspect of society. The power of money and exchange was not just in the physicality of goods but rather in the way they expressed hopes, dreams and desires within the social spaces of modernity. According to this view, the practice of power is therefore exercised through money and its exchange. Power does not simply flow through money, but through exchange in the economic, social and symbolic senses.

The developments of modernity and late modernity produced an analysis of power that expanded upon Simmel's understanding of power and Weber's identification of governmentality. Habermas (1989), for instance, focuses on the public sphere to explore how power is transformed in modern societies. He considers how the growth of regulatory discourses impact on citizens and analyzes the legal process and their roles in democratic society. Therefore, he stresses upon the importance of the state, identifying two kinds of power – administrative and communicative power (which is often located in collective action). In the first, power is yielded *by* the state, and in the second, collective action is often enacted *against* the state. Although Habermas (1989) recognizes collective action, he considers communicative power to be 'subject-less communication circuits of forums and associations. Only in this anonymous form can its communicatively fluid power bind the administrative of the state apparatus to the will of the citizens' (Outhwaite, 1994, p.143). The dynamic of power here is in the creation and maintenance of consent in liberal democracies.

Another approach that views power as being situated within social relations is the work of Foucault (1977, 1980). Foucault regards power as pervasive or omnipresent and productive (Westwood, 2002), and he raises the issue of surveillance and ways in which the state controls citizens. However, he also developed the notion of 'technologies of the self', which refers to the fact that people are constantly putting themselves under surveillance and controlling themselves. Therefore, people are not just at the mercy of power inflicted upon them from the external forces such as the state, but they also internalize disciplinary regimes. Foucault argues that this internal monitoring is a characteristic of modern people's lives – subjects become inducted through discourses and discursive practices, which are organized by the state and by civil society (Westwood, 2002). Foucault's work on the late modern subject created a turning point in the analysis of power in late modernity.

The poststructuralist analysis of power follows on from Foucault in terms of technologies of the self and from Arendt, who distinguishes violence from power. Arendt (1969) argues that violence can break power, but it cannot produce power. As Westwood (2002) asserts, violence is enacted upon those who are seen as the 'other', whether at an individual or collective level. This is often done in a spectacular way – such as through mob violence, riots and war – which, they consider to be performances of antagonistic relations. Given this analysis, contemporary writers such as Bulter, Laclau and Mouffe seek to address power in late modernity.

Butler (1990, 1993) addresses power through her work on the performativity of gendered identities. Although gender identities appear stable and unified, Butler (1990) maintains that they are the result of a complex negotiation and reworking of aspects of gender identity. This approach allows for human agency, whereby people have a performative space to question and disrupt gender codes and registers, so that they can transgress established performances of gender identity. Laclau (1994) and Mouffe (1992) consider another aspect of the way power works in late modernity – viewing power in 'relational terms and as a sphere in which agonistic power relations are constantly producing the identities of politics' (Westwood, 2002, p.25). Mouffe (2005) uses the term 'agonistic pluralism' to suggest a different way of thinking about democracy from the liberal democratic ideal, which focuses on the negotiation of interests and the formation of consensus. Rawls and Habermas (albeit in different ways) work within the traditional democratic model, viewing democracy as a process in which rational individuals put aside some of their own interests in order to reach consensus. Mouffe (2005), however, argues that while a collective society may want to an end to conflict, some levels of conflict may appear if the society's individuals are free. In terms of democratic process, there should be space for conflict to emerge, where differences can be confronted. Agonism is different from antagonism in that agonism is based on a respect and concern for the other and it recognizes the importance of struggle, including what can be learned and gained from struggle. Agonistic discourse follows on from this position, being concerned not only with conflict in debate but also with a mutual admiration for each person in the debate. To understand the significance of this, it is necessary to recognize that politics has moved from a time when political identities were fully formed and in conflict to a contemporary politics, which involves the ongoing formulation of identities during agonistic interactions. This reformation emphasizes the making of political identities and involves reconsidering citizenship and radical democracy. Laclau and Mouffe's concern is to analyze the way that democracy and its landscape are changing at the end of socialist political strategies. They address the political sphere where power relations, negotiations and contestations move towards plurality, active participants and a radical democracy that generates these 'agonistic relations' (Westwood, 2002, p.25).

The way power is practised has changed over time and in different contexts – the practice of power can be achieved via charismatic power, legal-rational power, state power or and hegemony. In late modernity, certainly in the West, power is increasingly practised through the internalization of certain disciplinary discourses. There are, however, other practices that curtail power such as coercion and violence, and in contemporary society across all parts of the world, these practices are still prominent. This section of the chapter raises the issue that power as sociality is embedded in the dimensions of social change. As Giddens writes: 'an agent ceases to exist if he or she loses the capability to "make a difference", that is, to exercise some sort of power' (Giddens, 1984, p.14). He continues: 'power is not one thing but many, from the transactional level wherein power is constituted as transformative capacity, to the state and institutional level wherein domination is inscribed in institutions and the state' (cited by Westwood, 2002, p.17). This illustrates Abrams's (1982) point that social change is a process through time in which agency and institutions are in an active dynamic, which produces new sociality and social experience.

Conclusion

This chapter has explored the areas and dimensions of change. It has shown how the key areas of social life change in terms of their own internal dimensions, and in relation to change in each other interrelated and linked area. The complexity of change reveals that no single dimension or area produces change; rather, it is the relationships between the key dimensions of economic, political and cultural life that shape social change. Furthermore, these broader changes are not abstract from the change experienced in the details of everyday social life, nor do they determine the character and experience of that social life. The way that people create their individuality, how they work and manage their everyday and leisure times is through their own agency. This agency is shaped by the institutions that each generation's predecessors have created and which contemporary social actors create anew in ways that foster change as well as continuity. Further, agency changes social institutions through its actions and this relationship forms a process that generates social change over time. At the center of that relationship are the conditions of power that enable particular kinds of relationships to develop between agency and institutions.

5
Everyday Life and Social Change

Introduction

To further understand, and contextualize, the debates outlined in the previous chapters, this chapter now moves on to consider substantive areas of change and their manifestation within contemporary social life. By addressing substantive areas of change, the need to identify and understand change sensitively is thereby illustrated. The first area that is discussed is everyday life and social change, and, to do this, it is necessary to consider how everyday life is ordered. This means addressing both the structure – the changing routines and institutions of the everyday – and the agency in everyday life that shapes the meaningfulness and culture of the everyday. Together these form the circumstances of daily interaction and process – a process that is fluid, flexible and constantly changing and one that incorporates various forms of communication and media technologies.

In order to consider everyday life and social change, the chapter first outlines the way the study of everyday life developed in the academic community. It then explores aspects of the lived experience of the everyday focusing particularly on women's experiences before considering the culture of everyday life. The chapter then turns to communication in everyday life and discusses the use of the Internet in daily life. It focuses on the Internet in the routines and practices of everyday life that are part of the meaningfulness of everyday life. Lastly, it discusses culture in relation to social change in everyday life.

Addressing everyday life[1]

Everyday life was first studied as a discreet subject area in the early 1920s and 1930s. One type of approach focuses on the way in which people make sense of their everyday life, how they structure it through routines and how they give it symbolic significance through rituals. This approach emerged from the development of Symbolic Interactionism (SI) in the United States and from the development of phenomenology in Europe by scholars such as Schutz (1899–1959). The focus on meaning and agency was further developed by the Chicago School and scholars in the Chicago School tradition, which locates the everyday in urban social networks and ecologies and focus on the way that individuals and groups shape and give meaning to city life through their own agency. Chicago School scholars seek to understand ways of living in the city from the perspective of their research subjects. The city is shaped through the everyday lives of migrants, people living in ghettos, working in dance halls and other employment as well as those engaging in informal economies or criminal activity. These studies show how different people shape their everyday life through interpreting and using urban resources to craft out their daily lives (Shils, 1991). SI, phenomenology and the Chicago School approaches to everyday life all place a strong emphasis on agency, which is shaped and guided by the construction of daily routines that interact with the many social and cultural forms that make up and give meaning to daily life.

Another approach to everyday life was developed from a Marxist perspective and stresses the way in which the organization of the capitalist relations of production creates a condition of alienation for many people. How people manage this alienation in their everyday lives is by seeking to ameliorate the feelings they experience in this condition. Lefebvre (1984, 1991) recognizes the complexity of everyday life, in particular its material invisibility and its contradictions. Within these dynamics, however, Lefebvre (1984, 1991) also recognizes the vitality of everyday life and its scope for transcendence. He details the various ways that alienation emerges in the experience of everyday life. This includes the ways that people experience their relationship between anxiety and security; how people can be active or passive; their perceptions of the public and private; how people ascertain levels of dependence and independence; and the relation between production and consumption (Silverstone, 1994). Silverstone (1994) makes a useful observation in that he notes that although Lefebvre addresses the complexity of negotiating alienation, he does not consider the politics of everyday life. Silverstone observes that there is a limited sense of agency in Lefebvre's and other Marxist accounts, because they see the economic conditions of capitalism as determining individual and social experience.

In contrast, De Certeau (1984) focuses on the politics of everyday life by linking everyday life with popular culture, which he sees as sites of opposition (Silverstone, 1994). Not all theorists see popular culture as a force of emancipation though, instead viewing popular culture as indoctrinating the masses into a dominant ideology. Theorists from the Frankfurt School's critical theory perspective[2] were writing in the mid-1900s, at a time when the premise of a mass society was first identified. It was a period when new technologies of mass communication were being developed and, alongside this, was the rise of public opinion and strategies of political mobilization. In Germany, economic recession was threatening the legitimacy of existing economic and political relations, which also interacted with prejudice against the Jews. The mobilization of a national population through mass rallies and effective mass media influence on public opinion prompted Frankfurt School theorists to analyze the way that power was practiced in this context. From their studies, they concluded that culture was a key mechanism for influencing 'hearts and minds'. This involved the incorporation of the masses into social norms – not just in terms of a disciplined work culture and legitimization of the existing relations of production but also in terms of leisure, consumerism and, from this totalizing perspective, everyday life. What the Frankfurt theorists clearly identified was the way in which 'culture' as a vehicle of ideology could be manufactured and distributed. Those scholars recognized that there was a culture industry, one which was specific to mature industrial society and which was part of modernity (Steinert, 2003).

Not all scholars interpreted the social changes of modernity in such a totalizing way as the Frankfurt School. Simmel (1950) identified how modernity might be experienced differently, and how the characteristics of modernity generated new types of social relations between agency and institutions. For instance, he explored the experiences of modernity by considering how money formed part of the relations of exchange in everyday city life. He noted how this exchange opened up culture and consumerism to more people, especially those who lived in an urban environment, and stated that one of the new social forms of modernity was the development of the large metropolis[3]. Simmel (1950) observed that a money economy and the dominance of the intellect were connected, since they share a matter-of-fact attitude in dealing with people and things, which is expressed in terms of value, in terms of 'how much?' This exchange has its own formal justice, but it is inconsiderate in social terms because it lacks any regard for individuals' well-being or for emotional relations between people. The calculating aspect of a money economy requires a mechanism for coordinated action, and modern clocks structure the organization of time in the city – not just in terms of business but also in the routines of everyday life that underpin working and business life. Thus 'punctuality, calculability and exactness are forced upon life by the complexity and extension of metropolitan existence' (Simmel, 1950, p.413). This rational logic interrelates with the size of the city, with the large quantity of other inhabitants and with other interactions that make depth or familiarity in social relations difficult.

According to Simmel (1950), other significant factors of city life include the vast amount of entertainment distractions available and the diverse cultures and people within a city. These factors contribute to what he calls a 'blasé attitude', which forms a 'reserve' that city dwellers display to each other and to objects, and which is part of the loose patterns of association that characterize city life. This means that there is a perceived – and, in many ways, real – sense of freedom in cities which differs from that of small-town life. These dimensions of city life create the conditions that enable the development of individuality, and this may develop further once a city's connections increase, to encompass more trade routes and cultural networks. The dynamic of this networking creates transformations in the quantitative dimensions of city life as well as influencing the qualitative dynamics of the way people experience city life and acquire their own cultural sensibility, resulting in the possibility of cities becoming sites of cosmopolitanism.

To return to the focus on agency, Schutz and Luckmann (1974) sought to develop a philosophical underpinning of human agency for the social sciences. Schutz and Luckmann's (1974) point of departure was the individual's own definition of their situation. In defining their situation, the individual draws on a common stock of knowledge, which comprises social conceptions of ways of behaving that relate to material or symbolic things. It is through typifications that individuals develop routines and definitions of situations that are rooted in everyday life. Schutz's (1971) work brought to the fore the way in which everyday life is formed and, indeed, made possible through the way people define their situations and have structures of knowledge by which to navigate it. This focus is part of SI, which addresses the agency and symbolic meaning that is located in everyday life. According to this approach, everyday life is shaped through the way individuals act towards things on the basis of the meanings that things have for them. This meaning is not something that exists 'out there', just waiting to be grasped and captured – on the contrary, the meaning of things arises out of the social interactions people have with each other. By generating meaning through interaction, these meanings are understood and modified by an interpretive process which the individual uses to deal with the things they encounter (Blumer, 1969).

Agency and meaning is addressed by Goffman (1959), specifically in everyday life in *The Presentation of Self in Everyday Life*. Although he works within the tradition of scholarship that focuses on agency, he develops a dramaturgical approach to show how people manage their daily life by creating various performances of self that fit with a given situation[4] – the everyday life that he observes being middle-class life in the United States. He also reviews the way that gender roles are performed, and considers women's management of their self-image in everyday life (1979). The main social requirements for women in that particular time (1950s–1970s) and context were to look groomed and not to usurp men. This is illustrated in the way they were pictured in subservient and supportive role in advertisements. Goffman (1979) highlights this construction of gender by advertisements and outlines how gender is created through daily interaction and impression management.

The discussion in this section shows how different sociological approaches address 'everyday life'. Each approach emphasizes either institutions or agency in the relationship between these two areas of social life. The approaches that focus more on agency highlight how individuals and groups create the meanings of everyday life through their personal actions and interactions. There is a level of dynamic relation with institutions – sometimes this is in terms of urban ecology, and at other times it is achieved through the institutional shaping of gender relations, for example. Other approaches, such as the Frankfurt School, develop an analysis that highlights the totalizing aspect of capitalism that shapes both institutions and agency. One approach, namely the work of Simmel, seeks to be more sensitive to the form and experience of everyday life in the modern world, capturing the dynamism of modernity to reveal how social forms and substantive experience are related in aspects like a money economy and migrant city life. However, although these studies address social life during periods of social change, they tend to reflect the *effects* of that change rather than directly addressing the change itself. Furthermore, although the approaches considered in this section provide certain insights into everyday life, research by feminist writers provides another perspective on everyday life and offers a more nuanced understanding of the negotiation of everyday life.

Lived experiences of everyday life: Women's experiences

Hochschild (1983, 1989, 1997)[5] concentrates on one specific area of every-day life – the way in which dual-income families (i.e. where both parents are in paid employment) balance their family and work life, including the emotional aspects of trying to manage that balance. The development of both parents leaving the home to carry out paid employment is part of contemporary social change. In *The Second Shift: Working Parents and the Revolution at Home* (1989), Hochschild explores how parents manage their emotions when experiencing the stresses of sharing child-rearing and household duties. Hochschild asserts that most of the women she studied were grateful if their husbands or partners shared any of the least-valued housework.

In *The Time Bind: When Work becomes Home and Home becomes Work* (1997), Hochschild focuses on mothers who lengthened the time spent at work. She notes that many mothers do not take advantage of 'family friendly' employer policies such as flexible time, part-time work or parental leave. To understand why, she explores the way in which mothers juggle work and home in their everyday life. By understanding the patterns of daily life, she reveals that these mothers' supportive networks are formed at work rather than through a mother's home-based network, which would have been the case in earlier generations. Previously, mothers talked to each other in their neighborhoods to 'blow off steam' and to discuss family issues, whereas in late 20th-century society, she found that mothers tend to do this with friends at work. The mothers in Hochschild's (1997) study participate in 'feel good' sessions at work, including coffee breaks, lunchtime conversations and rituals to celebrate birthdays or preholiday events, all of which help them to share and solve their problems on the home front. Hochschild (1997) also finds in her research that parents have to notice, understand and cope with the emotional consequences of the compressed second shift. The cutting back on family time means that more emotional work has to be done in the reduced amount of time that parents are at home. She says that the mothers in her study tend to carry this burden, and that:

> Parents are then obliged to hear their children's protests, to experience their resentment, resistance, passive acquiescence ... and in general to control the damage done. This unacknowledged shift only adds to the feeling that life at home is hard work.
>
> (Hochschild, 1997, p.218)

What Hochschild identifies is the tension being played out in families who are trying to manage the pressures of two institutions – work and home. Collins (1998) states that Hochschild is pointing to the cutting edge of social change and writes that it 'is a way of making sense of what has happened to the entire complex of work-and-home as we pass a historical watershed' (Collins, 1998, p.6). Hochschild's work shows how the tension of social change is being managed by people – as social agents – in their everyday life, as the institution of the family is changing in relation to changing patterns of work.

Collins (2000) explores the interconnections of race, social class and gender in African American women's lives, which are rooted in the everyday life of work, family, motherhood and sexual politics (as well as political activism). She explores the way that black women define themselves, noting that the relevance of self-definition is that many images of African American women were generated in the period of slavery and include stereotypes such as 'mammies', matriarchs, welfare mothers and sexually denigrated women. These images are controlling, and designed to make racism, sexism and poverty appear to be a normal and inevitable part of everyday life. Collins (2000) finds that most contemporary black women reject these types of definitions, suggesting that this rejection is mobilized through the women's relationships with each other, their blues musical tradition and the influence of black women writers who offer alternative definitions of black women's identity. Collins cites Dill's study of the child-rearing practices of black domestic workers, which shows how they pushed their children to avoid domestic work and 'discouraged them from believing that they should be different to whites' (Collins, 2000, p.78). She points to the rise of black feminist thought in social institutions such as schools, churches and the media. Collins locates this agency as an alternative vision of power, which is based on a humanist vision of self-actualization, self-definition and self-determination and which is played out in the complex interactions of the personal and the institutional within the politics of everyday life (Collins, 2000, p.224).

Both Hochschild and Collins' research provides insights into the way women including 'black and ethnic minority' women experience everyday life. In both contexts, the agency of women becomes apparent in their struggles with institutional frameworks and settings. In some cases, namely those of working mothers, women's agency is one of adapting to a set of conditions. Even though there are institutional policies in place to support women, these do not account for the informal support networks of everyday life, and hence they are not used. In the context of 'black and ethnic minority' women's lives, Collins illustrates how the agency of these women is influential in generating changes to their daughters' aspirations, and how the women's agency was also supported and channeled through supportive institutions.

Everyday life and culture

The social sciences and humanities started to address everyday life as a distinct category in its own right when it became identified as a site for political and social engagement in the 1960s. Radical and countercultural movements in that decade began in universities but were also located and played out within society more broadly. At that time, some genres of mass entertainment began questioning established conventions, social and gender orders. The uncertainties about how everyday life is changing are often related to developments in a culture of mass entertainment and are therefore distinct to the modern era.

As discussed in Chapter 4, Chaney (2002) notes that radical democratization and cultural fragmentation shape a key characteristic of everyday life, informalization. Chaney (2002) uses the term 'radical' in relation to democratization to indicate that forms of populism are dominant in public discourse but that, ironically, this rise in populism has not resulted in any substantial popular emancipation. He employs the word 'fragmentation' in relation to culture – not to imply that culture is becoming less important, but to suggest that the authority of culture is increasingly dissipated and discredited. Both of these processes are aspects of a broader process of informalization: one which refers to the blurring of many authority structures which were dominant in earlier phases of modernity. The processes of radical democratization and cultural fragmentation are located within the flow of everyday life, and everyday life is becoming more dominant in cultural discourse.

Chaney (2002) argues that it is important to consider the culture of the everyday because culture is influential in the organization of social life. This means that our culture depicts specific way of doing things – such as painting a picture, making and eating a meal, expectations of children – which are characteristics of a particular social group (Chaney, 2002). This is not to say that culture is determining or somehow preformed – rather, as Clifford Geertz (1973) writes, culture is created through human action. This action creates webs of significance that give meaning to the symbolic worlds of people and communities, and creates ways of life. Chaney (2002), working within the same framework as Geertz, points out that these distinctive forms of life are usually imbued with moral force, often as traditions, and that they constitute a central element of group identity. He states that the idea of culture is significant because it is profoundly effective – culture makes sense of the variety of social life, provides a level of collective existence and is explained and understood through everyday experience. Furthermore, given that everyday life is shaped by the routines of ordinary experience, it has form as well as content. Form (structure) includes the institutions and structures of change such as the social forms of networked individualism, as well as content such as the creation and engagement (agency) in social media which, together, represent the two sides of contemporary social life.

The way that form and content come together as a node, a mediator and a site of articulation of everyday life is in the institution of the household. In a contemporary context, Silverstone (1994, 2005a) shows how the household, for example, shapes the way that television and ICT are appropriated and consumed within everyday life. Chaney too argues that the household is a 'crucial institutional framework for everyday life' (2002, p.58). The way people now use digital mobile technology is also changing the institution of the household, because the household is no longer one of the main sites for private or personal communication, since personal space has now expanded into the flow of everyday life (Haddon, 2004). Because of the rise of web-enabled mobile communication, individuals can carry their personal and global connections with them at all times. The boundaries of locality are now defined more arbitrarily, which is part of a fundamental shift in the institutional frameworks of everyday life, namely that of disembedding time and space from locality in late modernity (Giddens, 1984).

Everyday life is also shaped in relation to cultural change, and, since society has become more diverse and multicultural, this has led to the destabilizing of any cultural homogeneity or conventional experience (Chaney, 2002). When this is combined with an expansion in the means of entertainment available through (digital) television, popular music across a range of media platforms and web-based cultures for example, it is clear to see that everyday life has become a site of negotiation in terms of cultural mores (Chaney, 2002). Another dynamic affecting everyday life is the way that leisure time and flexible work patterns have fostered negotiations over the control of time and space, which have, on the one hand, changed the structure and rhythms of daily time and place and, on the other hand, introduced a new range of consumer goods and services for the management of time and location in everyday life.

Cultural frameworks and sensibilities enable individuals to gain understandings and aptitudes for a variety of activities. Culture, therefore, gives forms of life their distinctive characteristics, which are meaningful to the social group in which particular activities are created and embedded (Chaney, 2002). It is through culture – lived culture, popular culture and 'high' culture – that individuals can interpret the richness of their own experience and learn to understand that their experience is part of a more collective, or at least intersubjective, experience that shapes everyday life. The creative industries and digital and social media are also resources that people draw on as part of the cultural environment of everyday life. In fact, the ways in which users shape the Internet (as prosumers) is adding to the forms of participation available to people in the 21st century – ranging from engagement in what the creative industries offer to the rise of social networking (Wessels, 2012).

Chaney (2002) argues that people in their everyday lives adopt, use and reject aspects of popular and 'high' culture, selecting performances, services and artifacts from the creative and cultural industries in ways that shape their practical understandings, which then become institutionalized. As discussed in Chapter 4, the media and cultural industries do not determine people's core expectations, but they are, nonetheless, a key resource in the embodiment or materialization of cultural expectations and mores. It is therefore more productive to think of the 'products' of creative and cultural industries as being environments rather than texts, performances or services (Chaney, 2002). This is because when these products are used and brought together within cultural frameworks, they help to shape and constitute the everyday world. In a similar vein, Silverstone (2005b, 2006) asserts that the media are best understood as an environment that is made up of different media platforms, channels and types of audience participation. Current examples of the way the Internet is used in everyday life include the development of social media, which enable individuals to communicate with each other – something that Castells (2009) terms 'mass self-communication'.

Social media, which is user-generated media (UGM), is embedded within everyday life, and its different forms shape the characteristics of communication in different ways. UGM generally features some means whereby individuals connect to each other to document relationships and indicate their interest in user-generated topics. Users create posts or status updates, while services circulate these posts to the users who are connected. This formula encapsulates the general principle of UGM, which is adapted within different services. The characteristics of UGM are categorized by looking at their aims and foci, ranging across a spectrum based on the type of connection between users and how their information is shared (Bontcheva, Morrell and Wessels, 2013).

An example of this is given by Ravikant and Rifkin (2010), who show how interest-graph media can encourage users to form connections with others based on shared interests, regardless of whether they personally know the other person or not. Twitter, a microblogging service in which users share short status updates, encourages this model. The 'following' relationship is often one-way, whereby certain people can attract large numbers of followers who are interested in what they have to say. Social-graph media is different and encourages users to connect with those they have real-life or known relationships with. Facebook, for example, provides a way for people to keep in touch with friends who are remotely located as well as sharing information between friends who see each other regularly. It can also be used for marketing where

the individuals do not know each other but the brand identity is known. Typically, short contributions are shared which outline current events in users' lives
or link to something on the Internet that users think their friends might enjoy.
These status updates are combined into a time-ordered stream for each user
to read. Professional Networking Services (PNS), such as LinkedIn, aim to
provide an introduction service in the context of work, where connecting to a
person implies that you vouch for that person in the context of recommending
them as a work contact for others. Typically, professional information is shared
through these PNS, which tend to attract older, professional users (Skeels and
Grudin, 2009).

This media environment is intimately linked with everyday life, and its
elements are mutually constitutive of the mediated and situated life that is
characteristic of late modern everyday life. The way in which these social media
are used varies and, as Castells (2001) notes, can be used progressively and
respectfully or in discriminatory and disrespectful ways. Thus, social media is
used for hate speech as well as for human rights campaigning, and it is used to
groom young women for sexual abuse as well as in creating empowering networks for young women (Wessels, 2010). Thus, as Silverstone (2005b) argues,
media and its cultural content are not straightforwardly adopted, rather that
the process by which both the forms and content of media are interpreted
and embedded in social life constitutes its form within the broader media and
cultural frameworks and environments. This process – a negotiation between
agency and institutions in a media relationship – is given meaning through the
culture of everyday life.

The Internet and everyday life: Locating communication as a way of organizing everyday life

The development and use of the Internet in everyday life is a central feature of late modern Western society. A defining historical moment in terms
of social change was the point when the Internet became an integral part of
everyday life for a significant proportion of the population. This is evident in
the digital divide, whereby any individual or community not connected digitally is considered to be excluded from wider mainstream society – and this
is the case globally(Ragnedda and Muschert, 2013). The work of Wellman
and Haythornthwaite (2002) is important because they identify when the
Internet is in its 'second age' (since circa 2000), because it was then being
used routinely within the everyday lives of many people[6]. Their research concludes that at that time and continuing to the present day that the Internet
is embedded in everyday life, with almost all Internet users routinely communicating using social media and email, and with many people web surfing
and shopping online (Wessels, 2010). They state that, although a smaller
percentage of Internet users play online games, their numbers are enough

to sustain a sizeable industry. From these early uses of the Internet, other forms have developed through innovations found in social media. The development of Internet telephony is a clear indicator of the way the Internet has become embedded in everyday life: in 2012, there were 2.1 billion people using web-enabled mobiles (ITU, 2012, http://www.itu.int/en/ITU D/Statistics/Pages/stat/default.aspx). Furthermore, the number of individuals, groups and companies using social media continues to rise with Facebook announcing it had over 1.19 billion users worldwide in 2012 and the data analytical company Semiotics reported that Twitter reached 517 million accounts in 2012.

The rise of the use of social media in everyday life is clearly shown in the 2013 American Pew Internet Survey, which reports that 73% of adults online in the United States now use a social networking site of some kind. Facebook has more users than any other social networking platform, but a striking number of people are now diversifying onto other platforms, and some 42% of adults online now use multiple social networking sites. Facebook and Instagram exhibit particularly high levels of user engagement, and Instagram users are nearly as likely as Facebook users to check their site on a daily basis. The 2013 survey shows that, although Facebook is popular across a diverse mix of demographic groups, other sites have developed their own unique demographic user profiles. For example, Pinterest holds particular appeal to female users (women are four times as likely as men to be Pinterest users), and LinkedIn is especially popular among college graduates and Internet users in higher income households. Twitter and Instagram have particular appeal to younger adults, urban dwellers and nonwhite individuals, and there is substantial overlap between Twitter and Instagram user bases. Facebook has high levels of engagement among its users: 63% visit the site at least once a day, with 40% doing so multiple times throughout the day. Instagram and Twitter have a significantly smaller number of users than Facebook does, but users of these sites also tend to visit them frequently. Some 57% of Instagram users visit the site at least once a day (with 35% doing so multiple times per day), and 46% of Twitter users are daily visitors (with 29% visiting multiple times per day). These figures show how social media is integrated into the everyday lives of American people.

The figures above indicate that the Internet is integrated into everyday life in the United States. Wellman and Haythornthwaite defining study in 2002 is still relevant in its stress that the Internet is used in both old, familiar ways and in new, innovative one and that it is now an accepted part of everyday life. They argue that research needs to take an integrative approach to computer-mediated communication (CMC)[7] in order to address and understand how online activities fit with and complement other aspects of an individual's everyday life, as well as examining how convergence has materialized into cultural forms such as vlogs. Factors that influence ways that the Internet is being adopted in everyday life include increasing access, commitment to going online, the use of ICT in schoolwork, 'keeping up' with trends in technology and media use and longer working hours, which means that people have less time to visit shops and businesses.

Internet in the routines and practices of everyday life

Wellman and Haythornthwaite (2002) define the Internet as a complex land-scape of applications, purposes and users that interacts with the entirety of people's lives, including interaction with their friends, the technologies they have around them, their life stage and lifestyle and their offline communities. They assert that people's Internet usage is related to their non-Internet attributes and behavior. The patterns of behavior include the observation that Internet users in the United States consume more other media than nonusers. These patterns of media use may be a reflection of the higher education and income of Internet users, and may signify the characteristics of early adopters whose preexisting inclination to use all types of media, combined with familiarity and ease of media, may make it easier for them to adopt computing and the Internet (Rogers, 1995). It is not, therefore, surprising that people with higher incomes and education levels were the early adopters of the Internet, and that their lifestyles have set some of the norms ('netiquette') for online behavior. However, although there were early shaping factors, the Internet is nonetheless being adapted and located within multiple interactions and responsibilities, both online and offline, which comprise people's activities, relationships and communities in everyday life.

Time weaves through everyday life, and the increasing mobility and flexible schedules of everyday life means that time is something that individuals negotiate and manage daily. This is because adding another activity into everyday life means making adjustments to the shape of daily life. As Wellman and Haythornthwaite (2002) note, people cannot add 16 hours spent on Internet activities a week to their daily lives without changing some patterns of their existing behavior. One key area for time transference is from television viewing to Internet activity. Anderson and Tracey (2002), however, find that average use of the Internet only marginally reduces time spent gardening, going to the pub, doing nothing, writing letters and sleeping.

In relation to young people, Wagner, Pischner and Haisken-Denew (2002) note that teenagers' use of the Internet does not reduce their time spent on other activities such as playing sport. Boyd (2014) also notes that teenagers in the United States have integrated social media into their everyday lives in ways that combine both online and offline life. A different pattern of behavior emerges when the Internet is used at home for important undertakings such as studying or working online, with online learners dropping some activities first, while preserving others. The first activities to go are relatively solitary experiences such as needlework and gardening; the next activities that are curtailed are leisure activities with friends and working for volunteer groups; in the last instance work, sleep and eating are compromised. Time with family (especially children) is maintained until the end, as well as work on the educational program itself (Wellman and Haythornthwaite, 2002; Haythornthwaite, 2006).

This discussion shows how the Internet has become integrated into the routines of everyday life and how people adapt their time management and existing activities in ways that integrate the Internet into their daily lives. The types of changes they make relate to their interests and priorities through which they not only take up the Internet and ICT but also shape it. The use and ongoing development of the Internet provides an example of the tighter relationship evolving between agency and institutional processes in the networked digital age. These negotiations between agency located in the everyday and the formation of new networked institutions is ongoing; however, companies such as Facebook are a strong presence in contemporary society, and to some degree act as a new institution.

Placing the Internet in the meaningfulness of everyday life

Although there is some evidence that the network is emerging as a social form, social life and changes in social life require a change in institutional terms, because the routines, practices and meanings of everyday life are performed in the institutions of everyday life. The household and the domestic sphere are important institutions and sites in the domain of everyday life and they interact with wider social and public life. Innovation occurs in the everyday, both in terms of a range of practices and products, and in forms of communication and their technologies (Wessels, 2010). Very often the interpretation and appropriation of goods and services by the diversity of everyday users is itself a source of innovation. As Chaney (1994) suggests, engagement with cultural products is social action and – in relation to the innovation of digital technology – the processes of the ways in which these technologies are used (or not) and shaped shows that the innovation process does not stop once a product leaves a supplier's shelves (Hirsch and Silverstone, 1992).

Digital technology enters the everyday through the institution of the household, the key site for the domestication process, which involves fitting and fixing the new digital technology into the familiar and the secure, while molding its novelty to the needs, desires and culture of the family or household (Silverstone and Hirsch, 1992). The shaping of digital technology in the relations of the household passes through four nondiscrete phases: (1) the appropriation of digital technology, (2) its objectification and (3) incorporation into the household, through which it is meaningfully (4) converted into domestic use (Silverstone and Hirsch, 1992). They assert that this process is one by which consumers incorporate new technologies and services into patterns of their everyday lives in ways that maintain both the structure of those lives and their capacity to control that structure. Domestication of digital technology shows how changes around patterns of communication are contested within sociocultural and institutional frameworks. Silverstone (Silverstone and Hirsch, 1992) argues that consuming digital technology is a struggle between the familiar and the new, the social and the technical. It is situated in the contested space between the revolutionary potential of the machine and the evolutionary demands of family and household. Furthermore, this concept considers the struggle within households in the appropriation of digital technology, seen for instance between parents and children, between male and female siblings, between sexual partners and between levels of computer 'experts' and 'novices'. In all these relationships, individuals seek to manage space, time and technologies without losing their existing position or identity within the complex and uncertain politics of age, gender and status in the household.

Silverstone (with Hirsch, 1992; also in Berker, Hartmann, Punie and Ward, 2005, pp.229–247) posits that the domestic sphere is a 'moral economy', a distinct social and cultural space in which the evaluation of individuals, objects and processes which form the currency of public life is transformed and transcended once the move is made into private life. In these domestic spaces, individuals are more or less free – depending on their available material and symbolic resources – to define their own relationships to each other and to the objects and meanings, the mediations, communications and information that cross their thresholds. Households are both economic and cultural units within which their members can define for themselves a private, personal and – more or less – distinct way of life. The materials and resources they have at their disposal come from both the inner world of family values and the public world of commodities and objects. This moral economy is constantly changing, affected by the 'relentlessness of the human life cycle, as well as the buffetings of everyday life, historically specific yet uneven in their consequences' (Hirsch and Silverstone, 1992, p.230).

The dynamics of this moral economy are defined through an eternal cycle of consumption and appropriation, in which a commodity is accommodated into the spaces, times and functional requirements of the home. New hardware and software technologies and services are brought into the home to be placed, displayed and incorporated into the rituals of domestic and daily life, in order to enhance efficiency or increase pleasure (Silverstone and Hirsch, 1992). New skills may be developed, meanings generated and new conflicts raised and resolved (or not) – all of which are expressions of the constant tensions between technological and social change within the household. The novelty and achievements, the significance created and sustained in the ownership and use of new technologies, access to new computer software, digital channels, social media and mobile media then become part of the currency of everyday discourse – discussed, displayed and shared in the social gossip and talk in neighborhoods, schools and workplaces. Silverstone's (in Hirsch and Silverstone, 1992) explanation of the domestication of digital technology makes a significant contribution to understanding the Internet in everyday life. In particular, he shows how institutions change as part of technological change. Therefore, although networks might be gaining greater and more particular relevance in late modernity, the social relations of households and the moral economy of the domestic sphere remain significant institutions in shaping digital technology and the characteristics of communication in everyday life. Furthermore, these processes are intrinsically cultural, and, therefore, the everyday and the shaping of the Internet are both informed by the culture of everyday life in its routines and its engagement with cultural activities – whether they are networks of friends, public culture or cyber culture.

The significance of the institution of the household is often neglected in conventional discussions of the diffusion of digital technology, which fail to acknowledge the work that households and the public at large do in 'domesticating' digital technology to serve their own particular values and interests. This impact also results from people's patterns of consumption and their everyday choices in consuming digital technology (Silverstone and Hirsch, 1992). The producers of digital technology, however, have significant power and influence in creating and managing the use of digital technology through the way they shape and frame consumer choice (Mansell and Silverstone, 1996). Nonetheless, the rejection of some digital technology, the early example of the videophone, demonstrates that consumers also play a pivotal role in the uptake of digital technology developments. Woolgar (1996, 2001) explains that the degree of influence exerted by producers depends on their ability to 'configure the user'. Producers can position digital technology in relation to users long before they reach the marketplace, however, as research by Silverstone (2005a) shows, the 'everyday is not biddable to the desires of technology' (Silverstone, 2005a, p.13) or that of its producers.

Members of households shape technologies and their cultural usage by deciding how to consume them and how to interpret the messages they convey. These decisions are diverse and include the ways that households consciously regulate access to communication technologies and media other than TV, such as using answering machines and services that screen and return landline and mobile phone calls. Parents regulate the use of Internet technology by installing software that allows children to use computers while preventing them from destroying electronic files or accessing pornographic sites on the web.

The culture of everyday life extends out into numerous forms of households and patterns of living the everyday. In a culture of everyday life influenced by neoliberalism – whether embraced, managed or resisted – individuals negotiate the socio-technical environment creatively in relation to the specificity of their lives. These negotiations are diverse and produce distinctive fabrics and flows to the everyday, and different patterns emerge in diverse studies. For example, in the established community life of a small seaside town in North County Dublin (Ireland), digital communications are mainly used to support the organization of local community events (Ward, 2005). In contrast, mobile cosmopolitan scientific researchers at the University of Trondheim (Norway) use digital communications to enable them to communicate in their global professional networks (Berker, 2005). Another example is the way in which mothers who have to commute to work use their mobile phones to stay in touch with their children and those caring for their children while they are travelling. This has been termed 'remote mothering', and it shows how mobile phones are a feature in the management of travel and parenting in everyday life (Haddon, 2004).

Another pattern of everyday life is where those living in diasporic communities find that communication is intrinsically linked with the dynamics of inclusion and exclusion. These transnational communities have always been reliant on networking to communicate with, and maintain their relationships with, dispersed friends and relatives from around the globe (Georgiou, 2005). In contemporary society, these communities often use Internet cafés in cities to communicate on a regular basis with relatives at home, and they structure this communication into their everyday life. Apart from the Irish example, these contexts, in differing ways, show how communication extends domestic space, as it is traditionally understood, to a range of public and semi-public spaces and publicly accessible media outlets.

The way in which the Internet becomes meaningful in everyday life is through the relationship between the agency of people and the institutions of everyday life. Further, this relationship is part of the process that is producing change in all its complexities as it materializes in everyday life.

Intimacy, family and social change in everyday life

So, some characteristics of the processes that are influential in shaping change in everyday life are populism, the fragmentation of culture, and a general informalization of life, which is blurring many of the authority structures of earlier phases of modernity. These trends underpin changing routines of everyday life. The flexibility of work, the inclusion of women in the workforce and peer-group leisure networks of young people all mean that the routines of everyday life are no longer structured through industrial time but instead have to be managed by networked and mobile individuals. The character of the family as an institution and family life itself is changing, with moves to serial families away from the nuclear family and routines being structured through networks of familial and friendship configurations.

In relation to these changes, Beck (cited in Bauman, 2000) asks what comprises a family in contemporary society, noting that parenthood is changing.

One example of change is that grandparents are playing an increasing role in child care, but in this they are restricted to taking on a caring role, not being in a position to make decisions about their grandchildren. Thus, care and authority are being reconfigured in some contemporary families. In what Bauman (2000) terms 'liquid modernity'[8], institutions such as lifelong marriage are being changed to the practice of serial marriage and cohabitation. Another dimension of this change in family life is the late modern expectation of the 'pure relationship' (Giddens, 1991). The pure relationship moves away from marriage, comprising a contract to relationships that only exist for their own sake.

Although Giddens' argument is critiqued by writers such as Jamieson, Lewis and Simpson (2010) and Jamieson (2011)) and Smart, Davies, Heaphy and Mason (2012), who argue that intimate and family relationships are not as fluid, flexible and individuated as Giddens and Bauman suggest. They question whether 'families of choice' and the assumption that friendships are always supportive and positive. They point out that the cultural, emotional and material aspects of intimate relations form aspects of relationships and influence how they are experienced and understood. The constant emotional work undertaken in family and friendship relations is experienced between senses of self and the other, which at times can be experienced as an emotional burden – not a light, fluid relationship that can be dropped easily. It is in this complex arena that family life, kinship and friendship are continually being negotiated. Nonetheless, individuals do choose to negotiate the end of relationships and they can achieve this through the legal and institutional structure of divorce.

Analyzing the rates of marriage and divorce in England and Wales reveals a marked change between 1930 and 2010. The Office of National Statistics' (ONS) UK trend analysis shows a marked change, with the number of divorces increasing between 1930 and 1990. The ONS (2010) suggests that this can be explained as a result of changing social attitudes and behavior. The ONS furthermore propose that the big increase in divorce rates from the late 1940s onwards (after the Second World War) correlates to the higher number of women going into paid employment, reducing women's financial dependence on their husbands. The large increase in divorce rates in the 1970s relates to the Divorce Reform Act 1969, which made the legal process easier for couples to divorce (ONS, 2011). The table below show the numbers and trends of marriages and divorces between 1930 and 2010 (Figure 5.1).

Attitudes to sexuality and sexual mores have also changed, with developments in contraception, feminism and gay activism producing a context in which individuals understand and negotiate their sexuality and gender identities reflexively. These negotiations are embedded within everyday life, link senses of identity and, in many ways, give new meanings to old institutions such as marriage. Sexuality is seen as being more fluid, and its negotiations are part of everyday life, seen in, for example, in the way that people feel able to publicly declare their homosexuality. Although much of Queer Theory focuses

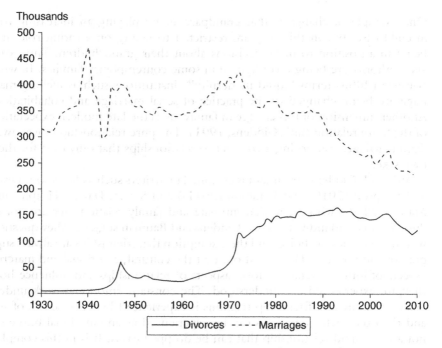

Figure 5.1 Divorce rates between 1930 and 2010
Source: Office for National Statistics (2011).

on the performativity of gay practices, such as drag and cross-dressing (Stein and Plummer, 1994) and readings in literature (Sedgewick, 1990), it has moved on to consider the everyday mediation of 'queerness' (O'Riordan and Phillips, 2007). Given that the Internet blurs the public and private spheres and that it is embedded within everyday life, the realm of 'cyberqueer' is both a part of everyday life and a part of cyber cultural space. In some ways, this space of the everyday points to a postmodern sensibility of play and irony on one level, and to strategies to celebrate difference, distance and incongruity on another (Ross, 1989). These encompass and express the experience of the everyday in terms of alienation and of agency, as well as a complex negotiation of institutional frameworks, such as sexuality.

These negotiations and processes are shaped (cf. Abrams, 1982) through everyday cultural frameworks. For instance, in the United Kingdom, civil partnerships were sanctioned and institutionalized by the Civil Partnership Act of 2004, which granted homosexual couples many of the same relationship rights as heterosexual couples. Shipman and Smart (2007) explore some of the everyday reasons why gay couples wanted partnership recognition. The main reasons are as follows: to express their love; to acknowledge mutual responsibility; the importance of family recognition; legal rights and recognition;

and the importance of a public statement of commitment. They found that, although the issue of legal rights is important, the significance of entering into a civil partnership was not driven purely by instrumental reasons, but was couched within the everyday cultural frameworks of love, recognition and commitment.

Conclusion

Communication within these new forms of everyday life is increasing through the use of mobile information and communication technologies, through which individuals create the structures that give shape to the fluidity of contemporary everyday life. The use of digital technology in these everyday contexts is also part of the way that meaning is interwoven within daily life, since the activities they help organize relate to institutions such as family units and the culture of ordinary life. They also act as a cultural medium in the way that they allow for, and indeed create, cultural artifacts and representations of contemporary everyday life.

Developments in everyday life such as fragmentation, informalization and the networked organization of the flexible and fluid character of the everyday all signify social change. The rise of networked individualism, the increased use of social media that, in part, extends the undermining of cultural authority as well as the incorporation of people into social media networks, provides new ways of participation, which at the same time acts as a new means of control and discipline. These processes of everyday life provide an understanding of people's experience of the everyday and the way in which they engage with and negotiate the institutions of contemporary everyday life, which interacts with the other spheres of social life. The way the Internet has developed is through people's usage, demonstrating how agency has shaped its development (Castells, 2001). However, in generating change through use, that agency has also constructed new forms of institutions, which are characterized as networks and can be civic, commercial or public. Meanwhile, the everyday is something that is often experienced in intense ways, such as negotiating family and friendship relationships. Thus, the agency that shapes changes in everyday life and the attendant institutional change form a relationship and the process of that relationship through time generates change in everyday life – as is evident in the way that personal relations have changed through time and the way the Internet has become part of everyday life over time.

6

Work, Production and Social Change

Introduction

Work, and the understanding of work, has changed over historical time. The characteristics of work are economically and socially shaped and organized through time and the meaning of work and its characteristics provide insights into the way that society is structured and ordered. The social organization of work creates hierarchies of reward and prestige. This can be expressed not only in terms of occupational hierarchies but also in broader social ordering such as social class. The study of work in certain periods also provides insights into the social actors and their agency that produce material, social and symbolic goods for society. The character of agency varies, and it includes particular skills, gender relations, ethnicity and attitudes to work. It involves a range of people's perceptions to work – from acceptance of their working conditions to resistance or protest over their working conditions. The organization of workers – of labor – is also a political process. This political dimension works on two axes: the development of unions and the ways that the state aligns with economic production and philosophies of workers' rights. The changes wrought by the use of digital technologies and the increasing individualization of societies have also brought immense changes to the understanding and organization of work.

To start to understand how work has changed, the chapter first outlines some of the way in which work is defined. It then describes some of the characteristics of work during the industrial period. This is expanded into a consideration of trade unionism as a form of agency in industrial relations. To explore how workers engage with change in how they work the chapter explores aspects of cultural change in adapting to new work patterns. The development of globalization involves the restructuring of work globally, and to gain some insights into this division of labor the chapter then focuses on work in the Global South. It moves on to discussing changes in the working practices in postindustrial society and information society before considering work in the e-economy. Lastly, the chapter discusses issues of gender and work, particularly, gender inequality and work.

Defining work

It is difficult to provide a precise definition of 'work' because what is defined as work depends on the social and historical context of the way an activity is understood and interpreted as work. Grint (2005) argues that it is important 'to consider past and present definitions of work as symbols of culture' (Grint, 2005, p.6), which also reflect the social organization of power within society. Using case studies, Burawoy's studies of work highlight the specific social relations of work under different economic regimes and the way in which the processes of work have been negotiated in different historical periods (1979, 1985, 2009). The value given to different types of work is one example of how power is distributed through work, as is the gendering of work, and the negotiation of what constitutes 'work' within the workplace itself.

There are, however, some key concepts to consider. One distinction that is often made identifies the difference between work and labor. Arendt (1958) argues that labor is bodily activity that is necessary for survival, and its results are consumed immediately. Work, on the other hand, is activity that is undertaken by humans to produce something that has 'objectivity' in the world. Although this distinction is difficult to apply socially, it does emphasize the point that people may labor for subsistence, whereas the notion of work is situated in a wider process of production and consumption. Work can be thought of as having transformative power, being located within the dynamics of the market system – socially, economically, politically and culturally. Work gives meanings about employment – within the domain of work there are occupations that locate individuals within the market (Brown, 1978, p.56). There are many different forms of employment, but during the industrial and postindustrial periods, the theoretical focus has been on studying paid employment[1]. Brown (1988) argues that it has only been the norm for 'employment' to mean full-time wage labor through an occupation within an industrial setting for the last two centuries – and only in a few countries. Another aspect in defining work is to understand the meaning of work from the point of view of workers. Richard Sennett (1998) in particular describes the way in which work changed from early industrial capitalism to the developments of new capitalism in the late 20th century. He focuses on the cultural and emotional aspects of work, which generates an understanding of how work is defined by how workers experience work (2006, 2008) (see the section 'Work in the e-economy' below). In particular, he notes how work in late capitalism involves individuals having to reinvent new work personas in order to develop portfolio careers in the flexible labor market.

Exploring Social Change

Work during the industrial period

An analysis of work in its historical context reveals how its characteristics are embedded in social life. The shape of that social life varies, especially in terms of frameworks of agency and the institutional structures of society, as discussed in Chapter 4.

The first industrial revolution began in Britain, where various forms of factory work developed, along with other forms of mechanized labor. Samual (1977) points out that the development of industrial capitalism in the 19th century was uneven and swift. He describes how, in the iron-making sector, huge furnaces in the Black Country (in England) sat alongside many small blacksmith's shops. In Sheffield, an early industrial city in England, between 30 and 40 rolling mills provided materials for 60 handicraft trades, which were organized via subcontracting and outworking arrangements. Although the textile trade was largely mechanized by the mid-Victorian period, there was nonetheless a rise in employment in dressmaking between 1841 and 1861 (Samual, 1977). Workers' terms and conditions varied among the different types of factory and other forms of work, with one of the key divisions being between men and women. Even if they worked together, the value of their work was highly differentiated. For instance, book binding was seen as a craft when undertaken by male labor but considered to be sweated, low-grade work when undertaken by women. Children were also employed in textile factories, brickyards and coal mines, often working for 12–14 hours a day (as did the men and women) for about 10% of the low adult wages. This was raised as a concern during the mid-1800s when Parliament started to investigate the conditions of child labor[2].

Industrial working conditions were awful. There is a consensus that Engels's *Condition of the Working Class in England* (1887) conveys a realistic sense of the working conditions in Manchester during the Victorian period, specifically 1842–1844 (Hobsbawn, 1971), depicting the lives of men, women and children who worked long hours for six days a week. The factory work was dangerous, with many workers being injured by the machinery and with insufficient ventilation. Furthermore, workers were at the mercy of the cycles of recession that form part of capitalist economic dynamics (Hobsbawn, 1971). This meant that many people were unemployed for periods of time and earned very low wages when they were employed. As well as these poor working conditions, most of the working class lived in slums where they were at risk of highly contagious diseases such as cholera, typhus and smallpox. There was some public sanitation, the pernicious safety net of the workhouse and some charities that provided meager support. Together, the working and social conditions of the poorer sectors of the working class caused concern for both the working population and for some philanthropists, evidenced by a series of legislative acts such as the Ten Hours Bill (British Parliament, 8 June 1847), which restricted working hours for children and women. There were also a number of secondary reforms that, to some degree, undermined totally free-market competition by imposing limited social requirements on capitalist employers.

Trade unionism

Another response to the working conditions within English manufacturing capitalism was the rise of trade unionism, which developed as an organized response by workers to negotiate better working conditions following worker protests in the early 1800s. The history of unionism stretches back to the guilds of medieval England, but trade unions were not officially recognized until 1871 (Grint, 2005), when a Royal Commission decreed that the establishment of these organizations would benefit both employers and employees. To some degree, the trade union movement from 1871 onwards was the vehicle of working-class agency. However, it was also a vehicle through which manufacturers could manage worker disputes. The strongest unions of the mid-Victorian period were the skilled workers' unions, such as the Amalgamated Society of Engineers (Hobsbawn, 1971). Trade unionism among semi-skilled and unskilled workers made little progress until the emergence of the 'new unions' in the late 1880s. Unions played a prominent role in the creation of the Labour Representation Committee, which effectively formed the basis for the UK Labour Party.

As industrialism developed, there were several periods of worker protest. For instance, between 1910 and 1914, there was serious industrial unrest and an enormous increase in trade union membership, which affected all industries, although to differing extents (Hobsbawn, 1971). The First World War resulted in a further increase in union membership, as well as widespread recognition of unions and their increased involvement in negotiations with management. However, following the General Strike of 1926[3], the government passed sweeping antiunion legislation under the Trade Disputes and Trade Union Act. This imposed major curbs on union power, including outlawing sympathetic strikes and mass picketing, and ensuring that civil service unions were banned from affiliating with the TUC.

The history of the trade union movement and worker protests provides an insight into the negotiation of working conditions and related social conditions (Pahl, 1988). England led the development of industrial capitalism, and the exploitation of workers within that system led to antagonistic relations between workers and manufacturers throughout the industrial period. By the 1850s, France, Germany and the United States were catching up with the English dominance of industrial productivity, making rapid developments while the newly industrialized workers began to struggle for better working conditions. In the United States, where the working classes were differently placed and configured, the struggles focused on shorter working days and for a legal framework to limit working time in factories (especially for children and women). There was a truck system[4] in place and, in rural areas, a cottage system[5] that enabled bosses to dominate the workers (Gutman, 1988). The strength of unrest was illustrated by a strike by 12,000 coalminers in the Connellsville district in Pennsylvania in 1886. Such protests were not only about working conditions – in many ways they provide pointers to the cultural changes that were part of the industrializing process.

Trade Unionism became a key part of industrial relations during the industrial period, and it played a key role in many of the corporatist settlements in European industrial relations (Fernie and Metcalf, 2005). Unionism remained strong during the post–Second World War Corporatist settlements that formed among labor, capital and the state. However, with deindustrialization and the rise of neoliberal politics, the regulation and organization of labor changed. The deregulation of markets and with the rise of flexible labor within a global market meant that unions started to lose their power and relevance in the workplace. A key period of the decline of union power was in the 1980s (Disney, Gosling and Machin, 1995), and this decline has continued to the present day. This is particularly so in terms of an Internet-based global e-economy that created the conditions for casualized labor (Castells, 2001). The role of unions has changed over time, reflecting the different, changing relationships between institutions and workers. Thus, during industrialization, when there was a relatively collective workforce, unions acted as a powerful collective voice to negotiate workers' right with managers. Changes in the role and status of unions occurred during postindustrialism and the rise of a globalized e-economy.

Fernie and Metcalf (2005) show how union membership has continued to reduce, because of the complex interaction between changes to the regulation of unions, reduction in state support, the rise of a liberalized market economy, individualism of work and society more generally. The role of unions has changed through time in relation to historical changes between institutions and workers. Thus, during industrialization when there was a relatively collective workforce, unions were a force in negotiating workers' right with management. Change in the role and status of unions occurred during postindustrialism and the rise of a globalized e-economy. The changing organization of the economy and its attendant neoliberal ideologies and an individualized workplace all configured to produce a decline of the power of unions and support for them fell.

Cultural change in adapting to new work patterns

Gutman (1988) argues that it is necessary to consider cultural change in order to understand working conditions during the industrializing process. He asserts that there were several phases and recurrent adaptations – and resistances – to changing working habits and practices, and therefore change was therefore an integral part of this ongoing negotiation. Gutman (1988) illustrates this by looking at the first generation of factory workers in the years before 1843, the United States' early industrial period, and later factory workers between 1893 and 1917 when the United States was a leading industrial nation in the international arena. What was common to both periods was that workers who were new to factory work often had habits that did not fit well with factory work discipline. During the first phase of industrialization, the kinds of behavior that were not seen as appropriate included smoking, any kind of amusement and drinking alcoholic drinks. A cotton factory in New Hampshire specified a set of working rules in order to alter these habits, while a firm in Massachusetts insisted that young workers who did not go to church had to stay inside the factory to improve their reading and writing (Gutman, 1988). Workers who were seen as troublesome, or did not turn up for work, were fined and they were prohibited from taking nuts, fruits, books or paper into the workplace. Furthermore, some US factory owners thought that long working hours had a moral imperative because they prevented the evils that were believed to accompany idleness. There was therefore a strong element of inculcating modern norms of work discipline into workers during the United States early industrial period.

During this early period, first-generation immigrant workers became employed at factories in the United States, many of whom were East and South European migrants or native Americans. They also had to adjust and become socialized into factory discipline, and it is evident that there were ethnic differences in the ways they adapted to, negotiated or resisted factory discipline and the industrial work ethic (Gutman, 1988). For example, skilled Jewish migrants brought with them town and village employment patterns, which they integrated into their production patterns in New York. This *landsman-nschaft* economy and small shop-based production method was often at odds with larger factory production processes, but reflected the Jewish work sensibility, which favored a more craft-based approach to production, rather than specialization. The Chicago glovemakers, for instance, chose not to specialize their trade even though specialization might have provided better wages. Workers appreciated variety in their work, and they did not want to spend nine hours on 'fingersides', instead enjoying the mental stimulus of moving between 'five leather pieces' and 'fingersides' in order to complete an entire pair of gloves (Gutman, 1988).

Another area of conflict between the US factory work ethic and the Jewish work ethic was religious festivals and other ritual events. For instance, Orthodox Jews celebrate the birth of a son when he is eight days old, but US working practice did not allow time to be taken off work for such celebrations in the working week, which meant that the festivities had to be rescheduled for a Sunday. The Jewish participants deplored this break in tradition, being aware that their celebration was being held on the wrong day (Gutman, 1988). Slavic and Italian migrants also brought some work habits, which did not fit into modern factory discipline, with many Italian peasant migrants unable to adjust to factory discipline and regimes. These groups informed new industrial sub-cultures (Gutman, 1988). Their resistance may not always have been directly expressed – there were numerous cases where men who had worked hard in factories for many years began having minor accidents or just gave up and stayed at home (Williams, 1938). Therefore, the adjustments that workers had to make in the move to factory work were cultural as well as socioeconomic.

Cultural adjustments in working patterns continue to the present day. Sennett (1998), for example, explores some of the cultural changes of work in late capitalism. He notes how disorienting the dynamism and flexibility of late capitalism is for workers. The speeding up of innovation in late capitalism results in the rise of corporate worlds that constantly reengineer their business operations. Work in this environment involves workers being able to network, undertake short-term teamwork and manage risk through being flexible. However, flexibly work and being a flexible worker is experienced in cultural and emotional ways. Sennett (1998) argues that in this dynamic economy, workers find that many of the aspects of flexible working are destructive in that it erodes a sense of sustained purpose in work. Furthermore, the constant need to accrue new skills and reinvent work personas undermines an individual's sense of integrity. Another aspect of the flexible and competitive work environment is that workers lose trust in others in the drive to get the next contract or project. The focus becomes one of the 'short term' and on potential ability rather than on accomplishment (Sennett, 2006). Workers find it hard to adjust to these demands and many workers experience a sense of use-lessness in a working environment in which there is 'no long term' (Sennett, 1998, 2006).

In the industrial organization of work, custom-based and individual responses to factory work gave workers some sense of control; this control was often resistance based in subcultural and individual agency and did not challenge in a direct way working conditions or lobby for change. The experience of work in late capitalism is often experienced in terms of uselessness that leaves little room for workers to negotiate there working conditions. There is, however, a similar pattern of managing work in the e-economy that is only effective as an individual response to working conditions rather than a collective response that can foster change (see the section on 'Work in the e-economy' below). The rise of trade unionism maps the development of industrial capitalism in Western society, with the current situation where unions are being undermined in the context of a 21st-century, neoliberal political economy and the emergence of a postindustrial society in the Global North. During the 1960s and 1970s, however, production and consumption were being reconfigured on a global scale. In the Global North, production moved from manufacturing to the service sector and the production of material goods moved to the Global South.

Work in the Global South

In proposing a World Systems approach, Wallerstein (1974) argues that the economy is global and that it is based on a worldwide division of labor. From this perspective, nation-states have little power to shape the economy or the conditions of work. The World Systems approach addresses the interregional and transnational division of labor, seeing this division as being shaped by core countries, semi-periphery countries and periphery countries. Core countries focus on higher-skill, capital-intensive production, while the rest of the world focuses on low-skill, labor-intensive production and the extraction of raw materials.

A key group of workers in semi-periphery and periphery countries is women workers. A stereotypical image of women workers in the new international division of labor is rows of young women in South East Asian electronics factories. Most of the research into women working in the industrial sector centers on work in export platform factories (Pearson, 1988). This reflects the specific demand for female labor for assembly processes in factories owned by foreign capital, which are producing goods for the global market. These trends are part of a new international division of labor that started to emerge in the 1960s and 1970s. The relocation of manufacturing production to low-wage countries was, and remains, part of a wider process of capitalist restructuring at a global level. One of the assumptions of this global restructuring is that there is an untapped pool of cheap, highly productive female labor available for work (Pearson, 1988). However, this notion presents a homogenous picture of women in developing countries, which fails to consider the complexities and contradictions of creating a new sector of waged labor.

In this model, the preferred female worker is young, single, childless and unskilled, with no previous experience of paid employment, although these characteristics vary in relation to the culture of the peripheral region or country. Thus, the period when a woman is considered suitably childless and single varies between cultures and countries. In Barbados, for example, the age of childbirth is relatively early and marriage occurs later (Standing, 1981), so, in this context, women tend to be recruited once they have completed early childrearing care. Pregnancy tests and declarations of childlessness are part of the recruitment process in some countries, such as Mexico, where there is a large pool of women seeking work at export factories (Instituto Nacional de Estudios Sobre el Trabajo 1975).

In Malaysia, there is a varied and differentiated cultural mix that shapes women's lives and, in response, another recruitment strategy is used. In the Malaysian social classes from which women electronic operatives are recruited, there is prejudice against married women working in factories, in part due to the perceived value of women's roles in maintaining a cohesive family structure. Therefore, recruitment focuses on single, female high school graduates (Pearson, 1988). There is, however, an added complexity to this process in that many men are antagonistic towards factory work, fearing that, as fathers and brothers, they will lose the control over their daughters and sisters that they have in the indigenous culture. One multinational company's response to these Malaysian cultural concerns is to reinforce patriarchal power within the factory setting, rather than fostering what is perceived to be modern Western independent behavior. Lim (1978) found that the company had prayer rooms, that its female workers wore traditional attire instead of factory uniforms and that it enforced a strict and rigid discipline in the workplace.

What all these examples show is that women working in peripheral countries are recruited in different ways and are encouraged to adapt to factory working life. There are similarities to the ways that men have to negotiate factory discipline, although women also have to contend with patriarchal attitudes – both in the workplace and in their everyday lives.

A combination of management practices and employment conditions located within the exploitative social relations of capitalism have created a position for women as cheap labor. Not only is the composition of the female workforce controlled (via age, single status and childlessness), but women's contracts tend to be short term and/or temporary, thus further reinforcing their lowly position and lack of job security. They do not have any long-term employment rights, so they can be dismissed if demand for labor drops at any point in the business cycle (Lim, 1978; Pearson, 1988; Green, 1980). Furthermore, women in these factories do not have any opportunities for promotion, increased earnings or technical advancement (Blake and Moonstan, 1981; Ong, 1984), which maintains their position as cheap labor. These women are also subjected to poor working conditions, including being exposed to health hazards in the workplace due to the specific types of work that women undertake. This includes myopia caused by constant close microscope work, feeling nausea and developing cancer from regular contact with chemicals and solvents or bronchial and respiratory disorders from working in textile halls (NACLA, 1975; Cardosa and Khoo, 1978; Grossman, 1979). Firms do not take any formal responsibility for their workers' health, so workers are obliged to withdraw from paid employment once they cannot meet the company's productivity demands.

Women in the Global South are still subject to exploitative practices in the contemporary workplace. Balakrishnan's (2002) studies of the gendered dynamics of subcontracted work in the global economy, which she calls the 'hidden assembly line', show the same inequalities and exploitation as that described above. The rise and strength of neoliberalism and the highly innovative global economy has only compounded the poor conditions of women workers in countries such as Pakistan, India, Sri Lanka, Bangladesh and the Philippines. Very often, local and national markets cannot compete with the competitiveness of the global market, which results in many women having to take on subcontracted work set by global companies.

Thus, the changing character of capitalist production, the increasing flexibility of work and technological changes has made the decentralization of work commercially viable and efficient for large corporations. As in traditional modes of work, women are often forced to accept unstable and vulnerable work in order to incorporate their reproductive roles (Balakrishnan, 2002). Although the organization of capital has changed, there is nonetheless continuity in the conditions of women's work in the Global South, because the women have little power to negotiate better working conditions or to question patriarchal structures. Nongovernmental organizations such as the International Labour Organisation (ILO) and local community-based groups seek to empower women in these situations; however, progress is slow and variable. Although the International Labour Organisation seeks to improve the conditions of workers it does not always have the power to radically improve working conditions. The context in which the ILO negotiates policy involves the increasing power of the World Trade Organisation (WTO) and the development of 'free economic zones'. In the 'free economic zones', companies only have to pay low (subsidized) tax or no tax at all. This policy seeks to encourage economic activity. However, the zones create an ever-increasing need for flexible labor, which is likely to perpetuate existing gender inequalities in the workplace, unless new institutions are established, which can effectively improve the lives of female workers.

The example of women workers in the new international division of labor illustrates the way in which industrial factory work has shifted to peripheral geographic regions. It shows that there is continuity in how people negotiate factory work and the ways that management seeks to control their workforce. One further factor is that this aspect of working life is coterminous with developments in core countries in the Global North, such as deindustrialization and the development of a postindustrial service sector economy.

Work in the postindustrial society and information society

As already mentioned, Bell (1973) argues that advanced Western economies have moved from a manufacturing base to production that is based on 'knowledge' and the use of knowledge in service and other industries. Therefore, knowledge is driving the economy, and so the workforce has to be highly educated and skilled in order to work creatively with knowledge in service sector environments. Bell thought that this type of economy and the work that was involved in it would create a more harmonious relationship between management and workers and between genders in the workplace. Although Bell's work serves to highlight a change from industrial society in the West, commentators such as Braverman (1974) and McLoughlin (1999) have criticized it for not addressing the complexities of knowledge economies, the specifics of the organization of production or the different experiences of work in such economies.

Bell has mainly been criticized by labor process theorists critique the postindustrial theorists' optimistic and positive scenarios about a knowledge-based work economy and ICT-enabled work in an information society paradigm. In general terms, critical commentators question whether the emerging use of ICT within new forms of production is, in reality, different from the predominant post-Fordist mass production paradigm (McLoughlin, 1999), raising issues such as the use of ICT to usher in new forms of electronic surveillance in the workplace. Many of these critical perspectives stem from the work of Braverman (1974), who develops a Marxist approach to changing trends in modes of production and related patterns of consumption. Whereas Bell (1973) concentrates on the internal logic of the move from an industrial mode of production to a postindustrial one, Braverman (1974) locates this change within the external capitalist mode of production (also see Wimott and Collinson, 1985; Knights and Wilmott, 1988; Thompson, 1989a). Such critical approaches identify continuity in many aspects of work, rather than any radical transformations in the social relations of economic and working life.

One key theme within these critical perspectives is to stress the ways in which management seeks to maintain its control over workers, based on the principal Marxist conviction that there is fundamental conflict between labor and capital. They argue that this conflict is structural and is located in the relationship between the few who own the means of production and the masses who do not and who are, therefore, forced to sell their labor. The private owners of the means of production want to maximize profits, and part of ensuring good returns from their investments entails controlling the workers and their levels of productivity. This means that the main role of management is to have 'control over the labour process' (Braverman, 1974, p.63).

Labor process theorists argue that, given the need to control labor within the capitalist process, relations between labor and management have not fundamentally altered in the new organization of work in the information society (McLoughlin, 1999). They suggest that the process of relabelling jobs into an expanding stratum of information and knowledge workers merely hides continuity within labor and managerial relations. Therefore, although economists such as Porat (1977) produce statistics based on changing job titles, labor process theorists address the ways in which work continues to be controlled through conventional means such as deskilling (in which work is fragmented so that workers lose the integrated skills and comprehensive knowledge of craftspersons) – noting that modern skilled job titles actually mask deskilled jobs.

Labor process theory posits that ICT is being used to enhance ways of controlling the workforce. In industrial contexts, control of the workforce was achieved through the scientific management techniques of Taylorism[6] and

Fordism[7]. These techniques were based on the separation of 'conception' – the mental labor of planning and decision making, from 'execution' – the exercise of manual labor. Those systems required direct personal supervision of workers. However, the use of ICT can eliminate the need for such supervision. This is because managers can use ICT to control and deskill their workforce by either automating out the need for direct human intervention or by using ICT to break down jobs into fragmented work processes that hardly involve any conceptual ability. When viewed from this perspective, it becomes apparent that the developments of ICT have not produced any radical break from the past. On the contrary, it shows how management has maintained and continued to exert centralized control over labor by using contemporary methods and technology (McLoughlin, 1999). Through networked technologies, this control is extended outside of the factory or office to mobile workers, homeworkers and outsourced functionaries (Dutton, 2001). Braverman (1974) recognizes that the use of ICT can negate 'the control functions of the worker, insofar as is possible, and their transfer to a device which is controlled, again insofar as is possible, by management from outside the direct process' (Braverman, 1974, p.115).

The materialization of labor relations, ICT, and work in the relations of production, is evident in organizational forms. A significant aspect of the postindustrial global economy is e-business, which is 'any business activity whose performance of the key operations of management, finance, innovation, production, distribution, sales, employee relations and customer relations takes place predominantly by/on the Internet or other networks of computer networks, regardless of the kind of connection between the virtual and physical dimensions of the firm' (Castells, 2001, p.66). Castells asserts that 'by using the Internet as a fundamental medium of communication and information processing, business adopts the network as its organizational form' (Castells, 2001, p.67). He defines the network enterprise as a 'lean agency of economic activity, built around specific business projects, which is enacted by networks of various composition and origin: the network is the enterprise' (Castells, 2001, p.67). The firm continues to be the unit of accumulation of capital, property rights and strategic management, but networks perform the business practice. Networks are flexible and adaptable and can, therefore, meet the requirements of continuous innovation as well as the rapidly changing demands of the global economy. The role of the Internet in these kinds of network enterprises is to enable 'scalability, interactivity and management of flexibility, branding and customization in a networked business world' (Castells, 2001). These trends emphasize the circulation and use of information, networking and the renegotiation of time and space, all of which require new kinds of worker sensibility.

The development, application and use of ICT have stimulated economic growth in numerous countries. In advanced countries, the ICT industry has fostered growth in employment of highly skilled workers. Demand for these skills is rapidly growing in East Asia, where ICT is an important element in generating competitiveness and growth (Senker, 2000). Software markets are attractive prospects for developing countries including Chile, India, Singapore and Taiwan, which have entered the low-value segments of the international software market with the expectation that cheap labor will secure them competitive advantage (Millar, 1998). Senker (in Wyatt, Henwood, Miller and Senker, 2000) argues that ICT production in the 'tiger economies' of Singapore, Hong Kong, Taiwan and South Korea has significantly reduced poverty, noting, however, that this is not the case for all developing countries.

Work in the e-economy

A recent landmark text is Castells' (2001) *Internet Galaxy: Reflections on Internet, Business and Society*. In this book, he argues that companies depend on the quality and autonomy of labor. The e-economy needs workers who can succeed in a digital informational environment. Workers, therefore, have to be able to navigate – both technically and in terms of content – vast amounts of information, organize it, focus it, and transform it into specific knowledge that is appropriate for the task and purpose of the work process. Castells (2001) suggests that this kind of labor needs to be highly educated and able to take the initiative. Labor in this context must be able to reprogram itself – in skills, knowledge and thinking, according to changing tasks in evolving business environments. This type of labor, defined as 'self-programmable', requires a certain type of education through which the stock of knowledge and information accumulated in a worker's experience can be expanded and modified throughout their working life.

The combination of these factors is resulting in what is termed the 'knowledge worker', which involves ongoing, self-directed 'e-learning' in professional life. The heightened levels of autonomy and involvement in project-based patterns of work are often combined in a light-touch form of cooperative ownerships. These factors often induce workers to have an intense commitment to business projects that extends well beyond their contractual arrangements. For example, professionals working in and around Silicon Valley in the United States regularly complete around 65 hours' work per week, and, at times of project delivery, these professionals will work around the clock until the deadline is met (Castells, 2001).

Not all labor, of course, is within the professional strata. For instance, untrained migrants provide a key source of low-paid talent across the labor market, while many people are carrying out 'generic' forms of labor, which are not 'self-programmable', including, for instance, those employed in call centers or routine manual work. In most domains of labor, the characteristic of labor relations is flexibility – and the notion of 'flexibility' is a key element in the narrative of work in the e-economy. Carnoy (2000) argues that flexibility within the labor market manifests itself in several forms of employment relations, such as self-employment, part-time work, temporary work, subcontracting, consulting and in new contractual forms of commercial employment. These various employment patterns and the differing character of working practices, as well as the individualization of working life, mean that there is no one homogeneous group of workers (Huws, Korte and Robinson, 1990, p.103). Flexible working, therefore, has different impacts on elite flexible workers who can dictate their terms of employment compared to the lower-level teleworkers who are on lower incomes and have less power to dictate their terms of employment (Galpin and Sims, 1999; Osterlund and Robson, 2009). Reich (1997) labels this distinction in the contemporary labor market expressively as that of an 'elite' and a 'peasantry'. In less subjective terms, the European Commission (1994) categorizes teleworkers in two groups: middle-class, self-motivated individuals or low-wage relatively unskilled workers who are desperate for work and, therefore, potentially open to exploitation. Galpin and Sims (1999) allude to this distinction in terms of a skilled elite core, referred to as 'knowledge workers' and an unskilled group, known as 'operatives'.

Changes to notions of what constitutes an ideal worker in the high-tech sector serve as a good template for understanding the skills that underpin telework. The rise of the 'hybrid worker' – someone who has both social and technical skills – in software organizations in the mid-1980s signifies a changing narrative of the characteristics of workers (Woodfield, 2000). The rise of key words such as 'flexibility', 'service', 'customization' and 'communication', which are found in the discourse of the market, is generating a rethinking of skills and aptitudes (Woodfield, 2000). For example, Deakin (1984) argues that the soft skills of 'advice, the translation and communication of ideas and the provision of intelligent information' are important in the high-tech sector. Woodfield (2000) asserts that progressive organizations need to use these 'soft skills' in pursuing commercial success because these intangibles are an important part of the value chain within the ICT and service sectors.

One consequence of this change is that these skills are seen to match gendered characteristics. Woodfield (2000) suggests that women's socialization makes them more empathetic, more willing to share information and foster cooperative working and more likely to have better interpersonal skills (cf. Hochschild, 1983; Tannen, 1995; Frenier, 1997). Turkle (1984) adds to this view from a programming perspective, asserting that women have a 'soft mastery' of computing due to their gendered development path, which enables them to learn the softer skills of negotiation, compromise and 'give and take' (Turkle, 1984, p.108). The narrative of work in the new economy is one of softer skills, flexibility and cooperative working, which manifests itself differently across levels of knowledge workers and operatives.

The positive concept of teleworking – that is, working from home – is located within the popular narrative of a rural idyll in which the work–life balance is regained through evoking a romantic notion of the tele-cottage or electronic cottage (Toffler, 1980). The imagery behind this is that teleworking reduces costs for employers by transferring overhead costs to employees, while enabling greater flexibility in the workforce. The restored work–life relationship promises that workers will have less commuting time, more flexibility, greater adaptability of working hours across their life course and a better ability to balance working life with their domestic life. It is also argued that these adaptations increase productivity, lower office and travel costs and generate a higher morale among employees.

However, this optimistic view is only one side of the story, as there are constraints and disadvantages to teleworking from both management and worker perspectives. Managers are concerned that they will have less control over their employees when they are not physically present in the office, which also raises questions about the ubiquity of electronic surveillance in the workplace. Workers, however, often feel isolated, and many are anxious about being overlooked in the allocation of assignments or promotions because they are less visible. Furthermore, many homeworkers find that they work very long, and extra uncompensated hours due to the difficulties of managing the work-home boundary. Thompson (1985) defines the industrial era cottage industry as: 'not only roses and thatch, but also long hours of toil by the dim light of rush candles for inadequate subsistence wages', which he updates to the postindustrial era as: 'backache and eyestrain of long hours keying-in at the visual display unit' (Thompson, 1985, p.22). These concerns can lead to a resistance to teleworking, with both managers and employees wanting to retain more place-based patterns of work.

The trend towards flexibility in labor relations and the emphasis on softer skills within an information society context is characterized as the rise of 'flexible woman' bringing the demise of 'organization man' – representing a move from an industrial pattern of work to a postindustrial, or information society, system (Castells, 2001). Evidence of this trend can be seen in California, United States, an area with one of the highest levels of ICT-related work, where only 33% of workers fit into old industrial patterns of work (Castells, 2001). Although European labor markets are less flexible, the overall global trend points to this labor marker heading in the same direction as that of the United States (although California is not typical of the whole of America). The narrative of work in the information society is composed of flexibility, variable employment patterns, diversity of working conditions and the individualization of labor (Castells and Cardoso, 2005; Huws, 2006). Castells (2001) states that these are systemic features of e-business, while flexible labor practices form part of a new social structure, which Castells characterizes as the 'network society'.

The case of telehomeworking is one example of new forms of work. Haddon (1998) and Haddon and Silverstone (1993, 1994) differentiate telehome-working from traditional homeworking. Traditional homeworking describes small-scale manufacturing or the provision of services in the home, whereas telehomeworking involves some processing of information, ranging from pro-fessional tasks to clerical ones. However, and in relation to the problem of defining informational work, Haddon and Silverstone (1993) explain that this is only a guide because the boundaries of telework are not clear. They demonstrate how the roles and responsibilities of professional and managerial hierarchical levels are becoming blurred by telework. On the one hand, cler-ical work is becoming increasingly professionalized through the expansion of skills and training required for clerical roles; on the other hand, many profes-sionals, such as academics, work from home, so are 'teleworking'. Therefore, information processing using ICT is part of a wide range of work, including small businesses and traditional homeworking.

Haddon and Silverstone (1994) identify three main terms of employment in telehomeworking. There are employer-organized schemes, which are appeal-ing for female employees with children who wish to spend more time in the home. The second is when individuals make a request to telework in organizations that do not have standard schemes, and they are granted an individual teleworking arrangement. The third type of employment is where workers become self-employed and undertake contract work for one or more organizations (Haddon and Silverstone, 1994). Often, older workers choose to become self-employed as a strategic response to feeling marginalized or overlooked in the job market. All of these terms provide flexible working arrangements but, apart from the employer-organized schemes, they leave many workers without adequate union protection or job security.

Goddard and Richardson (1996) argue that a significant aspect of the use of ICT in work is the 'spatial re-organization of the functions and personnel' of a firm or organization (cited in Dutton, 2001, p.152). As Moss (1987), Goddard (1994) and Goddard and Richardson (1996) explore, this process of spatial reorganization started in the 1970s, primarily in the banking, finance and insurance sector, when organizations relocated their clerical staff from 'back offices' in their headquarters in city center business areas, to sites farther away. Out-of-town sites are less expensive than business districts within city centers, so this move lowered their estates costs. Salary levels can be reduced in out-of-town areas, so this also resulted in lower human resources costs.

This spatial reorganization, underpinned by its economic rationale, is being played out beyond cities and their peripheries – on wider global geographical dimensions. This often involves organizations based in Western economies using labor and space in less-developed economies because both of these resources are cheaper there. For example, Dutton (2001) cites the way in which companies located in the West employ computer programmers in India where wages and site costs are lower than in Western advanced economies. The distribution of call centers follows a similar logic, albeit involving more routine work and less skilled labor. This type of arrangement is usually understood as 'outsourcing' and is a form of the decentralization of organizational functions. Some geographically distributed firms also centralize administration functions, such as accounting and billing, by outsourcing these aspects of their work to a central hub (Dutton, 2001).

Call centers are also part of the broader trend of 'distributed work' (Dutton, 2001, p.152) and the spatial reorganization of work. Call centers originated to support the finance, insurance and travel industries, and then spread into many other areas, including the public sector. The development of telephones and ICT in teleworking is clearly visible in call centers, which are enabled by ICT infrastructure providing access to information, customer interaction and, increasingly, email and web-based transactions. This ICT automation enables call centers to handle large volumes of interactions and, often, to operate every day of the week at all hours. They can do this partly because of being located in less-developed countries where labor is plentiful and relatively cheap, and where there is an appropriate ICT infrastructure, such as India (Taylor and Bain, 2005), or deindustrialized regions in Western economies, such as Northern England (Richardson and Belt, 2001).

Gender inequality and work

The previous sections have shown how women are part of the labor market and that in many cases they experience inequality in the workplace. Feminist writers such as, Beechey (1982), and Knights and Wilmott (1986) note that conflict within the workplace is based not just on labor and capital but also on gender inequalities. In the context of a wider sexual division of labor, feminists argue that managers use technology to maintain men's control over women in the workplace, thus sustaining women's subordinate position in labor relations (Cockburn, 1983, 1985; Barker and Downing, 1985; Wajcman, 1991). Management techniques, for example, use technology run by cheap female labor, to redefine some types of work as being 'unskilled' rather than 'skilled'. Technology is thus being used in workplace negotiations about the relative value of labor power, as part of the way in which men may seek to retain control of their status in the workplace through reasserting or redefining traditional images of what constitute 'man's work'. Moving on to address gender and work in the e-economy means considering the interaction of gender relations in the workplace and the dynamics of gender and technology. Given the rise in telework, the development of networks and flexible forms of work, the role and position of women in the labor pool is significant. More opportunities for flexible work might help women to balance their domestic and working lives; however, in reality, achieving this balance is found to be difficult.

Women have relatively low rates of participation in the labor market for designing and developing computer-based systems. Precise rates vary, but illustrative figures include 20% in the United Kingdom, 15% in the Netherlands, 24% in Sweden and Denmark, 30% in Finland, 25% in Australia and 30% in the United States (Webster in Dutton, 2001, p.167). These figures suggest that policies aiming to propel women into high-value ICT jobs have failed (Millar and Jagger, 2001). Whereas participation rates in the research, design and creative sectors within ICT are low, women form the majority of employees in ICT manufacturing and assembly jobs. These jobs are highly routinized, and not well regarded or rewarded, being distinct from higher-value research, design and creative work. Furthermore, there are few opportunities to develop higher skills in these assembly-type jobs. This type of work is also undertaken in distinct geographic areas, since the bulk of ICT assembly is done in developing countries and free trade zones, or in pockets of homeworking, where cheap female labor is available (Webster, 1995).

Woodfield's (2000) study on women working in high-tech companies shows how the need for softer skills, communication skills and flexibility may be advantageous for women. However, existing managerial conventions such as job evaluations and career maneuvering are still biased towards male-oriented work practices, since many organizations are unclear as to how to measure and reward these capabilities. So, even if women are socialized to provide better softer skills, reward and promotion structures tend not to measure or recognize these attributes. Instead, the male-oriented culture of many organizations works through more established practices such as presenteeism, 'old-boy' networking and production-related outputs (Woodfield, 2000). One exception is public sector employment in the United Kingdom, whose equal opportunities policies support women working in telework or in ICT-based departments and centers. This is reflected in the fact that women in the public sector are more positive than men about ICT in the workplace. Apart from this exception, opportunities for women to advance in the high-tech sector are generally undermined by patriarchal structures, regardless of their own skills and abilities (Woodfield, 2000).

Finding ways to manage work and domestic duties in the home are especially problematic for women (Haddon and Silverstone, 1994), so they are more likely to seek or accept telework, which gives them some flexibility over their working hours. Much of women's telework is based in the home, and it is low paid and casual with little support from management or from organized trade unions (Webster, 2001). In addition, many women do not like working at home all week because they find it isolating, experience difficulties in maintaining work relations with colleagues and lose motivation through a lack of professional interaction and stimulation. Many labor and trade unions are opposed to the increase in home-based teleworking, believing that there is risk of underpaying workers for the amount of work completed – 'sweated labour' – and stressing the difficulties of monitoring wage levels or working conditions within homeworking environments. These are very important issues for women, and they also extend to men. Lipsig-Mumme (1991) raises the concern that flexible employment patterns may lead to the gradual break-up of full-time unionized jobs, as more fragmentary employment patterns enable employers to shift responsibility for some of their costs onto the workers. This affects the whole workforce because, as well as threatening workers' rights; the whole trade union movement may be jeopardized in the longer term, thereby undermining standards of working terms and conditions.

These dynamics underpinning and shaping telework are producing an inequitable and insecure context for those in the information society workforce. Producer and user organizations are both failing to provide a supportive culture for women (and other less powerful groups in the economy, such as younger or older people and minority groups). A further consequence is the risk that women's talents and creativity may not be recognized or valued, limiting opportunities for them to participate in the higher value and creative sectors of the economy. Taking all these trends together, it is evident that ICT and flexible work processes have not generally improved the quality of women's participation in the labor market. Instead, industrial forms of capital relations persist, using ICT to exploit women's position in a form of society that is still influenced by patriarchy.

Conclusion

The character of work is a driver of social change, at the same time that any new forms of work are the result of broader social change. Change in the ways that people work, the organization of work and how that is expressed in broad socioeconomic terms, is multidimensional. Change within work relates to changes in the relations of production (including the technology); how labor and work is defined and organized; and how work relates to the broader dynamics of social formations and hierarchies. The way these factors are configured in particular historical periods give societies their distinctive modes or ways of production, which means that sociologists need to understand production in relation to social formations, political culture and broader cultures of everyday life. The study of work clearly shows the dynamics of agency and institutions that create change through time. For instance, during the industrial period, a collective factory-based workforce could organize to lobby for improved working conditions through the trade union movement. However, such an organizational response has been undermined because of the emergence of a neoliberal global economy with flexible working and workplace deregulation, and because of the wider individualization of society. Changes in both the way that work is experienced and the way it is organized clearly shows that change is a process resulting from relationships between agency and institutions. The main changes and continuities are fully detailed in the discussion above (and are not summarized here). Despite this, some exceptions remain, notably the fact that women often still experience inequality in the workplace.

This discussion shows that what work means in society varies over time, place and context. In many ways, social life involves various types of work and the nature of that work is differentiated via perceptions of gender, age and social status, and its place in the global networked economy.

7

Social Change and Consumerism

Introduction

This chapter addresses the history and dynamics of consumerism. The rise of consumer society is often seen as a modern phenomenon that arose after the Second World War in Europe and the United States. It does, however, have a far longer history – going back, for instance, to Tudor Elizabethan England, and, in terms of trade, it extends back to the ancient Amber Trade Route and the Spice Route of the Middle Ages. The characteristics of consumerism are distinctive and specific to different historical periods, and they vary in accordance with the social relations in which it is embedded. The focus on the dynamics of these relations means that analysts can identify the way that consumerism has changed, and its historical specificity.

The chapter first addresses consumerism and social change by tracing the historical context of changing forms and characteristics of consumerism. This is then followed by a consideration of fashion and the rise of fashion, which is a significant aspect in the dynamics of consumerism. The chapter then focuses on the relationship between consumption and economics before considering the way consumerism developed through the developing of marketing and how taste became increasingly ascribed through broader cultural processes. The way consumerism continued to change is then explored further by addressing the spirit of consumerism that is informed through Romanticism and a consumer ethic. The way consumerism is embedded within everyday life in late modernity is described through the notion of lifestyles. The chapter then addresses the relationship between consumerism and production and explores the rise of prosumerism in late modernity.

The historical context of changing forms and characteristics of consumerism

McCracken (1988) traces the historical background of consumption to show how consumerism can spring from political dynamics rather than economic ones. He studies the period of the Court of Elizabeth the First and the consumer boom in Elizabethan England. He and McKendrick, Brewer and Plumb (1982) also study the 18th-century explosion in the fashionable use of consumer goods. Both of these English dynamics influenced the development of consumerism in Europe.

McCracken (1988) situates consumerism in the last quarter of the 16th century, when Queen Elizabeth the First insisted that noblemen had to attend her court, which was driven by her desire to centralize her power. The underpinning of this type of consumerism was political, with Queen Elizabeth seeking to express how successful and impressive her rule was. She achieved this by presenting her court as a theater of splendid ceremony and spectacle, demonstrating her political legitimacy through the visibility of power (McCracken, 1988). This presented her noblemen with the problem of how they could stand out and gain the Queen's attention. To this end, they wore extravagant clothes and presented gifts at court, and this need to be conspicuous created a competitive dynamic that drove consumerism. The noblemen were constantly trying to outdo each other, which drove them to ever greater expenditure. This was shown by ever more magnificent clothes, their sumptuous feasts and the endless competition to give the Queen more gifts than their rival noblemen. This dynamic meant that each nobleman was drawn into a constant pattern of consumption (McCracken, 1988).

This process of political consumption, enacted through the institution of the court, had implications far beyond it. The consequences of a centralized and splendid court were felt in relation to family life and to ideas of community. The motivation for buying goods prior to the Elizabethan period was that purchases should establish the honor and prestige of a family across the generations. This rationale and practice of consumption was, however, disrupted and undermined by noblemen having to go to the Queen's court in London, which required them to spend a significant amount of money. This expenditure had to focus on gaining prestige in the 'here-and-now', so that each nobleman could compete for position (McCracken, 1988). This left each nobleman with less money to spend on establishing a legacy of honor for future generations, because they had to spend on themselves to remain competitive at court. This was a significant move in the basic unit of consumption, which changed from being the family unit, to being the individual (McCracken, 1988).

McCracken (1988) argues that the notion of the 'here-and-now' marks a break from older valuations of time to the rise of a new temporal sensibility. Before this central court, goods were bought to obtain transgenerational family honor – the longer the goods remained in a family, the more honor they conveyed. However, the social competition at court meant that there was no time to accrue family honor because of the fast rate of consumption demanded by noblemen trying to gain individual recognition. This change meant that the prestige items were no longer family heirlooms with their connotations of ancient honors, but became the new, the up-to-date and the different. This change gave rise to the birth of one of the most important phenomena of consumerism – fashion.

This politically induced consumerism, based on a centralized court, created new consumption patterns. Contemporary noblemen developed different consumption patterns to those living in the country seat, such as their family or subordinates. In pre-Elizabethan days, noblemen and those in his community had shown similar understandings of consumption. They also shared the same conceptual universe of consumption, more or less agreeing on the sorts of goods that were considered relevant and valuable (McCracken, 1988). However, with the new split between court and country life, noblemen, their families and serfs now inhabited completely different conceptual universes: 'what the nobles got up to in court seemed odd to the folks back home' (McCracken, 1988, pp.14–15). These different consumer cultures also fed into increasing social distances between lifeworlds, material culture and geographical regions.

The rise of fashion

The dynamics of consumerism in the need to assert social status meant that fashion displaced patina[1] as the mechanism for expressing status (McCracken, 1988). The growth of fashion meant that old wealth could no longer be easily distinguished from new money in many areas of consumption – anyone could now purchase consumer products, providing they had enough money to afford it. This meant that the lower classes could imitate the upper classes more closely, since signs of newness mattered more than signs of awe. McCracken (1988) argues that there was an 'explosion of imitative behaviour on the part of low-standing consumers' (1988, p.40). This in itself fed into the cycle of fashion, because this imitation by the lower classes led to the upper classes having to differentiate themselves again by buying new goods. These upper class goods would, in turn, be imitated by the lower classes, so that the upper classes had to differentiate themselves once more through consuming new goods – hence, the cycle of fashion and consumerism became self-perpetuating (McCracken, 1988).

This historical move underpins the contemporary relationship between culture, taste and fashion. Bourdieu (1984) explores this relationship in his work on cultural capital. He starts from a similar position to Velben (1975), who states that people are taught to consume in an 'appropriate' way, and that learning how to consume correctly and tastefully takes time and resource. Bourdieu (1984) develops this concept to assert that the time and money spent on gaining an understanding of the correct way to consume is a type of capital, which he calls cultural capital. In modern and late modern society this cultural capital is gained through education, and the longer a person experiences education, the higher their cultural capital is. Thus, an individual who

is well educated is likely to have better taste (if not good taste), than someone who has not accrued a cultural sensibility to taste through education. This
relationship does not necessarily equate taste with money though; rather, there
is a struggle for distinction in terms of taste (Bourdieu, 1984).

The significance of the struggle for distinction is based in Bourdieu's (1984)
argument that in modernity and late modernity cultural roles are important
in achieving dominance in influencing how hierarchies of power are situated
and reproduced across societies. These roles outstrip the power of economic
forces in determining social and cultural position and power. He argues that
status is as necessary as economic capital in maintaining dominance in a system.
In Bourdieu's analysis of hierarchies of power social actors need to possess
symbolic capital in addition and set apart from financial capital. The power of
cultural roles is practiced in the form of symbolic power, which is expressed
though distinction and taste. For example, power can be exercised through
the exchange of gifts in the interpretation of the value of the gifts and in the
relative status of those involved in the gift exchange. Bourdieu (1984) argues
that in this context symbolic power is practiced in the way the gift involves the
imposition of categories of thought and perception on the individuals who
are being dominated. The way symbolic power works extends further into
the cultural framework of individuals because they then begin to observe and
evaluate the world in terms of the categories embedded in a gift exchange, for
example. The individuals might not be aware of the change in their perspective
and they start to perceive the existing social order as just. Through the exercise
of symbolic power, the dominant elites maintain their influence, which ensures
the reproduction of the social structure that is favored by them and one that
serves their interests. Symbolic power, according to Bourdieu (1984), is a form
of violence, and it is powerful because it is embedded in the modes of action
and structures of cognition of individuals, and imposes a sense of legitimacy
of the social order.

The struggle for distinction is therefore more than a negotiation of taste;
taste itself is part of a broader struggle for power, power which is realized as
symbolic power. This raises the question of power and symbolic violence is
exercised and legitimated in social life. Bourdieu (1984) points to a process in
which taste emerges through social and cultural negotiations. The struggle for
distinction and the social, yet differentiated, sense of taste emerges in a homol-
ogy between production and consumption, which creates an objective link
between the two (Bourdieu, 1984). In looking at fashion, Bourdieu sees that
there is some element of logic in the internal struggles between those in production and those in the dominant consuming class in creating distinction –
that is, something that is objectified and can be seen as taste. In fashion, these
struggles are organized according to the opposition between the old and the
new. This extends to oppositions between the old and the young, as well
as contrasts such as expensive and cheap, and between practical and classical
(Corrigan, 1997). These dimensions create a logic through cultural capital that

objectivizes how 'people and things are brought together' (Bourdieu, 1984, p.241). Through this logic, taste is made and remade. Bourdieu (1984) suggests that taste is a 'match-maker ... [the] decoding of one habitus by another is the basis of ... affinities which orient encounters ... through socially innocent language of likes and dislikes' (Bourdieu, 1984, p.243). In this way, consumption conveys social meaning and distinction, and identities are formed and reformed through these struggles of fashion and taste. This process is a clear example of the way in which social processes can objectify a subject, a key point in considering social change (Abrams, 1982). The objectification of subjects through the process of taste formation gives some indication of how consumerism can be alienating for individuals while, at the same time, drawing people more deeply into market relations (Robins and Webster, 1999).

In Tudor Elizabethan society, high-status goods were only attainable for those in the wealthiest echelons of society. As consumerism developed in mercantile, early industrial and industrial society, people in the upper, upper-middle, middle and working classes also started to engage in status competition based around fashion. The fashion process created a class of consumers whose members wanted to own goods that were different in kind – not merely in value – to those desired by the subordinate classes. Distinctions in social status therefore began to be signified and expressed through the types of goods consumed. The rise of 'taste' – whether good or bad taste – was part of the way that distinctions became socially and culturally created, managed and controlled (Gronow, 1997). Ultimately, the rise of fashion across a wider population of consumers formed a ready market for the expansion of in the availability of consumer goods in the modern and late modern era.

Consumption and economics

Looking at another historical period, Corrigan (1997) writes that England's economic prosperity in the 18th century supported a consumer culture because people from a broader range of backgrounds and classes had more disposable income. This meant that fashionable goods were more accessible for many people. McKendrick et al. (1982) claim that 18th-century England was a period and place that fostered and generated an early consumer society based on the masses, instead of elite consumption. They assert that this development of wider consumerism across society related to changing economic conditions rather than to political factors – as had been the case in the earlier Elizabethan court. McKendrick et al. write that: 'the consumer revolution was the necessary analogue to the industrial revolution, the necessary convulsion on the demand side of the equation to match the convulsion on the supply side' (1982, p.9).

The industrial organization of production created some of the conditions required to develop this mass consumption across society. At the end of the

18th century, consumption was recognized as being a central feature of the English economy. The rising demand for consumer goods stimulated increased production efforts and output, and the higher levels of consumption across most groups and classes in society further stimulated economic production and profit (McKendrick et al., 1982). However, the expansion of consumerism was not solely a consequence of the changing processes of production or the development of capitalist industrial economics.

Another factor in the development of consumerism was the way that distinctions between social classes shaped their possibilities for emulative consumerism through fashion (McKendrick et al., 1982). The specificity of the English class system during the emergence of consumerism is significant. In comparison to other European nation states, the distance between social ranks in England was relatively close, which made it easier for some (limited) social mobility. The closeness of some social ranks and the transition between them resulted in a demand for distinctions between ranks to be unmistakably expressed and represented. One way for individuals to display their social standing was through the goods they owned, such as clothing, houses, cultural artifacts and domestic interiors (McCracken, 1988). This also meant that, if individuals were able to obtain goods associated with a social class above their own, they could easily and publicly claim to have a higher position and status in society.

The closeness of social ranks and the possibility of mobility were influential in facilitating the growth of emulative consumer expenditure (McCracken, 1988). Whole families were employed in certain growth areas of the economy, such as manufacturing and textiles, and the added income this provided enabled working-class families to participate in consumer society. McKendrick et al. (1982) raise a further point: because many more women were in paid employment, there was an increased demand for goods that had previously been produced in the home. This led to the rise in some domestic goods being produced and supplied to households by manufacturers. In addition, women were – to varying degrees – more in command of the money they earned in the workplace, so they had access to greater total family income. Women thus became consumers too, generating a market that was shaped by female consumer choice. This was shown by the growth in production of clothes, curtains, linens, pottery, cutlery, furniture, brass and copper for the home; and buckles, buttons and fashion accessories for women. The role of women in developing consumer markets is significant because they generated profits for the producers and suppliers, while giving women more opportunity to personalize their home and appearance to their own preferences (McKendrick et al., 1982).

The expansion of consumerism across mass society is open to interpretations that focus specifically on the way in which capitalist social relations shape the consumer. This focus emerged strongly in the early to mid-20th century in Western Europe. The development of mass media and the cultural industries interacted with mass society in order to inculcate individuals into market relations through a dominant capitalist ideology. Observers from the Frankfurt School argue that, during this period and into the present day, consumerism pulls people more tightly into capitalist relations and stops them from critically engaging with public issues. Even though individuals might feel that they are making choices by participating in status competition, they are, in reality, being enticed into the dominant relations of capitalism through a pervasive type of mass deception (Adorno and Horkheimer, 1973). From this perspective, consumer choice is not about individuals and groups seeking to engage in status competition and the social relations of taste. Consumerism is instead about incorporating people into a dominant ideology and into market relations. The role of culture acts to entice people into consumerism and into accepting a capitalist-based social order.

Choice in this context is enacted through commodity fetishism. Commodity fetishism refers to the exchange value of goods and services, and it points to the way marketing generates false needs. The gratification of these false needs unconsciously makes individuals in mass society believe they are in some way fulfilled. This also serves to divert attention away from the basic injustices of capitalist society and to reconcile people into accepting the dominant order. In this condition, people's needs in terms of emancipatory expression are not met and freedom is just an illusion. Freedom in capitalist society, from this perspective, is reduced to the choice between different consumer goods (Marcuse, 1964).

So far, this chapter has discussed the way in which certain contexts – political and economic – cultivated consumerism. Consumerism is related to, and interacts with, the dynamics of social status as well as class. Individuals' needs to express their social status became increasingly significant as the traditional ties of feudal relations and family position began being undermined by political and market dynamics. It is evident that the competition for status and recognition generated a consumer dynamic. Individuals at court competed by drawing on consumer goods, where their traditional status achieved through resources such as land and established family prestige were no longer sufficient. This meant that they had to buy goods from the market and keep engaging with the market, because this competitive element assigned a value to the 'novel and the new'. In this way, fashion emerged as a force that enabled individuals to compete.

The next stage is to consider how consumerism moved from the elite world of the Elizabethan court to wider society. The development of merchant classes and the availability of more goods, combined with a loosening of social positions, resulted in more people using consumer goods to express their social status. Again, there was a competitive and emulative dynamic, with individuals using fashionable goods as indicators of status. There was a general aspirational culture, with many individuals seeking to climb up the social hierarchy. Acquiring consumer goods was one way an individual could attain the appearance of status. In seeking to improve their social position, individuals copied the tastes of those above them, and this process of emulation produced a dynamic that created a constant need for new and fashionable goods. This more general consumerism had its own dynamic, just like that in court society, which resulted from the need for new and novel products.

For the Frankfurt School scholars, this need for novel products was part of the dynamic of capitalism, and consumerism from this perspective served to seduce people into the dominant ideology. From this perspective, there is little space for agency beyond choosing between particular consumer goods. Putting aside any normative judgments about consumerism, it is a complex activity that involves a dynamic interplay between marketing, taste and the ways that individuals seek to express their status and identity in different historical societies.

Marketing and taste

This chapter has so far examined how consumerism provided a way for individuals to obtain the socially 'correct' goods that enabled them to gain the appearance of a certain social status. The upper classes decided what was correct and tasteful in the world of consumer goods, setting the boundaries of taste and leading or following court fashion trends. In turn, those in lower positions copied the tastes of the upper classes. With the expansion of consumer goods and the higher levels of production, people started to question where taste might be set. They queried whether good taste should necessarily be set by the upper classes or if taste could be influenced through other means. These questions triggered the development of marketing and advertising, which subsequently became part of the dynamics of consumerism and gained a very significant role in consumer society (McKendrick et al., 1982).

One early industrialist who used marketing and adverting was Josiah Wedgewood, the owner of Wedgewood potteries in Staffordshire in England (McKendrick et al., 1982). He sought to influence taste and fashion, using marketing as a tool to constantly set new and fashionable tastes in products. He focused on promoting his pottery to the upper classes, deliberately positioning his goods as status symbols. By doing this, he continually fuelled the interest in, and desirability of, his pottery by producing new designs and lines, thereby using marketing to shape upper-class taste. Although the upper classes were still seen as trendsetters, 'good taste' was no longer seen as originating within their sphere; instead taste was being set through marketing that aligned with upper classes' tastes in consumer goods. However, it was still seen as the right thing to emulate the upper classes, which influenced those in the middle and working classes to buy the kinds of products that the upper classes were buying and, in doing so, endorsing themselves as being tasteful. This then locked the lower classes into a cycle of consumption, such as buying Wedgewood pottery, to display their status and an appropriate cultural sensibility. This created a dynamic between upper- and lower-class consumption, which was being fuelled and shaped through marketing. Then, consumer goods and the construction of taste more generally became shaped through advertising and marketing (McKendrick et al., 1982).

One effect of marketing was that local and traditional ways of consuming started to be deconstructed, as they were loosened by the new avenues of advertising such as the spread of magazines and the work of sales representatives across regions and provinces. This gave consumerism and the shaping of taste a wider, national scope, which subsequently expanded into global markets. Another consequence of marketing was that ever more goods gained a consumer value – for instance, 'functional goods' such as cooking pans became subject to fashionable variations in style and, in the late 20th century, brands become recognized as signifiers of taste (Tomlinson, 1990). This resulted in the use value of a product becoming less important than its fashion value, which, as McCracken (1988) argues, was a radically new way of viewing products. The dynamic of fashion created a constant cycle of desire to purchase products and services. This was, and remains, an important dynamic for manufacturers because it maintains ongoing demand for their products. Fashion affected more and more social classes until, towards the end of the 18th century, mass consumption emerged in contrast to the elite consumption that had characterized the Elizabethan court (McCracken, 1988).

This overview of the way in which mass consumerism developed over time shows the importance of material culture and class dynamics. It also highlights the cultural dynamics of change in the way that taste was shaped and shows how consumers became aware of, and discriminated between, a range of fashionable products to express their own status among their respective social groups and taste publics. This review provides insights into the dynamics of consumerism, but it does not fully explore the way in which individuals today embrace consumerism – beyond the desire to express their status among their peers. Furthermore, this analysis does not consider the entirety of the experience of consumerism for people, or why they value that experience. This gap in the analysis means that any conclusions to be made about consumerism remain only at the level of consumers being incorporated into a material and symbolic logic of status competition and coerced into a dominant capitalist ideology, according to the Frankfurt School perspective. Consumers may have some choice about what they consume and how they configure particular lifestyles, but this may not produce any active or critical engagement in broader cultural questions. There is, however, another aspect to consumerism, such as shopping as an activity, which is how people may use consumerism as a way of engaging in social life and of conveying cultural meaning, however limited that might be.

Romanticism and the consumer ethic

Campbell addresses this point in his book *The Romantic Ethic and the Spirit of Modern Consumerism* (1987). He takes an idealist approach to consumption, mirroring Weber's approach to production. Weber's (1930) perspective differed from Marx's approach to production, which was based on historical materialism by considering production at the level of ideas embedded within religion, in particular Protestantism. Campbell (1987) explores consumerism using the possibility that there might be an ethic of consumption based on an individual's particular cultural beliefs, which relate to how 'personhood' is socially and culturally created and made meaningful. Campbell (1987) enquires whether consumption could be both an ethic and an end in itself and, if this is the case, how has this ethic emerged. The reasoning behind Campbell's argument was that Weber had found an ethic based on religious ideas and beliefs, which led to the accumulation of capital – so, similarly, there could be an ethic of consumption prompted by a set of ideas or beliefs.

A point common to both modern production and consumption lies in the fact that they represent breaks with tradition. Traditional patterns of consumption were fixed and based on a perceived set of needs that people needed to satisfy. The various formations of 'wants' or desires were directly located from within a narrow needs-based lifestyle. McCracken (1988) observes that traditional peasants would regard anyone who worked beyond the need to secure subsistence as unusual, and they would think that this was damaging to a subsistence way of life. Aligned with that, traditional consumers would also raise concerns about anyone who was seen to consume beyond an established needs-based framework of consumption. However, following the rise of mass consumerism, contemporary consumers would be bemused by those who are not involved in an endless cycle of consuming, chasing new desires and following new fashions.

Campbell (1987) contrasts traditional and modern consumption further by examining how people learn to consume. He states that it is easy to understand how people in traditional societies learned – because there were only a limited number of goods and services available, people had less choice, as well as clearer cultural frameworks, which guided appropriate consumption. In contrast, he argues, a generational orientation to consuming is required in modern and late modern society. This means that there is (in theory) an unlimited and rapidly changing choice of goods and services for consumers, who have little cultural guidance in how to negotiate this arena. Campbell (1987) suggests that desiring goods is not, in fact, the nexus of consumerism, but the endless pattern of discontent which this demand for new things engenders. He argues that this pervasive wanting and desiring is a process separate from products and services that might be desired, and it defines a generalized mode of being.

Campbell (1987) understands and depicts this desire to consume in socio-logical, rather than psychological, terms. He argues that is there is no innate human disposition to consume (constantly 'wanting to want') but that the desire to consume is part of a particular form of civilization, namely indus-trial civilization, in which the processes of production and consumption have been split apart. Furthermore, he posits that the character of consumption in industrial and postindustrial societies is not embedded within any ratio-nal calculation of goods and services as economists might suggest, nor is it driven by irrational impulses in psychologist terms. Campbell's point is that consumerism is based upon a strong sense of social duty – an obligation to engage in 'want satisfaction as an end in itself' – as part of the Romantic ethic. Just as the Protestant ethic underpins production, he asserts, the Romantic ethic underpins consumerism.

Romanticism was a reaction against industrial society in terms of its lived reality, its attendant materialist and rationalist philosophies and its belief in the power of reason and science (key factors of the Enlightenment period). To counter what those in the Romantic Movement saw as the dehumanizing realities and beliefs of industrial society, they sought to touch upon the other senses and ways of seeing and being in the world. This was displayed in the way that the Romantics preferred 'feeling' to 'knowing' and valued the 'imagina-tion' over the 'intellectual'. They also attached more importance to the 'inner world' of individuals above foci that emphasized the outer (material) world. These countervailing ideas were influential – even revolutionary – in rethink-ing and reshaping what it meant to be an individual, because they replaced the established idea of the individual (Wessels, 2012).

The archetypal pre-Romantic period individual was based on an ethos of the commonality of humankind. The Romantics, however, developed a different idea – viewing each individual as a distinct and autonomous human being, stressing the uniqueness of every person, rather than the generalizability of people. This uniqueness of the individual became the dominant view of what it meant to be a person, and it extended through the relationship between the individual and society. Prior to the Romantic Movement, the individual was seen as being linked to society in formal ways, becoming shaped as an indi-vidual through these links. The Romantics, in contrast, did not believe in the continuous and interdependent relationship between individual and society. Instead, they saw the self and society as opposing, rather than complemen-tary, concepts. According to this view, the individual is divorced from society and he or she is obliged to develop their own uniqueness through a quest to become a unique individual (Campbell, 1997).

One way of achieving this was through the cultivation of many diverse experiences, which generally meant going outside the constraints of conven-tional society, which tried to limit experiential possibilities. The Romantic duty was to rebel against these limitations in the belief that, only without constraints could individuals freely experience everything the world had to offer – including all sorts of pleasurable activity (Campbell, 1997). Through this interpretation of self-development, the Romantics redefined individualism in relation to ideas of individual improvement and advancement. The Romantics advocated that people should develop as individuals by 'expressing' or 'realizing' themselves through exposure to powerful feelings and to various intense experiences (Campbell, 1997) rather than by hard work, discipline and self-denial. This pursuit involved seeking out new and more diverse forms of gratification.

This quest for individual fulfillment illustrates the link between the Romantic ethic of individual experiences and the practices of consumption. Central to this connection is the idea of the self, and although notions of self-expression and self-development are now taken for granted as being good, these are concepts that have only recently become valued (Campbell, 1997). Another aspect of the dynamic between an experiencing individual and the practices of consumerism is the idea of having 'autonomous control' – the notion that consumers are free to acquire things any way they like, selecting which products they desire (Campbell, 1997). Since production and consumption have become separated in modern consumerism, the remaining connection was between consumer choice and available products in the market. This maintains a link of some sort between production and consumption (a variant of this is prosumerism, which is discussed below). Part of this perceived autonomy is the way that consumers decide how they live and consume within a framework of both self-denying and self-gratifying activity – one where they make distinctions between necessities and luxuries.

A key characteristic of modern consumerism is a pervasive sense of hedonism (Campbell, 1997). This contrasts with societies before mass consumerism, where the search for pleasure was undertaken by trying new sensations. This search for new sensations was only really found among the wealthy elite whose everyday needs were already met. Because this small minority had the resources and power to strive beyond general satisfactions, they could search for more pleasurable experiences, which involved extending and deepening the pleasures of specific practices such as eating, drinking and sex. In modern consumerism, however, this aspect has changed in two main ways. First, hedonism is no longer the sole domain of wealthy elites, since it is found in different guises across many groups in society. Second, modern hedonism seeks pleasure in all social and cultural experiences, because the underlying ethos of contemporary life is to find self-satisfaction through pleasure (Campbell, 1997).

The central change in the shift from elite forms of hedonism based on specific activities to a pervasive hedonistic approach to everyday life is the move from seeking pleasure in sensations to seeking pleasure in emotions. Seeking pleasure in emotions can provide prolonged stimulation, which has a significant degree of autonomous control by individuals. This means that emotion becomes a form of 'willed control' that can be adjusted and separated from people's involuntary behavior (Campbell, 1997). It implies that individuals possess the ability to manage the nature and strength of their emotions. Whereas, in traditional hedonism, individuals controlled objects and events in the world in order to gain pleasure from them, and individuals find pleasure in modern hedonism through having control over the meaning of things (Campbell, 1997). The things that can have meaning ascribed to them by individuals are wide ranging and include objects and commodities, shopping, advertising, magazines, the home, food and drink, tourism, the body, clothes and fashion.

Lifestyles

This discussion shows how consumerism and senses of pleasure have become integral to modern social life by becoming embedded within the culture of everyday life. One significant manifestation of consumerism in advanced Westernized societies is through 'lifestyles', which Chaney (1996) argues is a late modern phenomenon. Although the word 'lifestyles' is used in various ways in popular discourse, there is a discreet sociological definition. Chaney describes lifestyles as 'patterns of action that differentiate people' (1996, p.4). This entails some relation to cultural forms, being about a certain 'style, a manner, a way of using certain goods, places and times that is characteristic of a group' (Chaney, 1996, p.4). Lifestyles do not, however, cover the whole of a particular group's social experience.

Lifestyles – which comprise sets of practices and attitudes – create, and are created by, sensibilities. These sensibilities are generated by groups who wish to distinguish themselves in terms of status and identity, and who, collectively in terms of lifestyle affiliations, shape the significance of their environment (Chaney, 1996). The choices that individuals make are, to a significant degree, informed by the culture of their social position, their everyday life and by broader public, popular and political culture. The dynamic of these processes creates sensibilities that frame and order the way that individuals seek to style the way they live – whether this means home decorating, ethical orientations or choices about social issues. Lifestyles also provide a way of connecting – or at least identifying with others – within the anomic late modern worlds of inner cities, suburbia and rural areas. Individuals can find ways to identify with others in mass society because they can read and interpret the way in which a particular lifestyle is expressed (Chaney, 1996).

This way of reading and interpreting the symbolic significance of material and nonmaterial goods, such as fashion or home furnishings, on the one hand, and ethics of living, on the other, are achieved through symbolic exchange and symbolic capital. Chaney (1996) asserts that both areas are part of the symbolic process through which lifestyles are developed, expressed and achieved. The way in which the Romantic ethic has been interpreted and practiced through imbuing Western everyday 21st-century life with pleasure is also transposed into lifestyle options. Chaney argues that one of the key factors in understanding lifestyles is to 'grasp the changing meanings and significance of goods in everyday life' (Chaney, 1996, p.71). This means that it is important to note that 'goods and services are being treated as symbols of attitudes and expectations that constitute a distinctive form of life' (Chaney, 1996, p.71). This symbolic relationship, which refers to the link between a symbol and the referent that generates its meaning, is changing through the contemporary and late modern development of lifestyles. During traditional, medieval and the early modern period, the link between a symbol and its referent was stable and located in the strong correlation between its production and use. Since postindustrial society to the current period, that link is being reconfigured because symbols have become more free floating by being taken out of their original context of use.

Although Chaney (1996) refers to late modernity in his analysis of lifestyles, there is some overlap with the notion of postmodern culture. Postmodernism can be summarized as an intellectual and social phenomenon involving the rejection of modernist thoughts, values and practices, along with a rejection of claims to identify 'truth' on the grounds that there are only 'versions of truth'. This general standpoint also means that any attempt to search for authenticity is pointless, because everything is inauthentic. Related to this is the perception that it is futile for an individual to try to identify meaning because there is infinity of meanings. Key postmodernist thinkers like Lytord, Baudrillard and Derrida celebrate difference, emphasize pleasure and take delight in the superficial, in appearances, parody, irony and pastiche. Drawing on postmodern writers, Brown (1995) notes how objects and meanings are reconfigured in various ways by people, and this relates to the way in which lifestyles are constructed in contemporary society through the practice of marketing and consumerism.

This means that the symbolism of goods is no longer necessarily connected to their original context of production, use or cultural provenance. A suburban European resident can buy and wear ethnic-style clothes either purely for fashion or as an expression of a particular ethos. The reason why that design of clothing, its fabric, color and dye were used – because of its origin from a particular culture – is no longer relevant. The processes of globalization and Western deindustrialization means that goods, services and meanings flow across the globe in diverse networks and channels (Lash and Urry, 1993; Lash, 1999; Castells, 2001). One result of globalization is that symbols and their meanings are becoming 'increasingly arbitrary and unstable' (Chaney, 1996, p.71), which might appear to create fragmentation or uncertainty in social life. However, interacting with this aspect of social change is the way that late modern individuals are highly reflexive and capable of interpreting symbolic goods and services from a range of sources. The networks that structure late modernity ensure that goods are exported across the globe, enabling those with sufficient money to purchase goods with a wide range of consumer choice. These consumers organize these choices through lifestyles, which also provide the orientating framework for reflexivity.

The development of lifestyles illustrates the way in which social forms and activities interact in historically specific ways, showing how individuals and groups negotiate their lived realities and their institutional frameworks. What is distinctive is the way in which these lifestyles are negotiated, suggesting that any argument that consumerism enables personal expression or, conversely, incorporates people into a capitalist exploitative system, is rather reductionist.

From this discussion of lifestyles, it is clear why Chaney (1996) defines lifestyles as 'patterns of action and as a distinct type of social grouping' that are 'embedded in the social order of modernity'. This definition offers a way to address both the structuring features and human agency in the creation and development of lifestyles. Although ideological influences are apparent in shaping lifestyles, they do not determine them – socially, economically or politically. There are, of course, hegemonic influences in shaping people as consumers, but individuals also contest existing attitudes, perspectives and institutions in choosing how they shape the way they live. Many people only shape a style of living through their economic and cultural capital as consumers. The cultural framework of consuming lifestyles is that it enables people to express their values – not just their status – in the contemporary social order. Thus, as with the dynamics of the creative industries (discussed in Chapter 8), lifestyles enable both integration into and resistance to, or ways to challenge, the social order. Chaney (1996) argues that the 21st-century proliferation of lifestyles results from the privatization of communal life in postindustrial society.

This review of lifestyles, just like the history of consumerism, shows how consumerism has a dynamic that creates change and ideas of autonomy and shows how individuals actively use it to compete and vie for position in society. However, this dynamic of consumerism also incorporates people into forms of capitalism by generating desires that fuel increasing levels of consumption. These desires are shaped by fashion and are internalized through an ethic of consumerism. This ethic has evolved from the principles of the Romantic Movement into diverse groups of consumers. For example, some individuals seek to create ethical or environmentally considered lifestyles. This sensibility is often shared with other like-minded people through expression of a certain style and range of consumer choices, as well as personal practices. At the other end of the continuum is the construction of lifestyles based more on fashion, with consumer groups who configure their symbolic meaning and the status that taste expresses through their purchase of particular styles and trends. This can be seen in the way that magazines shape levels of taste – from what is deemed to be 'higher'-status taste – shown through Vogue – to a 'lower'-level sense of taste – seen through Glamour magazine, for example (Corrigan, 1997).

Prosumerism

This consideration of lifestyles reveals that consumerism is used as a creative social practice to express status and sensibilities. It also incorporates people into the dominant economic system and social and cultural orders. The negotiation within consumerism between stances of resistance to – and acquiescence with – social order is political, since it refers to the political dynamic within everyday life (discussed in Chapter 5) as well as contesting social institutions and social order. Bauman (2007) identifies the way in which lifestyles and digital and social media combine to create a central ethos of contemporary life, which is a consumerist life in the West. As noted earlier in the book, there has been a shift in late modernity through which consumerism has become the main dynamic of social life, replacing production. Bauman (2007) extends this analysis to show how each consumer is now also a producer of consumer goods, services and sensibilities. In many ways, he follows Robins and Webster's (1999) proposition that ICT and digital technology would draw individuals more tightly into market networks.

Bauman (2007) extends this argument, pointing out that the notion of the 'customer' has changed, and that customers are now profiled and categorized according to their consumer behavior. For instance, supermarkets profile their shoppers and register their buying habits via loyalty cards, online shopping data and surveys. Each supermarket company then competes to attract the high-value consumers. Similarly, companies use computer ranking systems to prioritize their customer service calls, giving preference to those who spend more. Increased competition and consumerism on a worldwide scale means that the commercial sector realized it must be more aware of its segmented consumer base in order to remain competitive and profitable, breaking the segments down even more to target individuals accurately and individually. Bauman (2007) argues that these trends mean that the customer has become the commodity in contemporary society; as it is now the customer – the person – that is being bought and sold (or at least their data). The market has therefore truly penetrated individual and social life.

There is another layer that cuts across these dimensions, the notion of 'prosumerism'. Theorists have previously analyzed consumerism by separating the relationship between production and consumption (Ritzer and Jurgenson, 2010), noting that they were only linked to a small degree within industrial and postindustrial societies. Contemporary commentators, however, are beginning to challenge this idea of separation and reviewing the relationship between production and consumption. This renewed interest in the relation between production and consumption is based on developments within an information society framework, principally through social media and Web 2.0 technologies.

The term 'prosumer' refers to the closer link between producers and consumers in a 'third wave' of social and economic development, which is characterized by digital technologies, a strong service sector and pervasive consumerism (Toffler, 1980). The term reflects the way that consumers contribute to the production of goods and services – thus bringing production and consumption into a closer and more dynamic relationship (Ritzer and Jurgenson, 2010).

Although the current focus of academic research is on Web 2.0 prosumer culture, the trend of consumers being involved with production can be traced back to the mid 1950s. Ritzer and Jurgenson (2010, pp.18–19) cite the following examples:

- Drivers filling up their own vehicles with petrol
- Individuals serving themselves instead of using bank clerks, via ATM machines
- Shoppers processing their own shopping at a self-service check out
- Individuals working as booking clerks by buying holidays, travel and events online
- Patients working as their own care workers by using telehealth facilities
- Acting as a radio presenter by contributing to phone-in programs
- Being in a reality TV show

This trend is also evident in the use of social media based on Web 2.0 technologies (discussed in more detail in Chapter 9), which enables user-generated content to be circulated around networks of production and consumption because it allows users to produce content individually and collaboratively. Ritzer and Jurgenson (2010) suggest that this has produced an upsurge in prosumption, and that Web 2.0 is a key aspect in the development of the means of prosumption.

Examples of contemporary prosumption include:

- Wikipedia, where users generate, edit and comment on articles
- Facebook, MySpace and other social networking sites where users create personal profiles, interact with each other and build communities through the use of various media
- Second Life, where users create and enact virtual social characters, communities and environments
- The blogsphere, including blogs (web logs), microblogging (Twitter) and comments on other people's blogs
- eBay, where consumers (along with retailers) create a retail market
- Amazon.com, where consumers order products and write reviews
- Yelp! where users create online city guides
- GeoWeb, where users create and augment content onto online maps using Google, Microsoft and Yahoo tools

(Ritzer and Jurgenson, 2010, pp.19–20)

This type of activity can be viewed as empowering because it enables consumers to actively participate in shaping the market and the types of goods, services and knowledge that is networked among consumer groups or 'tribes' (Tomlinson, 1990). However, the wider question about consumerism remains – which is, whether the prosumer is being exploited. To answer this, it is necessary to consider the way that consumerism is negotiated. The development of the World Wide Web was based on a libertarian ethic and, for some, is considered as revolutionary and utopian. This idea of liberty is, however, based on a radical individualism and democracy, which can either be interpreted as being right wing, or, conversely, as digital socialism (Kelly, 2009). The symbolic aspect of exchanges using prosumption is that different consumer and producer groups or lifestyle tribes are actively shaping the digital marketplace – and the marketplace is a result of the politics of everyday life, late modern culture and social institutions.

Ritzer and Jurgenson (2010) extend the analysis of these trends in Web 2.0 by exploring the negotiation between capital and consumers in the spaces of digital production and consumption. They argue that are four distinctive new features in the relationship between capital and consumer in the context of Web 2.0. First, it is more difficult for capitalists to control prosumers than consumers or producers, and prosumers are more likely to resist tight control by capitalists. Second, the exploitation of prosumers is less clear-cut than in the case of traditional consumers. Third, they argue that a distinct economic system is emerging in which services are free and prosumers are not paid. Fourth, this context works with an orientation of abundance rather than scarcity and there is a focus on effectiveness rather than efficiency in prosumer capitalism. Ritzer and Jurgenson (2010) argue that these features are emerging and that they are open to debate. Furthermore, they point out that capital is extremely good at reorganizing itself and finding new ways to operate. However, they argue that in historical terms capitalism is confronting a new continually changing and uniquely resistant environment. These developments feed into the broader ongoing development of the types of negotiations that occur throughout the practices of consumerism and the institutionalization of consumerism. Whatever the merits or criticisms of Ritzer and Jurgenson's (2010) argument are, for the purpose of this book, they illustrate the way consumerism changes through time by the interaction of agency and institutions. They show in their focus on Web 2.0 that consumerism is continually changing and that it is historically shaped.

Conclusion

One of the defining features of consumerism is that it is a social practice and is institutionalized in different ways, and this relationship is shaped through the dynamics of negotiation. This negotiation has historically different characteristics, ranging from political to economic consumption through to the development of late modern lifestyles and prosumption. The development of consumerism clearly shows that it has been shaped and changed over time in accordance with Abrams' (1982) notion of process.

The history of consumerism shows how it first developed through political dimensions and the related economic and social dynamics that created the notion of fashion. During industrialization, consumerism became locked into an economic logic and it mainstreamed fashion for mass society via new social practices such as marketing. As mass markets developed alongside an ethic of consumerism, individuals and groups appropriated the symbolic significance of goods, services, styles and sensibilities into their own perceptions of self-development and the creation of lifestyle choices. People use consumerism to define their sense of self and its relation to society, negotiating this on economic, political and social terms through symbolic exchange and interaction. Whether consumerism allows people to participate in and shape social life, or whether it in reality incorporates people into existing economic systems is interesting – but not the fundamental point. Instead, the many characteristics of consumerism reveal the active relationship between social agents and symbolic institutions as they negotiate meaning through time.

8

The Creative and Cultural Industries

Introduction

The changes described in the previous three chapters are all aspects of what some commentators call 'the cultural turn' (Chaney, 1994). This refers to the way that culture has become more centrally placed within social life and the way it has contributed to the development of mass culture trades and industry, including the mass media industries that emerged in the mid- to late-industrial period (Steinert, 2003). The creative and cultural industries have undergone rapid transformations since the early 1980s and have moved closer to the center of the economy. In relation to this change, the meaning of 'creativity' and some cultural sensibilities have also changed.

The chapter first defines what is meant by the creative and cultural industries. It then discusses how the idea of culture and creativity has changed over historical time. It continues by addressing the various approaches that are taken in understanding the creative and cultural industries. It then explores the way the cultural industries have changed but also addresses some of the continuities in the sector, which in so doing highlights the way social change can involve both continuity and change. Next, the chapter explores a particular characteristic of the creative industries, which is that the meaning of some of the cultural texts that the sector produces express views that do not necessarily align with mainstream dominant culture. This helps to illustrate that in some cases of social change the relationship between institutions and agency is complex and contradictory. The chapter then moves on to discuss an exemplar of cultural texts, and it discusses an extremely popular product of the creative industries, namely 'soaps'. Lastly, the chapter explores the experience of work in the creative industries that addresses both agency and institutional perspectives.

Defining the creative and cultural industries

There is some debate about the precise meaning of 'cultural industries' and 'creative industries', however, in broad terms the term cultural industry tends to refer to the sector of museums, galleries, heritage sites and so on, which often have a public sector brief. This sector is traditionally supported by public sector funding, and its rationale is informed by national agendas of maintaining a strong cultural identity in terms of nation-state building and in terms of attracting foreign tourist and visitors. It is also often part of a widening access to culture and the arts and has been part of a drive to democratize access to culture. The term 'the creative industry' tends to refer to commercial companies, which are often vast global businesses that produce popular cultural texts and products. The ownership and organization of the creative industries has changed. The largest companies work across many domains of the cultural and creative industry, such as film, publishing, television or recording and form alliances, partnership and joint ventures to compete in a global market. Cultural products increasingly circulate across national borders, and images, sounds and narratives are borrowed and adapted from other places, not only producing new hybrids but also, for some, reaffirming the value of cultural authenticity. The long-standing domination of cultural trade by the United States may be diminishing, as seen in the rise of Bollywood, for example.

The way the cultural and creative industries conceive of their audiences is changing. There is greater emphasis on audience research, marketing and addressing niche audiences, and there has been a huge increase in the amount of money that is spent on advertising. The cultural tastes and habits of audiences are more complex, and the consumption of cultural products and turnover of fashions have quickened. Television programs, films, records, books, comics, images, magazines and newspapers have undergone radical transformation with an increasing penetration of promotional and advertising material in these products. In general terms, cultural authority is increasingly questioned and satirized in this commoditization of culture.

The question that is raised by these trends is, to what extent do these changes in the creative and cultural industries represent major epochal shifts in the way in which culture is produced and consumed? To address this means considering the way in which audiences and participants can engage in cultural activity and what those activities mean for people. The rise of celebrity culture, the development of the Internet and World Wide Web and the proliferation of user-generated content are all factors in the changing experience of culture. However, the culture industries are well placed to manage those changes and ensure the products and services they produce relate to the popular and niche markets of the 21st century. To address the above question means considering how culture is defined and analyzing what we mean by creativity in modern and late modern social relations.

Understanding culture historically

Raymond Williams traces the meaning of culture historically in relation to ways of life (1958). Building on the discussion in Chapter 3, Williams (1958) argues that the meaning of art and culture changes in relation change in economic, political and social life. He points out that the emergence of a modern industrial sense of culture was not just a response to industrialization but also to the new social and political developments of democracy. And within these changes, a third influence was the new emphasis of personal and private experience, which was also to affect the meaning and practice of art. Together, a particular mode of production, a framework for participation and the individual's interaction and sensibility to material and ideational lifeworlds constitute a culture.

Kroeber and Kluckhohn (1952) summarize many of the points made by Williams (1990). They argue that culture consists of patterns of behavior and action (both explicit and implicit) that are informed by, and expressed through, symbols. The process of culture constitutes distinctive achievements of human groups, including their embodiments in artifacts. Kroeber and Kluckhohn (1952) also highlight that there is a core of culture, which consists of historically derived and selected ideas and their attached values, which through culture may, on the one hand, be considered as products of action, and on the other as conditioning elements of further action. Thus, culture is historically embedded in social change both as an agent of change and as a subject of change.

Banks and McGee (1989) add another perspective into the consideration of culture and cultural change. They argue that many social scientists today view culture as consisting primarily of the symbolic, ideational, and intangible aspects of human societies. However Banks and McGee (1989) seek to emphasize the interpretative aspects of culture in late modernity. They suggest that a culture is not only its artifacts, tools or other tangible cultural elements but how the members of a group interpret, use, and perceive these elements of culture. It is, they argue, the values, symbols, interpretations and perspectives that distinguish one people from another in modernized societies; it is not material objects and other tangible aspects of human societies. This puts a focus on the way people within a culture interpret the meaning of symbols, artifacts and behaviors, and it is their culture that frames their interpretations. The active role of interpretation can foster change or it can be reactive and resist change.

These discussions indicate that the way society generates meaning and a sense of intersubjective and public senses of culture changes through time. The production and interpretation of culture is organized differently through time and culture itself is subject to change but it is also part of change. Culture can be an agency for change, and it can also be reactive and foster a resistance to change among people. Given that culture shapes and creates the meaning of change, one also sees that the meaning of creativity changes through time. This is discussed in the section below, which leads on into discussions about how culture and creativity is organized as industries or sectors.

Considering creativity historically

The term 'creativity' is used in several ways and has been understood differently in specific historical epochs. Liep (2001) addresses the idea of creativity in critical and anthropological terms, and he focuses on creativity within the incessant innovation of modernity (Liep, 2001, p.1). The contributors to his edited book seek to show how creative energy and creativity materialize when inventive people bring elements, which are already known but are separate together, in a novel way (Liep, 2001). Creativity is popularly celebrated, and it is not necessarily good or necessarily bad – it is how new artifacts and practices are used that defines its normative and moral position. Liep (2001) defines creativity as 'activity that produces something new through the recombination and transformation of existing cultural practices and forms' (Liep, 2001, p.2). This creativity is found on a continuum that ranges from small-scale everyday activity to intensive creativity concentrated in a single period or place. One of the conditions of creativity is that it involves the novel in a social environment, and Liep (2001) sees innovation as aligned with creativity, whereas improvization hints to conventional explorations of a set of possibilities within a framework of rules.

Liep (2001) asserts that there is a link between creativity and processes of modernity, quoting Miller (1994) in stressing that continuous change is part of modernity. This sets a precedent for humans to be creative because they and their social formations must 'forge for itself the criteria by which it will live' (Miller, 1994, p.62). Creativity has moved from being perceived as a divinely ordained order to one that is made in the present time and thus becomes a conscious human project. In the West, where modernity emerged, these conditions are linked to the rise and continuation of capitalism. The competitive capitalist marketplace saw the emergence of entrepreneurs who sought to adapt the means of production to create commodities to satisfy new desires, while engineers and scientists developed new ideas and materials, some of which could be used in mass and niche market innovation. Meanwhile, artists were freed from their dependence on various forms of patronage and were able to develop novel and individual styles to compete in the market. Within these conditions, creativity took two forms – secular and rational innovation – and a more emotional and spiritual creativity within the artistic realm.

These changes took different forms and were articulated in various ways within the global economic system (debates between what constitute the center and periphery are ongoing, cf. Wallerstein, 1974). However, in late modernity, deeper market penetration is entering further domains of social life alongside the decentralization of capital, the extension and intensification of an international economy and the globalization of the media, which, together, are transforming social and intellectual relations. In general terms, the decentralization of cultural production and authorization is resulting in a reworking of the cultural field, as evidenced by the undermining of high cultural elites who had the authority to judge what was authentic and whose tastes led to trends in popular and exotic cultural lifestyle choices (Liep, 2001, p.4).

The continually expanding commoditization of culture into late modernity has influenced views about creativity, with some commentators (such as Featherstone, 1991) arguing that the reification of culture within this process of commoditization has led to the aestheticization of everyday life and to the rise of a new class of professionals who are involved in the mediation of culture. This class focuses on the consumption of novelties, events and aesthetic experiences (Featherstone, 1991), creating new distinctions and sensibilities that are then adapted by broader society. Thus, where creativity was once consciously identified in the separate worlds of science and art, it has now become recognized within people's lifestyles. This has transmuted into new forms of distinction and elitism, with 'creativity' becoming a 'buzzword' that is applied to a range of contexts (Lofgren, 1994).

There are important aspects to consider in addressing creativity, which include 'creative destruction; modes of creativity; methods of creativity; and conditions of creativity and motivation and experience' (Liep, 2001). First, Liep (2001) reminds us that creativity is not necessarily good, for example in normative terms creativity can create military weapons that can kill thousands of people. He also counters the view that creativity is the weapon of the weak, which is a view often found in cultural studies. He points out that creativity is located within some of the contradictory processes of capitalism in which the bourgeoisie created, and continue to create, unforeseen forces of production and created new forms of communication and knowledge. However, the accumulation of wealth and the expansion of production and consumption are also accompanied by creative destruction on a huge scale (Schumpeter, 1934, 1939) in which many old forms of work and life were destroyed. The new forces of production also ushered in more destructive forces in warfare and environmental degradation. Thus, creativity can be used in projects of seduction, control and domination (Liep, 2001).

There is debate about the modes, methods and conditions of creativity (Wessels, 2000). In relation to modes of creativity, there is a distinction between explorations of conceptual space from the transformation of it. The process of creativity is also understood in different ways from the notion of the 'invention of culture' where practice always involves improvization in the adaptation and development of cultural forms in everyday life, which is never completely specified. In this sense, culture is always emerging (Wessels, 2009). At the other end of the continuum is 'true' creativity where highly unconventional forms emerge. There is also recognition of the diffuse, widely distributed creativity of everyday life. This ranges from concentrated bursts of creativity, which, in specific environments, under certain conditions and within particular periods, give rise to novel cultural productivity – to creativity in the more general activity of making lifestyle choices, for example (Liep, 2001).

If creativity concerns moments which 'involve the recognition of a novel analogy between previously unrelated field' (Boden, 1994), then creativity is seen as emerging in open spaces, gaps and interstitial zones (Rosaldo, Lavie, and Narayan, 1993). This approach focuses on the cultural field as characterized by discontinuities and discrepancies, which may be bridged in searches for new meaningful connections. Therefore, there is also a motivational and experiential sense to creativity. Friedman (1994) points out that both creators and their social groups are motivated by desires grounded in the socially structured experience space they inhabit, which suggests that creativity is located in realms of the habitus. Barth (1966) argues that creativity follows a dialectic process in which public representations become deeply personal symbols which 'give identity and direction' to subjects. The experiential aspect of creativity and the response to creations addresses the ways in creations are accepted. Peers in accordance with explicit paradigms and procedures judge scientific creativity. In relation to cultural creativity, more generally, the acceptance of a creation rests more with the dispositions of others that are embedded in their habitus. The experiential aspect of creativity and the response to creations both reflect the ways that various creations are accepted, which extends the meaning of creativity beyond intellectual and aesthetic spheres into deeply felt desires and emotions at the core of modern, late modern and postmodern experience (Wessels, 2009). These aspects of creativity are incorporated and organized by the cultural and creative industries in the production of cultural texts, artifacts and media.

Approaches to the creative and cultural industries

The development of the mass media in the mid-20th century was as key feature of mass culture. Early studies of mass media in society, such as Lazarsfeld and Merton (1948), viewed the role of the media in functionalist terms – believing that the media existed in order to fulfill certain needs in society. Thus, it could be argued that the taxonomy of the 'social functions of the media' could include a 'dysfunction' – that is, the 'narcotizing function', which renders 'large masses of the population politically apathetic and inert' (Lazarsfeld and Merton, 1948). Another early approach was that of the Frankfurt School[1], which addresses and emphasizes the way the media forms part of a capitalist industrialization of culture that serves to reconcile people to the dominating social order in a 'totalizing way'. Adorno and Horkheimer (1973) view culture as comprising more than just the media. Adorno and, later, Steinert (2003), consider the culture industry to be pervasive, molding the way in which individuals shape their lives and sensibilities – in both an historical mass society and in a more niche segmented mass society in late modernity.

In *Dialectic of Enlightenment*, Adorno and Horkheimer (1973) theorize that the phenomenon of mass culture has a political implication, namely that all the many forms of popular culture are parts of a single-culture industry whose purpose is to ensure the continued obedience of the masses to market interests. They review the production of cultural content and the content itself in a capitalist society, concluding that mass-produced cultural products and texts and the supply-driven aspect of cultural economics inhibit critical engagement in cultural life. This process reduces cultural goods to forms of entertainment, which, they argue, aims to appeal to vast audiences. This creates a different type of participation – or rather a nonparticipation – than that found in the intellectual stimulation of 'high' art or the immediacy of 'low' art.

They suggest that the mass culture industry is pervasive, and that it extends beyond both high culture and vernacular cultural entertainment. To illustrate this proposition, they highlight the predominance of mass-produced culture, created and disseminated by institutions such as the US film industry and consumed by passive, homogenized audiences. The cultural industries are seen as comprising part of a system of domination by a range of monopoly capitalist and state institutions in post-Enlightenment modern society. Adorno and Horkheimer (1973) draw attention to the problems associated with a system that 'integrates its consumers from above' and, in so doing, subsumes them into a dominant ideology. Both the Frankfurt School and the functionalist approach represent the focus of early media and cultural studies, which maintained that the media and culture affected society and individuals, and that individual agency was not influential.

Later theorists disputed this 'effects' approach, looking into the reception of media and cultural texts. Hall (1973) constructed a model for understanding how media and cultural products were negotiated within social relations, proposing that there are three 'moments' or components in the production and interpretation of cultural goods and texts. The first of these is the production of the text or product in which cultural meaning is encoded, which he called 'encoding'. The second is the text and its discourse. The third moment is reception – how audiences interpret the text or cultural product – which Hall called 'decoding'. He suggested that each of these components should be viewed as being relatively autonomous but nonetheless located within a wider process of cultural production and consumption. Hall situated the operation of mass media in society as 'articulated' moments, each of which was a site of cultural struggle or 'negotiation', over meaning. Hall's approach was within a broadly Marxian perspective, drawing on theories of ideology, in particular hegemony.

The concern about the reception of cultural texts produced an array of studies that consider how audiences interpret media and cultural texts[2]. This focus on understanding how audiences engage with texts stems from the contradictions emerging from Hall's use of hegemony. McGuigan (1992, p.76) asserts that the theory of hegemony has been exhausted by its attempt to straddle both the production and consumption of texts, arguing that 'hegemony theory bracketed off the economics of cultural production in such a way that an exclusively consumptionist perspective could emerge from its internal contradictions'.

Another factor in the development of audience studies was the realization that neither academics nor cultural institutions fully understood audiences (Ang, 1985). Public and private media organizations sought to make sense of audiences by constructing segmented audiences through the use of viewing figures and market research. There was a belief that audiences were ontological entities, which acted in particular ways, so media and cultural texts could be produced for, and targeted at, those specific audiences. There was also an acknowledgment that audiences were active rather than passive, only switching on a media program or visiting a particular cultural text or event if they found it interesting or pleasurable (Morley, 1986). The ethnographic research on television audiences, for example, showed that audiences actively interpreted television programs and revealed a shared intersubjective engagement with programs (Ang, 1985).

This shows how theorists have tended to analyze either the production or consumption of cultural texts. However, by using cultural forms to analyze the creative and cultural industries, it becomes possible to review both the human agency and the institutions that make up these sectors. This is useful in avoiding reductionist accounts of these industries and audiences. Cultural forms have, however, like most conceptual tools, been used in a variety of ways. The definition of the concept used in this book is the one developed by Chaney (1983, 1990). Chaney developed his concept from two main uses, namely those of Willis (1978) and Williams (1974). Willis and Williams developed the concept in different ways. Each approach provided an account of *necessary* factors in cultural phenomena; however, they did not provide a *sufficient* account of cultural phenomena. Willis uses cultural form to describe how objects, whether records, clothes, bikes and so on, are amalgamated as symbolic resources for a lifestyle. This cultural form is therefore a way of being in the world in which cultural phenomena are used to define and exemplify sociostructural relationships. A very different usage develops from Williams' concern to resist cruder forms of technological determinism. Williams pioneered an approach to the study of television in which the technology is employed within cultural conventions that partly stem from other narrative traditions and partly from wider cultural concerns. The cultural form is therefore both more than and less than a particular technology. Chaney's (1990) definition of the cultural form is made up of three interdependent dimensions: first, the relations of production – the social organization of producing and distributing cultural phenomena (including specific features of the technology); second, the particular themes, styles and narrative organization of each form; and third, the type of participative interaction between producer, performer and audience that is characteristically provided within a particular form – the social bonds that are implied and generated within a performance.

This definition identifies a relationship between the cultural industries, the cultural texts they produce and audiences.

Change and continuity in the creative and cultural industries

Hesmondhalgh (2007) points out that the creative industries have undergone a major transformation since the early 1980s. The key change he identifies is that they have moved closer to the center of national economies as well as the global economy. Creative businesses are no longer seen as secondary to a 'real' economy where durable or 'useful' goods are manufactured, and many of them are successful global concerns. In addition, the ownership and organization of the creative industries have changed radically. The largest companies used to specialize in one particular cultural industry – such as film, publishing, television or music – but they now operate across a number of different such industries (Hesmondhalgh, 2007). These conglomerates compete with each other but, more than ever before, they are connected – with each other and with other companies – in complex webs of alliances, partnerships and joint ventures. However, Hesmondhalgh (2007) notes that there is an growing number of small and medium-sized companies in this sector along with increasingly complex relationships between large, medium and small cultural companies.

There has been a move from nationally sold cultural products to an increasing export and circulation of cultural products across national borders. Hesmondhalgh (2007) notes how images, sounds and narratives are now being borrowed and adapted from other places internationally on an unprecedented scale, producing new hybrids but also, for some, reaffirming the value of cultural authenticity. This, he argues, might be an indication that the United States' long-standing domination of cultural trade may be diminishing.

These broader changes are interacting with more discrete developments in technological media, changing audience profiles, and cultural policies – particularly the Internet. There has been a remarkable proliferation of digital technology with a range of new applications, which has changed the way that cultural industries create products and engage with their audiences. These technologies have been adapted and appropriated by cultural producers, marketers and by diverse audiences. The interactive and networked character of digital media is changing the way that producers and consumers relate to cultural products and services (Wessels, 2012a). There is a dual process occurring, in which commercial companies can target their marketing and production strategies more closely to consumer trends, while some cultural producers are able to bypass traditional gatekeepers and release their products directly to audiences.

The latter can be seen in the rise of self-publishing for a range of cultural products – particularly books and music – where an author can release their work without the involvement of any established third-party publisher. The creator is responsible for, and in control of, the entire process including design, formatting, pricing, distribution, marketing and PR. The creator can either do all of this themselves or outsource all or part of the process to companies that offer these services. Another relevant change is the rise of crowdsourcing and crowdsourcing technology, whereby members of the public contribute towards funding production and influence or produce the content through collaboration. The use of crowdsourcing is varied, but, within the culture industries, it is being used particularly to create films. A growing number of film production companies are now using Kickstarter technology, which enables large corporations such as Warner Bros. to lessen the financial risk in film production by ascertaining that there is a clear market demand for their film from a niche crowd of avid fans. Studios that harness the power of crowds may be able to gain financial rewards by making films that audiences already support and want, that is, drawing on a 'prosumer' process to fund and make films. Although this might reduce the risk of financial box office disasters (such as Disney's $200m USD flop *John Carter*), it might also lead to a reduction of innovative stories or structures in filmmaking by giving the public what they already know they want, instead of providing new ideas on screen.

Hesmondhalgh (2007) also argues that cultural policy and regulation have undergone significant shifts since the 1980s. Long-standing traditions of public ownership have been dismantled, and there has been some deregulation of the media. Furthermore, important policy decisions are increasingly being taken at the international level. One example of the way that deregulation and internationalization of cultural policy is interacting with change is the program for television and radio 'digital switchover' in the United Kingdom in the late 2000s and early 2010s. Public Service Broadcasting (PSB) is a key institutional actor in political communication and, it remains so even in a more pluralistic media environment. Both the BBC and commercial television and radio in the United Kingdom are still regulated by government, albeit with different criteria (Gibbons, Thomas and Humphreys, 2011). This regulation is based on the role of public broadcasting in the United Kingdom's public and national culture, with regulatory requirements that include maintaining editorial balance and impartiality; preserving taste and decency; pursuing educational and cultural goals; and serving as a potential communication medium for the government during crises such as wartime (Starks, 2007). Research into the 'digital switchover' agenda shows the need to understand different forms of interactivity with citizens and to find ways to validate user-generated content to develop programming for more diverse audiences. Furthermore, it involves understanding how to shape the technological affordances[3] in line with the BBC's remit and its Charter and License (Starks, 2007).

One of the key aspects of creating a digital television and radio environment was that the British government had to go beyond itself and the BBC Charter to negotiate the terms and conditions of digital issues such as a spectrum policy. This had to be done in discussion with the International Telecommunications Union (ITU), which sits within the framework of the United Nations in shaping the scope and character of digital television and radio in the United Kingdom. This example shows how public policy and the consumer market now have to work together, and it demonstrates how television and radio producers and technology providers are having to shape their content and technology for more diverse audiences, who are seeking to personalize their viewing and listening experiences more, as well as having a more interactive experience with cultural content and media (Starks, 2007). This change shows the significance of both agency and institutions in shaping the television and radio experience.

This is part of a broader trend in the way that the cultural industries now regard their audiences. There is greater emphasis on audience research, marketing and addressing niche audiences that align with increasingly diverse and complex cultural tastes and audience habits. This is part of a social move away from class-based, mass audiences to smaller audiences that are differentiated through particular lifestyle and cultural interests, which are often partly shaped by identity. Furthermore, in a digitally networked economy and with the need for capitalism to maintain itself via increasingly rapid innovation, the production and consumption of cultural texts and the turnover of tastes and fashions have both quickened. Cultural texts, which Hesmondhalgh (2007) defines as cultural works of all kinds – such as TV programs, films, CDs, books, websites, comics, images, magazines and newspapers – have undergone transformations. For Hesmondhalgh (2007), these changes include the increasing penetration of promotional and advertising material into previously protected realms, especially in European television, but actually across other cultural industries. He notes that there are more products across a wider range of genres and across a wider of forms of cultural activity than ever before.

Hesmondhalgh (2007) argues that, despite these changes, there is some important continuity in the creative industries. For instance, television continues to play a huge role in cultural life and provides an important source of information and entertainment in people's lives. Cultural companies still use 'stars' to promote their products, and this has widened out into the contemporary landscape of celebrity culture with celebrities who endorse a wide range of cultural and consumer products. Although other countries such as India and Australia are emerging as major cultural producers, the United States is still considered the world center for popular culture and has a strong, if not hegemonic, influence on the shaping of entertainment and cultural texts. There is more user-generated content and participation in the development of some cultural products, along with a creative commons (open sharing agreement) in some areas of publishing, but copyright still remains fundamental to an understanding of the cultural industries because the intellectual property of their products has high commercial value. So, Hesmondhalgh (2007) shows that there are patterns of change – but also of continuity – within the cultural industries, explaining that they are interwoven with wider social change, which is also often characterized by continuity as well as change.

Ambiguity within the cultural industries: Meaning in cultural texts

The way that meanings are created and interpreted in cultural texts comprises one of the key ambiguities of the cultural industries (Hesmondhalgh, 2007). This ambiguity is that the cultural industries are made up of powerful corporations working within a capitalist framework but they produce alternative texts and narratives – including narratives that are resistant to the dominant ideology. The source of this conundrum is that the cultural industries need to make money to continue existing and, to do this, they have to attract audiences. Therefore, the cultural industries – like all other capitalist sectors – seek business conditions in which they can make money, by creating a constant demand for new products, minimal regulation by the state (outside of general competition law), relative political and economic stability and hardworking employees (Hesmondhalgh, 2007).

Despite this, many cultural texts appear opposed to this neoliberal philosophy, as Hesmondhalgh (2007, p.4) states that 'very often they orient their audiences towards ways of thinking that do not coincide with the interests of capitalism or of structured domination by men over women or institutional racism'. This may be because audiences are often seeking views and stories that run counter to mainstream depiction. There is a cycle in creating alternative or countervailing texts, which involves the cultural industries seeking to outdo each other in order to satisfy audience desires for the shocking, the profane or the rebellious (Hesmondhalgh, 2007). There is also a long history of social and cultural factors deeply embedded in societies about the role and position of art in cultural life, with art often accepted as a radical mechanism for transgressing established cultural and social mores. There is, therefore, an interest in, and expectation that, some cultural products will provide alternative views, which may prompt action or may simply provide a form of entertainment in which people can imagine different realities.

An exemplar of cultural texts: 'soaps'

The rise of mass media and (for some) expanded leisure time, as well as women acting more widely as cultural consumers, provides the context for new genres of entertainment. One example of new genres in mass media entertainment is the development of soap operas. Although television is a private domestic experience, the way scheduling used to work in the predigital period meant that the medium could attract audiences of particular types if it tapped into people's sensibilities and interests. During the era of terrestrial television broadcasting, audiences tended to be national audiences. A very strong influence in the creation of specific – very large – audiences was the soap opera, often called 'soaps'.

Moran (cited in Bowles, 2000, p.121) argues that the success of soaps on television is that 'television…works with a continuous open narrative', with each episode ending with a promise that the storyline will be continued in the next instalment. This is clearly seen in the United Kingdom's extremely popular soaps. In the 1960s, *Coronation Street* was first broadcast by ITV, a commercial TV company, and it quickly became a British institution, which remains extremely popular today. A later rival to *Coronation Street* was ITV's *Emmerdale*, which was based in a rural Yorkshire setting and began in 1972. It was initially shown in the daytime, but its high viewing figures meant that it was moved to a prime-time evening slot in the 1980s. In 1985, BBC's London-based soap opera *EastEnders* was created, and was an instant success with viewers and critics alike. The first episode attracted over 17 million viewers, and the Christmas Day 1986 episode was watched by 30.15 million viewers. *Coronation Street* and *EastEnders* currently share the most-watched position in UK television audience ratings.

Australia has been innovative and successful in producing teen-based soaps, with *Neighbours* and *Home and Away* achieving particular popularity internationally, as well as in their domestic market. The emphasis in *Neighbours* and *Home and Away* on young, attractive and charismatic characters enables them to find success in a middle ground between fantastical US soaps, which feature wealthy but tragic heroes and the grim, naturalistic UK soap operas populated by older, 'dowdy' characters. The casts of *Neighbours* and *Home and Away* are predominantly younger and more glamorous than the casts of UK soaps, and the stories exist within more realistic settings than the US daytime serials. This middle ground proved highly lucrative in the 1990s and early 2000s; however, by March 2007, Australian viewing figures for *Neighbours* had fallen to fewer than 700,000 a night; nonetheless, it continues to achieve significant ratings in the United Kingdom. This and other lucrative export markets, along with Australian broadcasting laws, which state that a minimum quota of drama must be produced locally for commercial television networks, help to ensure that both *Neighbours* and *Home and Away* remain in production. Both programs achieve higher ratings in the United Kingdom than in Australia (the United Kingdom has three times Australia's population), and the UK market makes a major contribution to the production costs. The continuing popularity of soap operas illustrates the way in which television as a cultural form forms an important role in modern and late modern culture and everyday life.

Research by commentators including Hobson (1982), Ang (1985), Radway (1987) and Scannell, Schelesginger and Sparks (1992) shows that soap audiences interpret the programs in relation to their own experiences, which they then share collectively, in terms of an intersubjective, and largely national, audience sensibility. This was found to be true for other programs as well, and these studies show that audiences have a high level of autonomy in how they interpret the media texts, so the meaning of the program is created by members of the audience. This is a significant move from understanding audiences either as passive or as people who decode meanings that have been embedded in the texts by the producers of the content and programming. To some extent, this argument de-emphasizes the role of producers as well as the way in which each medium shapes the content and engagement. This idea of total free play, however, provides a rather single-focused argument that does not take into account the different dimensions of cultural production in modernity and late modernity, and it lacks a framework to address the ways in which texts are produced and shared as well as being interpreted – thus linking structure and agency.

Work in the creative industries

The status of those working in cultural production has changed over time. Williams (1981) and Bourdieu (1996) assert that the management and circulation of creative and cultural products and texts have taken radically different forms in different societies. For instance, in 19th-century Europe, systems of patronage gave way to the organization of symbolic creativity through the market. It was at this point that the cultural industries began to emerge and, from the 20th century onwards, this market organization began to take a new and complex form. As social relations changed, individual artists gained autonomy from patronage as they entered market conditions, although support from wealthy elites remained important.

Hesmondhalgh (2007) explores the 'symbol creators' in the cultural industries, which redresses the dominant focus of sociological theory on the creativity of audiences, and those who do not, in general, work professionally as symbol creators. Hesmondhalgh (2007) makes a general observation that the invention and performance of stories, songs, images, poems, jokes and so on, in whatever type of technological form, involve a particular type of creativity. He identifies a key characteristic in this observation, which is that all creative work involves the manipulation of symbols for the purposes of entertainment, information and enlightenment. Therefore, he argues that instead of calling this type of work 'art', it can be called 'symbolic creativity', and that 'artists' are best referred to as 'symbol creators'. He notes that scholars in the 1990s such as Born (1993), McRobbie (1998) and Toynbee (2000) started to focus on the symbolic creators. This was important because cultural texts would not exist without their symbolic creators, although they rely on industrial systems for reproduction, distribution, marketing and remuneration for their work. Hesmondhalgh (2007) also raises the distinctiveness of cultural work – that it can enrich people's lives in various ways through items such as novels, music and films – even though different people gain different amounts of pleasure from various cultural forms and genres.

The way that the creative and cultural industries organize and circulate symbolic creativity reflects inequalities and injustices, which relate to existing social divisions along class, gender and ethnic lines in contemporary capitalist societies (Hesmondhalgh, 2007). There are vast inequalities in access and entry to work in the creative and cultural industries. Furthermore, working conditions and rights in the sector are generally poor, with many people employed on freelance or casual contracts, meaning that those seeking to create cultural texts often struggle to earn a living (Hesmondhalgh, 2007). Many people dream of becoming a successful writer, producer or artist, but failure is far more common than success in this competitive sector. In addition, many people are attracted to this sector believing that they will retain personal creative freedom but, in reality, there is commercial pressure to produce specific kinds of texts, which reduces creative autonomy. It is also difficult for aspiring symbolic producers to find organizations that can allow for high degrees of autonomy (Hesmondhalgh, 2007), since they are operating in a competitive capitalist system. The use of web-based publishing has developed partly because it enables symbolic creators to bypass gatekeepers to the sector, and it allows them more creative freedom. It might also provide bargaining power, as seen by the music group Arctic Monkeys, who broadcast their music online and established a fan base before negotiating a contract with a recording company.

Despite these constraints, the cultural industries need symbolic creators who have the social talent to understand what particular audiences will respond to and who can devise successful cultural products. Therefore, there is a specific need for the original and distinctive symbolic creativity that taps into cultural frameworks and audiences, and this cannot be controlled by the cultural sector itself. Because of this need for creativity, owners and executives will make concessions to symbolic creators by granting them more autonomy (self-determination) than they would to workers of equivalent status in other industries and to most workers historically (Hesmondhalgh, 2007). This freedom is only given for a limited amount of time and is only extended as long as the symbolic creators remain successful. It also acts as a control mechanism that helps to maintain the lure of working in the cultural sector, despite the reality of scarce and often poorly paid work.

Cultural businesses are the mechanism through which creative texts and products find markets and audiences. These industries have the challenge of finding and then creating audiences for the texts that the symbolic creators produce (Hesmondhalgh, 2007). Although some cultural events automatically attract mass audiences – such as the Olympics – companies' marketing departments usually have to identify and then appeal to niche audiences for different cultural texts, products and tastes. Since different groups of people tend to have different tastes, much of the work done by cultural businesses comprises linking texts with audiences, and creating awareness of cultural texts that are new to the private or public market. This requires clever marketing and a network of industry actors who can market cultural texts to niche audiences (Hesmondhalgh, 2007). No matter how accomplished the marketing of cultural texts, this is nonetheless a highly risky enterprise, because there is no certainty about which cultural text will succeed or fail.

In seeking to understand the cultural industries, Hesmondhalgh (2007) asserts that the central role of symbolic creativity helps to explain the patterns of change and continuity in the cultural industries, rather than change and continuity in texts or understanding how audiences interpret texts. By addressing symbolic creativity, he explores the relationship between the systems of production and cultural texts, which shape the cultural industries. This approach highlights how complex, contested and ambiguous the cultural industries are. They do not totally incorporate audiences into any dominant ideology, nor do they necessarily foster resistant or oppositional social action. The uncertainly about cultural production and interpretation raises questions about whether the cultural industries are agents of change – in social, economic or cultural terms.

In the mid-1990s, there was a general belief among policy makers and various commentators that the cultural industries would become more important in the economy, and that the sector would experience high rates of growth. Although the economic role of cultural production has grown, it has not done so as quickly as they predicted. In addition, the economic benefits this sector brings should be understood in terms of the cost of some poor working conditions. To understand the implications of this move in broader terms, it is important to consider the relationship between culture, society and the economy.

As discussed in earlier chapters, much of recent sociological focus has been on theories of transition, which have sought to understand the move from industrial to postindustrial societies, and then on to information societies. Most of the analysis – such as Bell (1973) and Castells (2001) – argues that these changes are characterized by the importance of knowledge as a commodity in economic activities of various kinds. The increased production and faster distribution of products, images and information are also reflected in changing social and cultural relations. These types of changes sit at the center of changing perceptions of modernity, late modernity and postmodernity. Some of the key characteristics of modernity are present, but these have been accentuated. For example, modernity is often characterized as being ephemeral and fragmented, which in postmodernity has become accentuated so that rationality and meaning seem to have broken down (Lyotard, 1984; Harvey, 1989). The rapid circulation of information, images and knowledge is also at the center of the creative industries, since it manipulates different symbols and symbolic systems in rapid innovation cycles.

Bell (1973) highlights the use of information in a range of information-rich industries, and some analysts such as Lash and Urry (1993) develop this to suggest that the ability to use information creatively is closely linked to symbolic creativity and is becoming increasingly central to social and economic life. This leads Lash and Urry (1994) to stress the importance of cultural industries to the economy, while claiming that the cultural industries are becoming more akin to other industries and losing their distinctiveness in the economy. This is because most economic activity involves some type of symbolic creativity, as seen in advertising and the specific design skills needed in the generation of digital content and products, for example (Hesmondhalgh, 2007). This argument is demonstrated through the increasing importance of brands, which are, in many respects, cultural texts that are developed by symbolic analysts (Wolf, 1999). Both social science commentators and business and management analysts have recognized the value of brand names in generating sales and achieving continued growth and innovation. To develop a successful brand, a great deal of work is required to develop product names, logos and rules for their representation and dissemination.

Hesmondhalgh (2007) argues that brands are only one aspect of the increasing role of information, culture and knowledge in late modern society. This trend was discussed in terms of a 'weightless world', which suggested that, in the future, knowledge economy workers would be living in a world separate from material goods (Leadbetter, 2000). Closely related to this is the idea of a 'new economy' (Castells, 2001), in which traditional business cycles of boom and slump would be replaced by continuous growth. ICT, branding, information and culture were all seen as being central to this new configuration. In the early 2000s, such notions were increasingly joined by a new concept, that of the 'creative economy' (Howkins, 2001), and, even after the dot.com bubble of the early 1990s, there is a belief in the knowledge revolution that includes a strong focus on the importance of 'creativity' (Florida, 2002, 2011). Some academics argue that 'creativity' 'will be the driver of social and economic change during the next century' (Hartley, 2005, p.1). Hesmondhalgh (2007), however, brings the debate back to asking critical questions about how much the role of creativity is becoming central to the economy. He comments that it is surprising how few systematic, historically informed analyses of changes of these industries have been carried out by those involved in transitions to the information or knowledge society, to economies based on brands, on signs and meanings and on creativity. Such analysis would help to identify the changes and the continuities in the cultural industries, and ways in which audiences engage in culture.

To assess the significance of these changes and to understand how they are embedded within broader social change, we need to understand what role the cultural industries play in society. Hesmondhalgh (2007, p.3) asserts that the cultural industries are the key producers and distributors of products and texts. The significance of this production and distribution work is that 'the making and circulating of products – texts – ... have an influence on our understanding of the world'. Therefore, the cultural industries shape individuals' understanding of the world to some extent and, although lived experience is felt and understood on personal terms, the cultural industries – and the media in particular – frame our knowledge and experience (Silverstone, 2006).

Debates about the nature and extent of this influence comprise the contested core of cultural and media research (Corner, 2000). Going beyond a reductionist analysis of the media and cultural industries' influence, many researchers paint a picture of the complex, negotiated and, often, indirect nature of media influence in particular, as well as other cultural products – an influence which is often pervasive. Webster (1995) argues that people are influenced by informational texts such as newspapers, broadcast news, documentaries and analytical books, but also by entertainment. Hesmondhalgh (2007, p.3) takes a similar view, stating that: 'films, TV series, comics, music, online gaming and so on provide recurring representations of the world, which in so doing act as a kind of reporting that both creates and reproduces our cultural imaginations'. In this way, people draw on cultural texts and products to constitute their private and public selves as well as their fantasies, emotions and identities. These products contribute strongly to people's sense of who they are, of what it means to be a 'woman, man, an African or Arab, a Canadian or New Yorker, straight or gay' (Hesmondhalgh, 2007, p.3). Even though these texts are influential in shaping our cultural landscape, they are interpreted and, indeed, produced by people through their own, unique life experience. Therefore, meaning is always being contested (Geertz, 1973).

Conclusion

The creative and cultural industries are a key part of modern and late modern social and cultural life. The sector, its audiences and its texts combine to create cultural frameworks for people and institutions in contemporary life. Scholars have tended to focus on either the structural and institutional aspects of the creative industries or agency and audiences. However, the way in which the cultural industries are embedded in, and shaped by, social life indicates that neither approach can address the meaningfulness of cultural texts in social life. Neither can they account for the way in which what creativity means has changed over time.

This chapter shows how the cultural and creative industries express the ambiguities of contemporary life and change. Creativity, texts and the institutions that shape cultural production combine with audiences in varying ways to provide a landscape of cultural goods in late modernity. The level of agency from audiences is open to interpretation; however, the way that individuals and audiences interpret texts is influential in defining whether a text is successful or not – in both commercial and critical terms. Producers are influential in creating and distributing cultural texts, but only in relation to audiences. Furthermore, the characteristics of the text and cultural products are a key feature in this relationship, because they are critically evaluated by producers, consumers and – indeed – prosumers.

Any review of the relation between structure and agency within the cultural industries, therefore, requires a 'cultural forms' approach. This analytical device can be used to explore the complex dynamics of changes in the cultural industries, in creativity and in types of engagement in culture. Cultural forms are 'systems' in which artifacts and materials are used, organized and given meaning through social and cultural conventions. This approach was used to address the processes through which the cultural form of television, and one of its genres – soaps, takes on its own distinctive characteristics.

Finally, the way the cultural industries are changing means studying culture, which Geertz (1973) defines as: 'those webs of meaning that man himself has spun', as well as seeking the significance of what is being said and done in ongoing social action. Geertz sees culture as an 'enacted document' – in whatever form – suggesting that the 'thing to ask is what their import is ... [what] in their occurrence and through their agency, is getting said' (1973, p.10). This refers back to Abrams's (1982) point that the study of change involves looking at meaning, at experience and how that relates to institutional change. The creative and cultural industries provide examples of the way that process is contested in contemporary society.

9

Changes in
Communication

Introduction

The way people communicate is a defining feature of society. Dewey (1939) argues that society is made in, and through, communication. The means of communication have changed historically, with key aspects of change in early modern and modern society including the invention of the printing press and the spread of literacy. A further significant innovation was the development of telephony, and then radio and television for mass communication. These were followed by another radical innovation, the Internet[1], which enables interactive communication across global time and space. This chapter explores one distinctive feature of modernity and late modernity: the media and media environment. It shows how the way people communicate is influential in shaping their social relations and public culture, as well as personal and popular communication.

The chapter first discusses the role and characteristics of the media in contemporary life. It then addresses the way in a communications environment is being shaped and explores both continuity and change and change in this environment. Next, in order to explore some of the new developments in new media, the chapter outlines some of the key concepts that are used in analyzing new media. It then moves on to discuss the social relations of a new communications environment, which forms the context with which to discuss the mediapolis and proper distance in communication.

The role and characteristics of the media in contemporary life

The media is a defining feature of modern and late modern life. Mediation (Silverstone, 2005b) and mediated discourse (Smith, 1988) are both distinct features of contemporary technologically advanced societies. Silverstone shows how different media interact with social and cultural life to shape experience, seeing mediation as an uneven dialectical process between media institutions (the press, broadcast radio and television and the World Wide Web) and the dissemination of symbols in social life. Silverstone uses the term 'dialectic' to explain how the processes of communication interact with the social and cultural environments that support them and the relationships that individuals and institutions have to that environment and with each other (Silverstone, 2005b). In contemporary everyday life, audience participation can be understood through the role the media play in social life and by the audiences' own experiences, which, in part, shape their understanding of the world (see Chapter 8). These processes are part of the communicative and interpretive practices of individuals and groups who are differently positioned, both socially and culturally, and in their relations to media institutions (Wessels, Anderson, Durrant and Ellis, 2013).

The media form a mediapolis through which questions of public culture and personal interest are articulated and mediated. Silverstone defines this mediapolis as a 'mediated public space where contemporary political life increasingly finds its place, both at national and global levels' (Silverstone, 2006, p.31), which has material outcomes for social life. This approach considers lived experience and recognizes that the media frame social life, which can either facilitate collective action or fragment understanding to undermine individual and community expression. The emergence of this new communications environment is shaped by the way that digital media are mixing with more traditional media. An analysis of the process of change within communication needs to situate changes in the relationship between media technologies and the social organization of media institutions with the experiences of participants and audiences in everyday life.

New media, which is characterized by digitization, convergence, interactivity and the rise of networks, is reshaping the communications environment (Wessels, 2010). The cultural contexts of new media developments show a relative underdetermination of new media when compared with traditional media, as the medium allows users to participate more interactively in media forms. However, although there are examples of innovative and participative new media, such as local digital television (Harrison and Wessels, 2005), these are nonetheless part of the media environment's culture of global capitalism, which reproduces media concentration as well as generating new media nodes in the communications environment. The ubiquity of interactivity and more individualized uses of new media raises questions about the quality of its content and online experiences. For example, although social networking sites (SNS) connect people with each other, they also produce arenas of personalized and individualized entertainment, rather than cultural critique in an active public sphere. YouTube circumvents the traditional media's organizational structures and uses a social networking format to produce semi-public spaces where user-generated content is shared among self-selecting audiences with varying degrees of privacy and publicness. The character of this semi-public realm is one which focuses on interaction and dialogue around affinities that are entertainment based and individualistic. This situates social networking sites away from a public sphere ethos and more towards a networked individualism of taste friendships rather than taste publics (Wessels, 2010).

What is still unclear about digital media is its potential for deliberative democracy via new forms of networking and for the formation of political discourse and action (Silverstone, 2006). This means considering civic networks and their media tools to explore the character of communication, as well as media organizations. The design of digital media varies, and each shapes a different kind of communication in terms of characteristics and social forms, which include individual, crowd, and community-based communication (Haythornthwaite, 2011).

Interest-graph media such as Twitter facilitate communication based on shared interests, regardless of whether participants know each other or not, and it is based on individual followers. Social-graph media such as Facebook facilitates communication between people who know each other (as well as those who don't directly know each other, such as commercial marketing pages or online fan pages) and allows them to share information and build shared understanding. Crowdsourcing uses technology such as Kickstarter to draw on the power of the crowd to gain contributions for projects; it is an anonymous response to a directive. Community-based digital platforms are configured using various digital media for specific communities – such as the Com-Me-Toolkit for use in developing countries. This toolkit is a collection of hardware and software components that support content creation and sharing in locations around the globe where there is low textual and computing literacy and limited power and network coverage. It includes a Com-Phone – a multimedia narrative application for a mobile phone; a Com-Tablet – a tablet-based media repository; a Com-Charge – a phone charging station; and a Com-Cam – a TVCam device for sharing mobile phone content on old TVs. Used individually or together, these components allow groups such as nongovernment organizations (NGOs), community associations and governmental organizations to facilitate digital content creation and establish community media sharing infrastructures within rural and other isolated populations all over the world.

These media are part of what Castells calls 'mass self-communication' (2009), in that individuals can communicate with each other in a networked public way without any intervention from media organizations. In many ways, this frees up open expression and enables more communication among individuals. The media have the potential to play a significant role in the public sphere, providing a space for debate in civil society; however, its potential and precise form is not, as yet, determined (Papacharissi, 2002). The notion of the public sphere is a contested one, but it points to a more or less autonomous and open arena for public debate in civil society and involves the use of various forms of media including pamphlets, the mass media and the Internet (Calhoun, 1992). Traditionally, public spheres were considered national in scope; however, the global reach of Internet-related communication is now interacting in the notion and practice of public communication globally through political, economic and cultural dynamics at local, regional and global levels.

Another defining feature of Internet usage is that it blurs the public and private spheres of social life, producing interaction and culture that has varying levels of publicness. The rise in the use of interactive and mobile communications technology for personal communication has resulted in changing experiences of the public and the private spheres. A further dimension of this trend is the growth of social networking sites and user-produced content, which is sometimes appropriated by mass media outlets (e.g. for news items), and which blurs private and public senses of communication (Wessels, 2012).

These dimensions are bringing a different dynamic into public communication by destabilizing the existing institutional understanding of differences between the private and public, producer and consumer, the rituals of reception in terms of place and time (daily, weekly and yearly), and audiences. These factors are reshaping the communication environments of late modernity.

Shaping a communications environment: Continuity and change

The ways in which people use media, including ICT, within various domains of social life are influential in shaping the communications environment. Culture is meaningful in domestic and public life, bridging both dimensions with each informing the other. As chapters 7 and 8 show, individuals and groups engage with cultural goods and, in so doing, produce meaning to their social life – acting as cultural producers as well as consumers. These activities feed into the shaping of the public sphere, and particular patterns of using, sharing and debating 'private troubles and public issues' (Wright Mills, 1959) illustrate the way in which information and its communication is used to develop public sensibilities. The patterns of communication change within particular historical social orders, which in turn influence the character of participation in a public realm. For instance, the emergence of the bourgeoisie in European nation-states saw the development of a reading public that generated practices of debate. This literary public sphere created and sustained the practice of debate through engagement with cultural forms such as the novel, as well as letters, pamphlets and newspapers. Using these forms, the bourgeoisie reflected both on themselves and on the role of the state in the formation of society (Wessels, 2009).

The sphere for public dialogue has changed since early capitalism, through organized and disorganized capitalism, up to the present networked system of global capitalism. The communication environment for public dialogue is changing in terms of both the technologies and institutions of communication and the characteristics of participation in public communication. The role of the media as critic and in framing political and cultural commentary is part of print journalism and public service broadcasting (PSB), with PSB regulated to varying degrees, depending on state frameworks in different nations. However, the development of the Internet in new media forms is challenging existing media such as audiovisual broadcasting, radio and print journalism as well as the character of the public sphere. Part of this challenge is changing the institutional relationship between producers and consumers, since networked new media offer consumers the potential to be more actively involved in the production of content, voicing their concerns and defining their own media agendas.

The possibility of circumventing public communication through social media is impacting on political communication. The research report, *Reading the Riots* (Roberts, 2011), shows how political communication is not fully aligned with the ways that citizens are communicating with each other and with public and governing institutions. Because of this, people's concerns are not being heard through conventional communication channels and, therefore, some significant issues are not being publically debated. Research by Lewis et al. (2011) on the use of Twitter in the United Kingdom's 2011 riots details how many 'civic information flows' are now outside conventional communication channels. This is related to the rise of a post-democratic society (where elites manage much of the public debate) in which the existing democratic process does not fully facilitate the expression of civic concerns (Crouch, 2012). Political communication is therefore being destabilized by a more diverse society that is self-organizing in new ways, and by the proliferation of media platforms and services, which allow for new networks of communication (Dahlgren, 2005). There is evidence of this pattern across the globe. For example, the Egyptian uprising in 2011 and, more recently, protests in Turkey and Brazil in June 2013 were organized via social media.

The development of new media reaffirms the ways in which individuals negotiate their mediated and situated worlds. It extends their activity into the realm of negotiating interactive communication, including user-generated content and varieties of alternative sociopolitical and cultural activity, in contrast to the mass media of commercial and PSB. However, PSB has a strong ethos of broadcasting that seeks to serve as a public good. New media reiterates the tension between the consumerization of the media (including the Internet), and its historical legacy of free and unregulated communication (Berners-Lee, 1999). Therefore, new media can be considered not only a tool for open and free communication to be used for the public good but also a tool appropriated by global capital for marketing and consumerist communication. Likewise, although Habermas (1989) recognizes the democratizing opportunities of the mass media, he argues that – through the commoditization of culture – the mass media are drawn towards populist programming in which publics comprised less of debate and more of consumption. The commercialization of the media (both new and traditional) and the commodification of culture are leading to private life becoming publicized and public life becoming privatized, with culture as a site of critical debate becoming emptied of meaning (Habermas, 1989).

Key concepts in analyzing new media

Two key characteristics of new media are digitization and convergence, which, in the communications environment, generally add to their recombinant characteristic – the way that:

> new media systems are products of a continuous hybridization of both existing technologies and innovations in interconnected technologies and institutional networks. The recombinant and hybrid metaphor suggests that, although ICT are influenced by existing technological contexts, and may have unintended consequences, to a great extent they are the result of human actions and decisions.
>
> (Lievrouw and Livingstone, 2006, p.23)

Digitization and convergence must be seen in relation to interactivity in mediated forms of communication, the rise of networks, virtual communities and identities in the context of political, economic and cultural globalization. The characteristics of institutional agency and people's actions are central in the definition of new media and new media is actively being configured at both levels. This relates to the fact that new media involves: 'artefacts or devices that enable or extend our abilities to communicate; the communication activities or practices we engage in to develop and use these devices; and the social arrangements or organizations that form around the devices and practices' (Lievrouw and Livingstone, 2006, p.23). These aspects of ICT and their social contexts interweave within cultural forms and, in so doing, produce specific forms and content for media production and use.

Part of understanding new media involves addressing three interrelated social and technological processes:

- Digitization and convergence
- Interactivity and networks
- Virtuality and globalization

(Lievrouw and Livingstone, 2006)

The convergent approach addresses the way that new media technologies arise out of interaction between digitized content, convergent media forms and global communications networks (Flew, 2002). Convergence initially arises out of the growing linkages between media, information technology and telecommunications. This approach posits that the consequences of digitization, convergence and networking include a shift in employment towards service and information in a new economy, away from agriculture and manufacturing (as discussed in Chapter 5). A further indicator is the rise in major corporate mergers and takeovers in the media, telecommunications and computing sectors, as well as the growth in global Internet access and computer-mediated communication (CMC). Digitization, convergence and networking manifest themselves in the growing significance of interactivity in all forms of mediated communication, in the rise of a networked society, in the increase in virtual communication as expressed by online communities, and through the adoption of virtual identities, as well as political, economic and cultural globalization.

Part of the academic debate regarding changes in the media environment includes the notion of a virtual culture and the emergence of digital media. Gauntlett (2000), for example, argues that social relations have become increasingly 'virtualized' through the development of the Internet and CMC. This perspective suggests that virtual communities have the potential to provide a basis for new forms of community and for a revival of democratic citizenship. Extended online participation is made possible by developments in digital media, including all the media that combine and integrate data, text, sounds and images stored in digital formats, and which are distributed across networks.

These features are further developed in social media, which allow people to self-publish and communicate with each other at mass and scale. There are different types of social media, and each type produces a particular type of communication. Interest-graph media (Ravikant and Rifkin, 2010), for example, enables users to form connections with others based on their shared interests, regardless of whether they know the other person or not. Twitter, a microblogging service in which users share short status updates, encourages this model, with users 'following' content producers in an often one-way relationship. Followers have no obligation to respond or participate in the Tweet. Social-graph media is different as it encourages users to connect with people they have real-life relationships with. Facebook, for example, provides a way for people to keep in touch with friends who are remotely located as well as share information between friends who see each other regularly, as well as more anonymous communication such as public commemoration and celebrity Facebook pages. Typically, short contributions are shared, outlining recent events in users' lives or linking to something on the Internet that users think their friends might enjoy. These status updates are combined into a time-ordered stream for each user to read. Professional Networking Services (PNS), such as LinkedIn, aim to provide an introductions service in the context of work, where connecting to a person implies that you would recommend them as a work contact for others. Typically, professional information is shared in these fora, which tend to attract older professionals (Skeels and Grudin, 2009). This type of selectivity provides interactivity through services and platforms that enable social networking and peer-to-peer communication. The proliferation and diversity of content and sources now available through new media have raised concerns about the quality of the content, namely, its authenticity or reliability, as well as questions about the nature of online experience and interaction. There are also some concerns about anonymity or identity in specific online interactions in cyberculture and new media contexts (Wessels, 2010).

Some aspects of new media development are influential in transforming mass media industries, one consequence of the changes being that they are leading to some level of disintermediation, or cutting out the intermediaries between content creators and users. The potential of any such change is dependent on a range of legal, economic and policy-related factors seen, for example, in peer-to-peer developments such as Napster shareware as well as in developments of interactive digital television. The trend, however, is actually towards reintermediation of information by new intermediaries (Verhulst, 2005). Verhulst (2005) argues that a new mediation ecology is emerging because the promise that ICT will decrease mediation has not happened. Rather than disintermediation, the trend is actually towards reintermediation, which is marked by new actors and methods of disseminating information and framing reality.

Silverstone (2005b) extends Verhulst's thesis by arguing that mediation is both 'literal and metaphorical' because 'technologies, institutions, messages and meanings all interact and influence each other recursively' (Silverstone, 2006, p.30). For example, Sarkar, Butler and Steinfield (1995) argue that functions such as 'needs assessment and product matching' are helpful to consumers, and this is a role undertaken by a digital intermediary, such as Amazon.com. It is questionable whether these processes of reintermediation in new media enable users to shape the media itself. There is a double purpose to this service, in that the service provider also receives valuable marketing information about their customers, which can be sold to the commercial companies (cf. Bauman, 2007). Nonetheless, some commentators such as Sarkar et al. (1995) maintain that new media has the potential to give users an unprecedented ability to modify and redistribute content – an example of this would be Tripadvisor.co.uk, where individuals share comments about hotels and leisure activities online, for others to interact with. In the example of Tripadvisor, repeated negative reviews may impact almost immediately on a business, driving potential customers away. This type of practice is an example of the way consumers and producers are tightly linked in an interactive marketing relationship. It is another example of the changing relationship between consumers and producers in the e-economy that Ritzer and Jurgenson (2010) identify, which is discussed in Chapter 7.

This capacity creates a situation of the underdetermination of new media in comparison to traditional media (Poster, in Lievrouw and Livingstone, 2006). The idea of underdetermination refers to the way that new media is malleable and open to user appropriation in terms of content, institutional frameworks and user participation. It does not, therefore, strongly determine content, programming frameworks or types of audience participation. In addition, the debate about user participation and influence leads commentators such as Livingstone (2005) to stress the need for reconceptualizing notions of 'the audience' and exploring audience characteristics in the digital age. Finally, each of these diverse examples shows the influence of an audience's role and character, as well as their patterns of participation, in shaping new media forms.

Robins (in Lievrouw and Livingstone, 2006) raises another point regarding new media – that new media have produced a new kind of 'knowledge space' or 'communication space' that is 'de-referentialized'. This means being disconnected from local, situated knowledge and experience. In contrast to Levy, who sees this as an emancipatory break from older, linear, hierarchical and rigid forms of knowledge, Robins (in Lievrouw and Livingstone, 2006) argues that the 'new relation to knowledge' serves to promote global corporate capitalism and the interests of a relatively small elite. In this environment, information and communication are not valued for their substance or meaning, but for their capacity to be processed, circulated or connected for their own sake: 'contemporary knowledge culture is regarded as essentially about the acquisition of generic information skills and competences' (Robins, in Lievrouw and Livingstone, 2006).

Two defining features of new media are that it is flexible and networked, which in practice facilitates the underdetermination of new media. The networked open source architecture of new media also means that the medium does not shape the use that communication is put to or the type of content it circulates (Castells, 2001, 2009). In normative terms, communication across the Internet can therefore be used for progressive purposes by social movements and NGOs that seek to address social issues such as human rights violations and environmental concerns. However, it can also be harnessed for other purposes that are harmful to human beings and to wider social concerns. There are many examples of this, such as the use of the Internet by far-right movements that seek to mobilize racial, ethnic and religious hatred (Castells, 2001). These media can also be used by individuals for ill intent, and examples include grooming young people for sexual abuse and being used by some people to bully others in the form of cyberbullying (Byrne, Katz, Lee, Linz and McIrath, 2013). Another example is cybersexual harassment, which is a relatively new trend in deviant online behavior (Ritter, 2014). These examples show how much individuals and groups shape the ways that social and digital media is used. They also illustrate that social and digital media (as new media) do not as a technical media shape the values or morality of what is being communicated and what is being facilitated via online communication.

New media's networked characteristic and the fact that it facilitates open communication mean that there is less institutional power and ability to regulate its communication environment (Wessels, 2010).

The networking characteristic of new media is creating new dynamics of power in contemporary society. Castells (2009) addresses the power that communication networks can generate and how that power is practised. He defines power as 'the relational capacity that enables a social actor to influence asymmetrically the decisions of other social actor(s) in ways that favour the empowered actor's will, interest and values' (Castells, 2009, p.10). For Castells (2009), power is a relationship and is not an attribute of individuals and groups. This view of power relates to the networks of communication as well as a networked e-economy of the network society. Castells (2009) argues that communication networks are central to the implementation of power making of any network.

Networks are pervasive across society and include the corporate, financial, cultural-industrial, technology and political worlds, which all operate as separate and interdependent networks. The fundamental sources of power are to be found in the programming of single networks and in the switching of different networks. These bases of power means that the holders of power in the network society are the network programmers (such as media companies, public institutions, publishers, editors, technicians) and switchers (such as Rupert Murdoch who link media, cultural, political and financial networks) (Castells, 2009, p.429). It is important to note that Castells does not mean that Murdoch as an individual holds power rather that the role Murdoch has as a programmer and switcher holds power. Both programming and switching are network positions that are embodied by social actors, thus 'Murdoch is a node, albeit a key node' (Castells, 2009, p.429). The actual form of power in the context of network making is the capacity to set up and program a network of multimedia or traditional mass communication. This capacity resides in the owners and controllers of new media and traditional media, namely the media corporations, whether they are capitalist businesses or the state. In this context, network programmers and switchers are the power holders in the network society. This power can be contested by the reprogramming work of mass self-communication, in other words the way in which users of the communication networks rework the content and its communication.

Castells (2009) defines the way in which individuals can communicate with each other via new media at scale as 'mass self-communication'. It is mass communication because the way people can communicate with each other across new media networks means that they can potentially reach a global audience made up of other individuals as an individualized audience. Castells (2009) gives examples to illustrate this: posting a video on You Tube, issuing a blog with RSS links and sending a message to a massive e-mail list. Although it is mass communication in this sense, it is also, nonetheless, self-communication, because production of the message is self-generated, self-directed and self-selected by using Internet sources. Castells (2009) argues that three forms of communication – interpersonal, mass and mass self-communication – coexist in contemporary society, interacting and complementing each other. He states that this coexistence is historically novel because it is 'the articulation of all forms of communication into a composite, interactive, digital hypertext' (Castells, 2009, p.55).

In his review of Castells' (2009) book *Communication Power*, Van Dijk (2010) argues that the concept of self-mass communication is important. Van Dijk (2010) points out that the concept refers to important new forms of communication, which are produced by digital media that are located between interpersonal and traditional mass communication. However, Van Dijk (2010) criticizes Castells for considering all new media as comprising just one category and making insufficient analytical distinctions between them, referring to the mix and convergence of communication forms. Van Dijk (2010) counters this by tracing the way that senders and receivers may be both public and private and, given this, it means that there is a fourfold table of new communication forms. Therefore, mass self-communication refers to private senders and public or semi-public and private receivers and new media takes many forms, such as public video and music exchange sites, blogs, tweets and profiling sites, instant messaging, video conferencing and social-networking sites. The different types of new media communication and the different configurations of senders and receivers are influenced by different user intentions, strategic opportunities and risks (Van Dijk, 2010). Although Castells does not fully consider the complexities of self-mass communication, he nonetheless sees opportunities for reprogramming communication networks, which would counter some of networking power of the main nodes of a networked communication system.

These debates about new media developments reveal a relative underdetermination when compared to traditional media, as users are able to participate more interactively in media forms and engage in various participant dialogues. New media within both situated and cybercultural frameworks can dereferentialize knowledge from its respective frameworks and sources, which, in some cases, facilitates a more open communication space. However, although these 'new relations to knowledge' offer possibilities for various forms of emancipation, they are also created within the culture of global capitalism, which, as discussed above, continues to reproduce media concentration as well as generate new media nodes in the communications environment. Furthermore, power within communication networks is still retained by wealthy corporations and has, to some extent, been enhanced because of the way they can create, switch and link networks. This not only concentrates power, but also makes it fluid and flexible.

To recap, the ubiquity of new media and its more individualized use involving interactivity and selectively raises questions about the authentication and reliability of content, as well as the quality of online experiences. These questions reflect some of the core themes about the social relations of digital technology in wider social and cultural change. To understand these changes further, it is necessary to explore the ways in which new media is materializing itself in cultural forms in everyday life and in broader institutional change within a new communications environment.

The social relations of a new communications environment

Harrison and Wessels (2005) address the social relations of a changing communications environment populated by traditional and new media technologies and institutions, looking at the ways in which the emerging multichannel and multimedia environment is reshaping the traditional broadcasting sector. Traditional broadcast programming offers limited, set choices for audiences and encloses pluralism within institutional frameworks. The modern development of niche channels may appear at one level to add choice to the broadcasting environment – but these channels often form part of a themed strand within a homogenous media package. In addition, the increasing numbers of television and radio channels, along with enhanced television and interactive digital television (iDTV) services, are resulting in greater audience fragmentation. However, within the new public communication environment, research by Wessels (2010) identifies some pilot developments in new media that are producing senses of audience cohesion, understood as communities of interest[2]. There is some evidence that nonmedia professionals and audiences-as-users are actively shaping the production and content of programs and modes of participation in them.

Figure 9.1 below shows how new social relations are mixing into the communications environment, being situated in the relationship between media technologies and the social organization of the media (i.e. media institutions), and the experiences of participants and audiences in everyday life.

Figure 9.1 outlines the characteristics of traditional, reconfiguring and new media. The reconfiguring media highlight various developments that are using new media technologies in new forms of media organization, as well as those that draw on the legacy systems of traditional media. Types of media reconfiguration include the reintegration of public service values into new aspects of form and content. It is necessary to trace the social relations of specific media forms and outline their respective patterns of usage in order to identify the emerging characteristics of some of these reconfigured media. Thus, for example, traditional media emerged within the ethos of mid-modernity and its focus on the nation-state and national identity. Here, for example, national PSB is couched in terms of reaching mass audiences while providing some niche programming to ensure that both majority and minority tastes and interests are served. In contrast, new media emerged in late modernity with an emphasis on individualization and choice within a culture of freedom

'TRADITIONAL MEDIA'	THE PROCESS OF 'RECONFIGURATION'		'NEW MEDIA'
Social Relations	**Social Relations**		**Social Relations**
Mass and niche PSB	Networks		Individualization and choice
Origins: Mid-modernity National and regional broadcasting	Origins: Late modernity Partnership and notes		Origins: Late Modernity Local, national and supranational initiatives
FORMS	**FORMS**		**FORMS**
Broadcasting	Informate, e.g. iDTV, community networks, weblogs		Internet and WWW, IS services, mobile phones, weblogs, social networking sites
	Automate niche channels VOD PVRs traditional media online		
USAGE	**USAGE**	**USAGE**	**USAGE**
National unity	Individual use of mass media	Nodes of participation	Global networks of interests
Audience fragmentation	Self-selection	Community of interests[2]	Networks of interests (various)

Figure 9.1   The social relations of a new communications environment
Source: Harrison and Wessels (2005). Reprinted by permission of SAGE.

(Castells, 2001, p.17), which resists strong institutional structures in order to encourage communication initiatives at local, national and supranational level. Also, as Figure 9.1 shows, developments in the communication environment are reconfiguring both the traditional and new media in similar ways. These reconfigurations are materializing as enhanced services for traditional forms of media, or transforming both traditional and new media into innovative media forms. These distinctions illustrate the divergent patterns of emerging media usage that emanate from different sets of social relations of media production and use, as well as new rituals of participation.

Contextualizing these dynamics means considering the ways in which different audiences engage with, and participate in, the media. In contemporary everyday life, audience participation can be understood through the role that the media play and by the audiences' own experiences, which, in part, shape their understanding of the world. Mediation (Silverstone, 2005b) and mediated discourse (Smith, 1988) are distinct features of contemporary societies. These processes are part of the communicative and interpretive practices of individuals and groups who are differently positioned – both socially and culturally – and in their relations with media institutions. It is through the interpretive practices of actors that various media intersect with, and structure, everyday life. The ways that audiences interpret, engage with and participate in, these processes are part of the sociocultural dynamics that relate to and feed into socioeconomic and political processes (Smith, 1988). Audiences tend to form around particular interests, tastes and life experiences, with biographical and cultural factors as well as individual motivation and aspirations shaping their participation in media forms (Wessels, 2000). These cultural dynamics are enacted in everyday life and demonstrate the ways in which audiences practise discretion in viewing, selecting and contributing within media environments (Chaney, 2002).

Contemporary processes of the fragmentation of culture and the undermining of cultural authority as traditionally understood provides a context in which the meanings of mediated views and their associated mediated discourses are interpreted and negotiated through the different cultural frameworks of diverse audiences. Each audience is motivated by various social, cultural or political goals and facilitated by the extension of choice and intervention in the reconfiguring media, potentially creating a new dynamic in the communication environment. In new media projects, audiences can voice particular views and foster new forms of local democracy through grassroot participation organized via digital technology. Such media forms coexist within an environment dominated by commercial media companies; however, some of these reconfiguring forms show that a distinction can be made between populism informed by commercial imperatives and genuine cultural pluralism informed by people's social, cultural and political experiences. The dynamics of everyday life, the roles of various media and forms of audience participation all generate the social and cultural context to institutionalize traditional, reconfiguring and new media.

Any analysis of technological change involves a consideration of institutional change (Mansell and Silverstone, 1996), particularly broadcasting and information society arrangements. The dynamics of these institutional facets vary across nations and provide an example of the institutional complexities of technological change in the media context. For instance, in Europe, the plurality of services and diversity of content of traditional broadcast media are linked to their legacy of ownership and funding arrangements and the particular nature of their PSB obligations. It is, as yet, unclear how far traditional broadcasters with public service obligations will be able to expand into many new media areas and whether these initiatives will be viewed as enhancing or overstepping their existing PSB remit (Harrison and Wessels, 2005). However, the aim of PSB is to ensure that citizens have access to a diverse range of opinions and that the freedom of expression is responsibly upheld. The European Union and its member states continue to support publicly funded programming for this reason and because of the fear that if the private sector media market was deregulated, it would only produce commercialized output (Harrison and Wessels, 2005).

In parallel, the EU's Information Society strategy shows how some policy makers are addressing new media technology in relation to visions of an
inclusive information society (Mansell and Steinmueller, 2000). Policy-making
instruments stem, to a degree, from some of the early ideas that drove the
development of new media – namely, free and democratic communication, as
seen in Ted Nelson's 1965 Computer Lib manifesto – and in the ethos of
Berners-Lee's development of the World Wide Web. The early rhetoric surrounding new media variously suggested that the Internet had the potential
to facilitate new political associations, a new libertarianism or new forms of
economic production. It also suggested that it could enable increased democratic participation, the provision of free information and communication, and
support for freedom of speech (Rheingold, 1993; Negroponte, 1998; Castells,
2001). The current EU Information Society and Media portfolio endorses the
understanding of economic competitiveness based on ICT in an information
society, by focusing on both the underlying communications infrastructures,
and the content and services they deliver. It encompasses telecommunication
networks, broadband Internet access and satellite communications, new communications technologies such as '3G' mobile communications and Internet
telephony, and digital material as diverse as cinema releases, channel strategies and portal services. This reveals how an Information Society and Media
perspective is beginning to bring a more convergent view to communication
within the European Information Society framework, albeit still from the viewpoint that ICT is a key enabler in facilitating a variety of cultural and political
initiatives (Wessels, 2009).

Who has access to new media is a fundamental consideration, with commentators discussing issues including the lack of access to technology, lack
of skills and capacities, the knowledge gap and the domination of elites in
online discussions (Jankowski and van Selm, 2000; Norris, 2000). These issues
have their own exclusionary dynamics, but, considered together, they point to
divisive trends in accessing and participating in new media forms (Freeman
and Soete, 1997). One constraint against universal access is that changes in
economic activity, education and symbolic work stimulated by new media
technologies occur 'within capitalist relations of production' (Papacharissi,
2002; Garnham, 2005), so the adoption of new media technologies is limited by price and market demand. EU policy makers have taken a stance that
embraces the dynamics of commercialization, but which also aims to address
issues of social justice. These dynamics question the character of emerging
media as cultural forms, including the respective roles these new forms take in
relation to the public sphere. This chapter explores this issue by considering
the dynamics of a social networking site and, then outlines some new media
projects that are engaging with 'public issues and private troubles' in fostering
public dialogue (cf. Wright Mills, 1959).

The development of social networking sites raises many of the themes surrounding media, new media and public communication. SNS are websites that

allow individuals to construct a public or semi-public profile within a system and visibly articulate their relationship with other users through this profile (Boyd and Ellison, 2007). Users build networks by developing contacts with whom they interact, called 'friends', 'contacts' or 'fans', depending on the site, and they leave messages – often called 'comments' – on each other's profiles. Some sites have privacy settings, some have photo-sharing or video-sharing capabilities; others have built-in blogging and instant messaging technology and others, such as Facebook, support mobile interactions. There are a variety of audiences on SNS (Boyd and Ellison, 2007). For instance, SNS can target specific geographical regions or linguistic groups, although this does not necessarily determine who participates – for example, Portuguese-speaking Brazilians adopted Orkut – an English-only interface launched in the United States.

Some sites are designed in relation to ethnicity, religious affiliation, sexual orientation, political views or other identity-driven categories. For example, Asian Avenue, MiGente and Black Planet are popular community sites that added social network site features six to eight years after their initial inception. QQ began as a Chinese instant messaging service, Cyworld was originally a Korean forum tool and SkyBlog was a French blogging tool before adding social network site features. Beyond profiles, friends, comments and private messaging, social network sites vary tremendously in what they do or do not support (Boyd and Ellison, 2007). Some SNS are designed to generate their own micro-social network using tools such as Ning. Ning (launched in 2005) is an online platform, which allows users to create their own social websites and networks. Ning seeks to compete with large social sites like MySpace and Facebook by appealing to users who want to create networks around specific interests or who have limited technical skills. The unique feature of Ning is that anyone can create their own customized social network for a particular topic or need, catering to specific audiences. It offers a single template aimed at allowing nondevelopers to more easily customize their copy of the social website, but it stills allows developers to have some source-level control of their social networks, enabling them to change features and underlying logic.

However, usage of SNS is overwhelmingly characterized by nationality, age, educational level or other factors that segregate society (Boyd and Ellison, 2007). The rise of mobile devices is another factor that impacts on patterns of SNS usage. To set the scene in terms of devices in the United Kingdom in 2008, mobile phones were widespread: 94% of Internet users had them, 18% of Internet users had handheld devices, 43% of Internet users with a mobile phone or handheld device used them to access emails and websites and 24% used them to access SNS (Haddon, 2008). Although social networking was not their main online use, nonetheless this 24% uptake is significant, given that SNS was relatively new in the mobile portfolio in 2007 and 2008 (Boyd and Ellison, 2007). The predominant users of SNS are young adults of ages between 18 and 24 years, partly construed through levels of mobility and accessibility of each user-group's life stage, as well as through the design of their mobile interface.

To explore in a little more detail some of the dynamics of SNS as new media, the discussion now focuses on the public video-sharing website YouTube. Research by Lange (2007) shows that YouTube participants develop and maintain social networks by manipulating both the physical and interpretive access to videos. The different practices of circulating and sharing videos reflect different relations between users. For instance, one common practice on YouTube is posting videos that only friends and family can see and respond to (Lange, 2007). Posting comments enables people to express their affinity for the video or the video maker. These practices reveal different levels of 'publicness' in sharing videos, with some video makers revealing their identity – often while sharing more private content among a limited network, that is, 'publicly private' behavior (Lange, 2007). In other cases, participants share content more widely with many viewers, providing only limited information about the video producers' identities, which Lange calls 'privately public' behavior. It is through these practices that a media circuit is created, in which memberships of social networks are negotiated. YouTube circumvents traditional media's organizational structures and utilizes the technology and social networking sensibility to produce semi-public spaces of sharing user-generated content among self-selecting audiences with varying degrees of privacy and publicness. The character of this semi-public realm is one that foregrounds interaction and dialogue around affinities that are entertainment based and individualistic. This places SNS such as YouTube away from a public sphere ethos and into a networked individualism of taste friendships, rather than taste publics.

The exploration of a new communications environment shows how complex change is in the media, and how change interacts with notions of a public sphere. Because of the centrality of communication in social life, there is a need to consider the normative aspects of this environment as a mediapolis.

Mediapolis and proper distance in communication

In considering the media and its role in late modernity, Silverstone defines the concept of a 'mediapolis' as:

> The mediated public space where contemporary public life increasingly finds its place, both at national and global levels, and where the materiality of the world is constructed through (principally) electronically communicated public speech and action. There is of course no integrity within the contemporary mediapolis. The public space which it constitutes is fractured by cultural difference and the absence of communication, as much as it is

by the homogenization of global television and genuine, if only momentary collective attention to global events, crisis and catastrophes.

(2006, p.31)

The development of a shareable mediapolis means that analysts need to address what can be termed the 'relations of communication'. These encompass the values and mores of the media within the production and reception processes (including the processes themselves) as they combine to define media outputs and their interpretations (Wessels, 2009). Many people who work in media institutions claim that their practices are objective, or that they express particular views overtly. However, the values of the media are involuntarily expressed through the reporting and production practices of its workers, and very often these values are concerned with what makes a 'good story' that will sell the products (Karvonen, 2009). There are good examples of investigative journalism such as exposure of thalidomide, the campaign to bring the killers of Stephen Lawrence to justice and the exposure of abuse in the operation of MPs' expenses (in the United Kingdom) (Leveson, 2012). However, a significant amount of the journalistic output focuses on sensationalist stories. Karvonen (2009) asserts that much media practice trades in positioning the 'other', in creating a culture of fear and of pointing at the spectacular.

However, if one takes Silverstone's point of a mediapolis seriously, which is that the media is the Fourth Estate in a public sphere, then an analysis of the media involves considering the way it respects those it reports on, which includes considering its editorial practices. A key aspect of this is to what degree – if at all – do those working in the media express 'respect' in the way they report and represent people, events and places in news stories and other reporting practices? If respect is lacking or partially expressed, then it becomes difficult for audiences in turn to feel respect for those being reported. Furthermore, it also influences the levels of respect that audiences might practice in their interpretation of media content and in any user-produced content they might produce themselves. This is equally applicable to the media, virtual communities and forms of cyberculture in which senses of identity and otherness are performed and played out. In addition to cyberbullying, cybersexual abuse and trolling discussed above (Ritter, 2014), there are also other forms disrespectful practice on new media. A concrete example of other forms of abuse is the way derogatory remarks about participants in reality shows are made in the media and in social media such as Facebook and Twitter (Biressi and Nunn, 2005; Turner, 2009).

A high profile example within the traditional media is the recent 'Leveson Inquiry' (2012) into the practices of the press. This inquiry builds on a growing distrust between the press (particularly the British tabloid press) and the public and the press and politicians (Bingham, 2007). Examples cited by Bingham (2007) include the insensitive reporting of the Hillsborough football stadium disaster in April 1989 and the libel damages awarded to Elton

John for libellous reporting by the *Sun* newspaper. Even though press regulation was tightened following these sorts of complaints about the press, further
misconduct resulted in another inquiry into the press in 2012. The Leveson
Inquiry (2012) was instigated because of the public revulsion about the way a
media company, News International, hacked into the mobile phone of a mur-
dered teenager. The inquiry illustrates the power of communication and the
lack of respect in media reporting. In terms of power, the position of News
International fostered a situation in which the police became too close to the
press. This close relationship resulted in a lack of rigor to an investigation of
phone hacking by the press. In relation to privacy and in respecting the lives
of citizens the inquiry noted the persistent lack of respect for people both
in terms of the stories published and in how stories were pursued (Leveson
Inquiry, 2012). These examples indicate that the way the media create, report
and share stories is not necessarily respectful and can result in personal tragedy
and in a lack of trust of the media and media-generated stories.

   In response to the work of the media, Silverstone (2006) critically assesses
the current media through the concept of 'proper distance', reviewing hospitality, responsibility and trust in the mediation of public and everyday life.
Proper distance means the degree of proximity required to mediate interrelationships in order to create and sustain a sense of 'other' sufficient for
reciprocity and for the exercise of duty of care, obligation, responsibility and
understanding. If proper distance is achieved in mediated communication,
it maintains a sense of other through difference as well as through shared
identity, hence proper distance is a prerequisite for, and part of, plurality.
Silverstone (2006) argues that: 'proper distance involves imagination, understanding and duty of care and involves an epistemological (Arendt) and an
ontological (Levinas) commitment to finding the space to express what is
experienced (Arendt) and essential (Levinas) in our relationships to the other'
(Silverstone, 2006, p.47).

   People's relationships and social knowledge are highly dependent on the
media as a key communicator within late modern society, but Silverstone
asserts that the current organization of the media fails to value and to practice proper distance (some examples are given in Chapter 10). He argues that
the media generally 'trade in otherness, in the spectacular and the visible'
(Silverstone, 2006, p.47), and they therefore limit the possibility of connection and identification. Identity, in this context, is a commodity that is traded,
which empties identity of its distinctiveness and connectiveness. It denies the
validity of difference and the irreducibility of otherness in social relations.
This approach to representation highlights the failure of the current media to
receive or represent different perspectives or the complexities of social life. This
method of communication can therefore be seen as sustaining modernity's
inability to engage with plurality and the rights of the stranger (Silverstone,
2006).

Silverstone (2006) argues that the culture of hospitality should inform the work of the media. From his perspective, hospitality is the ethos in which 'the other' can speak and 'the stranger' be heard. He differentiates hospitality from tolerance or toleration, as it is not a relation of sufferance or patronage of the powerful. In Derrida's terms, tolerance is 'scrutinized hospitality, always under surveillance, parsimonious, and protective of its sovereignty' (Derrida in Borradori, 2003, p.128). Silverstone's hospitality, in contrast, is unconditional, entirely innocent and devoid of judgment and discrimination. It is uniform and universal, and is an obligation whatever anyone's position in social or symbolic hierarchies. The culture of hospitality is therefore at the center of a plural and fair mediated world that informs and is constituted through a proper distance between ourselves and others (Wessels, 2009). Cultural critique is therefore an important aspect in the processes that inform an emerging communicative environment – an environment constituted through an array of institutions, organizations, people and technologies.

Conclusion

The mass media comprise a key social institution, an important aspect of the public sphere and civil society. They are a forum in which private troubles and public issues are articulated and debated. The development of new media spans both the public and private aspects of social and everyday life and is part of a broader communications environment. This environment is a complex arena of established media organizations, technologies and forms of audience participation, and new media is being shaped by – and is shaping – this environment. New media have the potential to undermine established practice and open up the possibility of a more pluralistic media and public sphere through their interactive capacities. It is, moreover, the activities of people who think creatively and find new forms of organization, which are central to the development of new media as cultural forms. In some new media projects, this means working to create open spaces of dialogue and participation, whereas others, such as SNS, are creating semi-public communications and forming privatized spaces of user-generated entertainment.

These cultural forms are part of a broader environment where there is an increasing tension between commercial media services and public service media provision. The contest between commercially based populism and responsible and pluralist media production is initiating a normative debate regarding the character of public communication in late modern culture. The call for a culture of hospitality within the media communication environment and mediapolis is timely, since the multiplicity and enhanced forms of Internet-based communication can provide opportunities for dialogue and cultural exchange that, if it is to be progressive, requires hospitality. This ideal is contested, especially in the current neoliberal environment and the commoditization of culture that run in parallel with multicultural, diverse and mobile experiences of late modern life. New media is changing the media environment, but the relationship between private and public media institutions and the ability of citizens and end users will shape the way that it frames public expression, culture and politics across localities within a global world.

10
Diversity, Difference and Contesting Power

Introduction

One of the key themes in sociology and, indeed, in other social sciences is that of seeking to define and theorize power. There is some similarity to the broader issue of how sociological analysis seeks to constitute the 'social' as an object of sociological inquiry, since the characteristic of social life change and are open to new modes of analysis. Power, and the practice of power, changes its characteristics through time. Furthermore, the way that power is constituted and made an object of inquiry has varied over time and by disciplinary approach. In order to address the issue of power with a sociological imagination, it is necessary to explore the social relations of power. Alongside this, it also requires developing an understanding of the human condition in sociological terms. In other words, it is necessary to understand how agency is empowered or disempowered in relation to broader institutional structures, frameworks and networks. The way that power has been experienced in sociological terms is often related to the ways that difference and diversity are experienced by individuals or groups, and the attendant discourses of difference. These discourses shape how power is practised and also how power is shaped by the social relations that shape those discourses.

The chapter first considers power in relation to the experiences of difference and how power is understood sociologically. It then moves on to exploring the way power works through various positions, access to resources and how power is negotiated in late modernity. The chapter then draws on two specific contexts of power to illustrate the complexity of the way power is institutionalized and how it is negotiated through agency. The first context is that of women's position on Latin America. The example illustrates how power flows across many dimensions, and in this case those dimensions are gender relations, racism and the politics of identity in Latin America. The second example addresses another context of the complex flow of power, which is the

167

development of media and communication systems in an enlarging and socially diverse Europe. Both these examples also illustrate the way social change is often experienced as messy, and is negotiated in multiple ways and involves different types of institutional change. The chapter then consider power through the concept of proper distance as a lens through which to assess how power might be negotiated through ideas about respect within social relations.

Considering power: Experiencing difference

In order to consider power it is necessary to explore the relation between power and social difference, taking into account the way that difference is experienced. In contemporary society, globalization and heightened levels of geographical mobility are producing societies that are more diverse. The experience of that diversity varies between different people, depending on their own situations and identities (Wessels, 2013). To move beyond racism, sexism and homophobia, some progressive commentators (Roche, 2007) seek to change the discourse around difference while ensuring that society is more open to diversity. Although multiculturalism aims to encourage diversity within a framework of tolerance, Beck (2002, 2003) notes how multiculturalism actually essentializes difference. The shortcomings of these types of discourse, aligned with ongoing social change, are producing contemporary debates around cosmopolitanism. Beck (2003) argues that there are many types of cosmopolitanisms and that their sensibility lies beyond multiculturalism, in a sense of common humanity lived out in different places, ethnicities, religions and regimes. Similarly, Silverstone (2006) suggests that the condition of humanity in late modernity is an empirically grounded plurality. The negotiation of diversity in society is, however, complex because it rests on entrenched historical and cultural positions and involves questioning the existing social relations of power (Touraine, 1981).

Understanding both the experience of power and how power is institutionalized in society requires some level of empirical description. The utilization of a sociological imagination in an exploration of power means that an analysis can address both agency and structure. This requires exploring power in context, which yields a rich understanding of the way power is experienced. It also provides an in-depth analysis of the different dimensions of power and how they configure in particular contexts. This chapter explores power in two different contexts in the late modern period – Latin America in the 1990s and the European Union (EU) in the 2000s. Each context explores the complex interplay between dimensions of difference and power in two different world regions. The Latin American example illustrates the way that power materializes through indigenous women's lives, how power relates to the formation of their identities and the complexity of power and its negotiation in recent historical terms (Radcliffe and Westwood, 1995). The second example explores diversity in an enlarging European Union and illustrates the complexity of acknowledging and assigning voices to various cultural groups within the dynamics of Europeanization. It investigates the role and power of media communications in the way this type of diversity is negotiated, discussing how difference may or may not be understood and respected in media communication. This example focuses on the time when the EU was enlarging, and the issue of European media and a European Public Sphere was being debated by academics (Harrison and Wessels, 2009). These examples illustrate some of the issues discussed in previous chapters, such as identity, gender, work in the Global South and the dynamics of media and communication. Both examples explore the way that power is exercised from innumerable points in the interplay of nonegalitarian and mobile social relations.

Understanding power sociologically

The idea of power, how to define it and how it operates is something that is debated across a wide range of academic disciplines, in the worlds of politics and policy making, in the media and also by ordinary people in their family, work and everyday lives. Very often in these contexts power is seen as a capacity – as something that 'contains the ability to intervene in the lives of others' (Westwood, 2002, p.2). This type of definition as Westwood (2002) points out suggests that power is a 'thing' (something conceptualized through capacity) and that the exercise of power is relational. In terms of understanding the relational aspect of power, most people understand and can see these dynamics in their interpersonal relations. However, what is more difficult to grasp is the power of someone such as Rupert Murdoch, who acts as a node in a form of networking power that is influential in many people's lives (Castells, 2009). When addressing the exercise of power, the focus is on the relational aspect of power, and given this focus, power therefore involves agency in the sense that some individuals or institutions are able to impose their will on others. This type of approach closely aligns with a Weberian model of power and power relations. Approaches within this perspective provide insights into various strategies of power that are based on an instrumental rationality schema of human agency. However, this type of approach does not fully deconstruct power and does not fully analyze how it flows through social life. To go beyond the approach to power that focuses on an agent's capacity to exercise power requires exploring how power is part of social relations.

Foucault (1980) draws on the work of Nietzsche to take into account the productive aspects of power. To this end Foucault (1980) argues that 'power is not something that is acquired, seized or shared, something that one holds on to or allows to slip away: power is exercised from innumerable points, in the interplay of non-egalitarian and mobile relations' (Foucault, 1980, p.94). This approach is different to the one discussed above that focuses on power as a capacity that is outside of and beyond social relations. The difference between Foucault's approach and a rational approach to power is that in Foucault's perspective power is seen as constitutive of social relations. Thus, as Westwood (2002, p.3) points out, 'power is everywhere and is always present rather than a thing to be fought for and over', which means that power is diffused throughout all social relations. In order to address this in sociological terms, there is a need to find ways to theorize power in the social realm.

Westwood (2002, p.4) develops the concepts of modalities of power and sites of power defining modalities of power as 'the different forms in which power is exercised, the qualities or attributes of different forms of power and the manner in which power is enacted'. She defines sites as 'social spaces [which are] locations for the exercise of power' (Westwood, 2002, p.4). These modalities of power include repression/coercion; power as constraint; hegemony and counterhegemony; manipulation and strategy; power/knowledge; discipline and governance; and seduction and resistance. Sites of power include racialized power; class and power; engendered power; sexualized power, spatial power and visual power (Westwood, 2002, p.4). Westwood suggests that linking forms of power with the ways that power is enacted in specific sites can reveal how power is constituted – both within the social and through social process. This relates to a Foucauldian analysis, which rests on the social as being decentered and on processes that are constituted and reconstituted in a variety of sites. According to this viewpoint, the social is thereby created, shaped, recreated and reshaped through the play of power in various contexts.

Although Foucault's work about power is open to criticism, it is useful because it focuses attention on the fluidity and ubiquity of power. He does not see power as in itself being either positive or negative, but rather existing as something that is omnipresent and productive. His view is that power is pervasive but takes diverse forms, including governance through state organizations; and managing and disciplining of populations by bureaucracies and institutions, including mass surveillance techniques. These forms are complemented by the way that modern individuals internalize and enact self-discipline – what Foucault calls the 'technologies of the self'.

For Foucault, this marks the lives of individuals in modernity and late modernity who are inducted into disciplinary regimes through the discourses and discursive practices of the state and civil society. Although Giddens and some feminist writers have developed some of Foucault's insights, Giddens criticized Foucault on this point of discursively induced self-discipline (Tucker, 1998). Giddens (1991) is concerned with the process and role of agency in late modernity, asserting that society is more individuated and yet power is still shaped through differences in class, gender and ethnicity as well as by prescriptive discourses about deviance. Although Giddens agrees with Foucault that power marginalizes some groups and that state surveillance plays a key role in the role of power socially, he draws back to concrete social formations to discuss power. He argues that power needs to be understood in terms of broader social change such as changes in time and space, in changing city and spatial forms and in changes from a class-divided to classless society (Tucker, 1998). This argument reinforces the idea that, although, power is omnipresent, it is realized through concrete social relations and ethnographies of power.

This discussion introduces the notion that power is relational and that it flows through social formations. It is in constant negotiation within social relations and is, therefore, a factor in social change. Although there is an aspect of decentering power in later modernity, Westwood (2002) argues that power has certain modalities and is enacted within various sites. This therefore situates power within social relations, something that Giddens identifies as important. To address the omnipresence of power, its social formations and the way it is experienced, it is necessary to consider the way that diversity is negotiated in social life and enacted in the modalities and sites of difference.

Positions, resources and negotiation in late modernity

The negotiation of identity in terms of historically prescribed difference is multidimensional, ranging from gender to class and 'race'. Western colonization of the Global South produced a distinctive discourse about the 'other', which was built on a Western – more specifically, European – perspective. This perspective was established through the dominant position of European colonizers and was based on a position of power that produced material consequences in terms of poverty and unequal access to resources. It also created cultural oppression, with local cultures being discredited as 'primitive', as well as social and ideational oppression with indigenous populations being subjugated to, and excluded from, the colonial regime, culture and resources.

Theories of domination often originate from perceptions of difference – mainly along the lines of gendered identity and ethnic identities. The way in which difference becomes articulated is through the discourses of the powerful who are in a position to define difference in ways that ensure they maintain their control over the 'others'. The perception of difference has changed over historical time, and yet the definition of difference remains contested, including ideas of the 'native', racial difference, multiculturalism, ethnicity and, more recently, diversity. The term 'diversity', and its related discourse, seeks to move beyond the term 'multiculturalism' towards an understanding where difference is respected in an equal way. This is different from the notion of tolerance that is part of multicultural discourse. Multicultural discourse advocates that difference should be tolerated. However, the use of the word 'toleration' indicates that there is a dominant position from which others must be tolerated. Difference in this context, therefore, indicates a power relationship in which a dominant group maintains its cultural legitimacy and 'others' are accepted in the terms of the power relationship. Diversity, on the other hand, seeks to support a genuinely open and inclusive society.

Across many world regions, difference has been suppressed in varying ways, and, currently, two opposing trends are emerging in contemporary society, which challenge how diversity is understood and engaged with. One view is that the breakup of many world regions is allowing some countries to regain their independence and some indigenous groups to reassert their own cultural identity. The other trend, which is also part of a global reconfiguration, is the strengthening of national identities, which are often based on some racial purist mythology that sees those who are different (in their eyes) very much as the 'other' (Smith and Wright, 1999).

These trends are historical and show how difference and its negotiation are complex, dynamic and multidimensional. Across the globe people are seeking various ways to participate in social life through forming social identities, creatively imagining space and interpreting, resisting or engaging with narratives of difference. The opportunities they have to do so – and to what effect – is dependent on the social relations of power in society, which can be played out at local, national and global levels. One aspect of these negotiations of difference and diversity is social geographies and locales, which act as sites of material and cultural resources for action. These locales can be situated and mediated, and can comprise grounded spaces, broadcast spaces, interactive digital spaces or a combination of online and offline spaces. In this context, Westwood (2002) refers to modalities of power, which are sites in social life where power is negotiated in relation to particular contexts. She states that these include the way power – in terms of gender, 'race' and class identities and positions – is negotiated. These modalities also include how power is contested through the dynamics of space, time and how power is represented and challenged in visual terms. These areas of power are not necessarily discrete, but may interact with each other in specific ways and in different contexts. To understand this in context, the discussion now addresses gendered identity in Latin America.

Gender, ethnicity and the politics of identity in Latin America

One example of the complexity of diversity, power and difference is that of gender identities in Latin America. Commentators such as Radcliffe and Westwood (1995) assert that the diversity of gendered identities in Latin America, and the 'complexity of a multidimensionality of situations of power, subordination and exploitation' (Vargas, 1990, p.9) is clearly addressed by Latin American scholars and activists (Vargas, 1990, p.1). These scholars take into account the historical shaping of contemporary situations in which identity, difference and power are being negotiated. Vargas (1990) argues that, in order to understand the gendered identity of Latin American women, it is necessary to review the history of their global conquest and colonization. She discusses how peasant women were coerced into submission, how African women were imprisoned into slavery and how European middle-class women suffered marginalization and isolation in their own societies. All of these events have affected women's identity and status in Latin American society, and the ways that they interact with other social dimensions.

Vargas (1990) points out the deeply engrained presence of the Catholic church across many Latin American countries and cultures has a significant effect on women. The conservative aspects of the Catholic church mean that women have little control over their own sexual reproduction and that they are positioned within the family. Writers such as Alvarez (1990) note the importance of taking into account the specific contexts of women's gender and political identities within *latina* culture. The focus of this type of research has mainly been on women's domestic and private roles and the impact of *marianismo*[1] and *machismo* on women's identities. It also considers the participation of women in formal revolutionary bodies and political structures (Collinson, 1990). These foci highlight the context in which women negotiate their identity and status, and demonstrate that those contexts are multidimensional, including historical ramifications, religious and patriarchal structures.

Certain additional dimensions need to be considered to fully understand the negotiation of difference within specific sets of power relations. These dimensions can be considered more internal to the ways in which women experience and negotiate their own identity within sets of power relations. They include the practices of everyday life, the characteristics of images that circulate within and across cultural communities, and symbolism and senses of place in political culture (Westwood and Radcliffe, 1995). To explore these more internal, but nonetheless powerful, influences means looking at '(self) representation', which is, as De Lauritis (1987) argues, part of gender identity formation. This entails analyzing the micro-politics of power to see how identities are forged through certain technologies of power, which Foucault (1980) calls a major feature in inscribing difference. These technologies, De Lauritis (1987) asserts, form part of the mechanism of difference, which operates through the ascription of racial and gendered stereotypes and positions, creating a certain micro-politics.

The broader context of the micro-politics of power in Latin America is diffuse and its layers of influence emerge from various phenomena. This complex social power includes the influence of a European-oriented elite, Latin high culture, an authoritative high church – Catholicism – and Western-based economic policies such as the structural adjustment programs implemented during the 1980s. Another key dimension is a highly differentiated popular culture, which has been created and shaped by the 'descendants of black Africans who were enslaved [and] by the descendants of pre-Colombian peoples', which also interact with 21st-century mass global culture (Radcliffe and Westwood, 1995, p.2). By focusing on both this context and on people's lived experience, it is possible to gain insights into the 'two sides of the social', which Abrams (1982) argues must be addressed in order to understand social change. Furthermore, this shows how the personal and public spheres are interlinked, as expressed in the feminist phrase that the 'personal is political'.

Teresa De Lauritis (1987) considers the various influences that women recognize in their own subject positions, and she argues that these are multiple rather than unified. This means that the engendering of people as women occurs through their individual experience of 'race', class and sexual relations and that each of these overlaps the public and private spheres. De Lauritis (1987) emphasizes that the multiple aspects of a woman's identity is often experienced as a series of contradictions, rather than divisions. This understanding is particularly pertinent for understanding women's positions, their negotiation of power and their actions within the Latin American context (although of course it has a broader, worldwide application). Its pertinence is because De Lauritis's approach places diversity, heterogeneity and local narratives at the center of women's sensibilities and actions. This sense of diversity is reflected by Gonzales (1988), who argues that the term 'Latin American feminism' hides the pluricultural and multiracial characteristics of the various societies, which are, together, labeled 'Latin American'.

Recognizing the diversity of women's lives in Latin America (and, indeed, other places) raises the importance of sites in which diversity is negotiated and played out. Tovar (1986) points out that in Limeno shantytowns the *barrio* is an important site in negotiating identity, as well as being a space of shared memory. The negotiation of identity within social relations is not tied to one site, but occurs in and across a multiplicity of sites. Political struggles, which are personal as well as organized, involve engaging in the power dynamics that are enacted out in sites which range between the worlds of the household and the worlds of the street. It is important to consider the geographical context of sites, and sites as discursive spaces in order to understand the meaning of sites in this context. Although the theorist Foucault did not address how space was gendered, his work provides a framework for understanding how sites act as mechanisms of social power as well as being spaces in which power and identity are negotiated. Driver (1985, p.426) draws on Foucault, writing that Foucault sees 'spatial organization as an important part of social, economic and political strategies in particular contexts'. Driver (1985) argues that Foucault points to different mechanisms of power, which he calls 'technologies', arguing that technologies of power and authority are grounded in the site-specific spaces in which they take effect, and through the organization of space by social groups.

De Lauritis (1987) also believes that spatial dynamics are significant in the shaping of gendered identities, ideologies and practices. She expands on this by stating that gender is constructed through technologies of gender and institutional discourses, which have the power to control social meaning. Nonetheless, she recognizes that women from different cultural and ethnic backgrounds do not just passively allow themselves to be constructed in discourse or through fixed spatial practice. She notes that 'a different construction of gender can be found in the margins of hegemonic discourses' (De Lauritis, 1987, p.18) and that this negotiation frequently occurs through resistance at the local level in terms of subjectivity and in self-representation. De Lauritis writes about Western society, but her attention to 'margins' is important in terms of the Global South. For example, low-income women in Latin America are placed at the margins of the global economy, at the periphery of gendered power relations and in the underclass of formal power structures.

Radcliffe and Westwood (1995) argue that the sites where these women can resist are those locales that are historically ascribed to women. These are the home and domestic sphere and the neighborhood networks where men are absent, so women can organize resistance to the dominant discourses. There are other sites and resources that women use, including public parks in cities and towns, or public meeting places in isolated villages. These sites provide the spaces in which women can organize themselves, often with the support of various institutions and organizations such as some churches, feminist groups or union organizations. The characteristics and levels of negotiation vary across different sites, both in and between different countries, because of cultural and ethnically framed differences. Thus, there are differences in gender politics between, for instance, Ecuador and Peru, and within Peru between coastal towns such as Guayaquil and highland cities like Quito (Prieto and Rojo, 1987).

These dynamics suggest a shifting account of politics in which women, in various ways, negotiate their difference as women and their diversity in different contexts. This is similar to Laclau and Mouffe's (1985) assertion that any kind of negotiation involves frontiers and interfaces across and within specific sites. This movement across and between frontiers and interfaces is a way of understanding politics that is allied to 'alternative, non-essentialist accounts of political identities' (Radcliffe and Westwood, 1995), which resonates with other nonessentialist ideas about postmodern politics (Boyne and Rattansi, 1999). This turn to postmodern politics is in part a response to Marxism. Marxism sits firmly within a modernist framework in which the grand narrative of class struggle and the end of exploitation through the development of socialism dominates. This view underpinned all the political agendas of the 20th century. However, historical changes including the demise of organized class politics (or its appropriation by the state) has moved analysis beyond Marxist-Leninism and builds on Gramsci's theory of hegemony, which foregrounds the politics of civil society. These changes have signaled the need for a new type of analysis that can address diversity from within the dynamics of civil society. To illustrate and support this claim, Munck (1990, p.ix), for example, notes that politics in Latin America are based upon a 'deep human will to surmount oppression'.

Munck agrees with Laclau and Mouffe (1985) in stressing the importance of plurality, stating that: 'in accepting the plurality of political spaces we are implying the centrality of democratic struggles' and 'a dispersion of subject positions' (Munck, 1990, p.12). From this perspective, it is no longer possible to view political struggles as being focused on one single issue, such as class politics or women's rights, but it is necessary to understand these endeavors in their full complexity. Struggles for recognition, for the right to assert one's own identity and to gain a better quality of life are all located in a complex set of life circumstances, identities and cultural differences. Fraser and Nicolson explain that, although 'some women have common interests and face common enemies' (Fraser and Nicolson, 1988, p.102), it would be a mistake to assume that these are universal. Instead, they maintain that women face various types of issues, which are all interlaced with differences and conflicts. In practice, then, struggles and negotiations comprise overlapping alliances within different types of context. Identity is not fixed – as Laclau and Mouffe (1985, p.85) state: 'unfixity has become the condition of every social identity'. Hall (1987) also recognizes that notions of coherent and unified subjects are being replaced by more contradictory ideas of 'the self', in which every self is made up of multiple selves. This is because individuals are experiencing themselves reflexively as being defined by multiple aspects or selves that are all suited within a multiplicity of discourses (cf. Giddens, 1984).

The struggle for recognition in social life is also undertaken within the broader political sphere. In political terms, this means that there needs to be support for progressive deliberation within democratic processes in which citizens can engage in the complex issues that arise in supporting a diverse society. Currently, many forms of liberal democracy rest on established discourses of participation, which are built on modernist discourses of coherent identities and homogenous societies. Latin American scholars comment how much this approach is being changed and shaped by the diverse peoples, religions and cultures within their region. Thus, the economic, political and cultural dimensions of social change are shaping the situation of women's lives in various parts of Latin America, and the ways that women as social agents are negotiating their own identities and situations within the social relations of their sites of struggle.

There is a colonial legacy to the struggles of those living in Latin America, and, although this is influential, it does not necessarily determine women's entire struggle. In Europe too, struggles are emerging as it, as a world region, recognizes its diversity in late modern society. In the European context, issues of difference are represented via communication media, and access to that communication media is an important aspect in negotiating identity and difference (cf. Chapter 9).

Communication, diversity and power: The case of Europe

The idea of Europe, Delanty (1995) writes, is reinvented in every age. He argues that a 'cultural construction cannot be regarded as a self-evident entity' (Delanty, 1995, p.1), which points to processes of change across the various dimensions of change discussed in Chapter 4. An example of this process is the recent reinvention of both the idea and the reality of Europe in enlargement of the European Union and in the desire by the European Union to create a European Public Sphere (Harrison and Wessels, 2009). The reconfiguration of alliances within the enlargement of the European Union has cultural implications, as well as social, political and economic consequences (Smith and Wright, 1999). The media play a role within these dynamics by reporting and representing European developments and debates to enable public debate and participation in democratic processes (Habermas, 1989; Calhoun, 1992). Participation, therefore, is not just at the level of individuals and groups voicing their own concerns, but it also involves the institution of the media. The key institutions responsible for building Europe within democratic liberalism are the European Parliament, the European Commission and the European Council, which all have to engage with the ideology of the market to promote social cohesion, inclusion and social justice. Within these dynamics, there is the rise of 'different partial arenas of cultural and social sub-politics – media publicity, judiciary, privacy, citizens' initiative groups and the new social movements ... [that] add up to forms of new culture' (Beck, 1992, p.198). This is especially complex because of the diverse populace of the European Union, which means that no universalistic or relativist argument regarding inclusion and participation in Europe will suffice (Borradori, 2003).

The provision of information and communication, whether via the mass media or the Internet and World Wide Web (WWW), is important to facilitate dialogue regarding European concerns and to foster participation by the inhabitants of Europe (Wessels, 2009). The media are influential in shaping public perceptions of events, public culture and civic space. This can be seen in the ways that community, identity and culture around European migration are played out in the media. To counter any established mainstream media bias within this context, minority media in the EU seek to acknowledge the rights of ethnic minorities by producing media output in their own languages and by acting as mediators between mainstream and minority cultures. This has the potential to contribute to the development of a genuine multiethnic civil society (Silverstone, 2005a). The economic, social and political conditions, along with forms of participation in the means of communication, give Europe its sense of public culture. These conditions form grounded empirical situations in which different groups can engage, in varying degrees, with European concerns and provide the basis for levels of participation.

However, this also raises questions about the formation of European publics.

The quest for participation in Europe requires a European public, which raises the question: 'who are the Europeans?' (Smith and Wright, 1999). Given the Western notion of *demos* as signifying (national) territory, common institutions, and a political community that binds people together, it is difficult to identify a clear sense of Europe as a single political entity and even more problematic to identify one group of Europeans. This differs from national identities, which are established, popular and widely believed, in contrast to any notion of a 'whole European' identity, which lacks any of these attributes (Grundmann, 1999, p.133). In an effort to envisage the development of a 'European', some commentators identify a progressive approach to envisage a 'New European', who is: 'as sophisticated as the merchants and courtiers of the Renaissance or the multinational and multilingual inhabitants of Central and Eastern Europe before Hitler and Stalin . . . S/he has to know foreign languages beyond the superficial and unreliable *koine*' (Picht, 1993, p.87). One approach proposed within this framework is to develop a European identity through some sort of intercultural training, which would not reject one's own identity but would adopt additional other identities in an open way (Grundmann, 1999, p.134).

However, as described above and previously in Chapter 4, this is a complex area, in which actors select and adopt multiple aspects of their identity in varying situations. Furthermore, although intercultural training might lead to greater understanding across Europe, it would not provide any formal routes for participation in Europe. Weiler (1997) raises the link between identity, national citizenship and European citizenship, suggesting that there is a flaw in the assumption that European citizenship could be an identity in the same way as national citizenship. He suggests a version of multiple *demoi*[2], in which individuals consider themselves to belong to two *demoi*, whereby their member state nationality and their European citizenship are understood as being interdependent. This is because it would be impossible for an individual to become a European citizen without first being a member state national. Weiler (1997) asserts that there is a civilizing aspect to this point, because:

> the acceptance by its members that, in a range of areas of public life, one will accept the legitimacy and authority of decisions adopted by fellow European citizens in the realization that in these areas preference is given to choices made by the outreaching, non-organic, *demos*, rather than by an in-reaching one.
>
> (p.510)

Although this ambiguity around the existence of a European union is problematic for the idea of 'Europeanization', the development of a public sphere within Europe is a prerequisite for public engagement across the region

(Wessels, 2009). Grundmann (1999) argues that the creation of such a public sphere involves two phases: first, a synchronization of key debates between national public spheres and then, a homogenization of national public spheres across European nation states. Grundmann (1999) sees this distinction as a way to build a public sphere for Europe, although he identifies some difficulties in achieving this synchronization and homogenization of national public spheres. First, despite the increased technological possibilities, there is no common media system across Europe and it would be difficult to develop one because of the heterogeneity of cultures and languages in the EU (Groze-Peclum, 1990; de Swaan, 1991). A second barrier is the fact that news correspondents tend to be nationally aligned and primarily interested in European topics that relate to their domestic policy agenda (Gerhards, 1993), and that member states tend to pursue a national line in European policy debates. Both these viewpoints strengthen national discourses about Europe instead of fostering a European perspective on policy debates. A further dimension is that member states may be focusing on 'looking to Brussels' and thereby reducing or limiting their bilateral discussions, resulting in less intersection of interests at the national level to form a European perspective. One outcome of these dynamics is that they do not emphasize cultural diversity or participation and representation in the media spaces across Europe (Silverstone, 2005a).

Silverstone (2006) addresses the mediapolis as a potential space for mediating multiple voices. He argues that the movement of people within Europe produces a context where cultures coexist both as a source of tension and misunderstanding and as a source of creative dynamism. The mobility of individuals and groups within Europe means that these actors have to balance identity and senses of belonging in spaces between their home and host societies. In these situations, individuals often have to negotiate senses of self and place in locations where there are a hybrid of cultural perceptions and mores within a latent 'in-between space' of established populations and influxes of strangers. However, rather than seeing these sites as 'either-or' spaces, Silverstone (2006) posits that they can be better understood as (nascent) 'both-and' spaces in terms of communication and, the author would add, in terms of experience. Any experience of 'both-and' spaces is varied, with some situations being more volatile and less supportive than others (Steinert and Pilgram, 2007). For some commentators, this mix of cultures represents a form of cosmopolitanism; however, the contemporary situation of merely colocating does not necessarily facilitate a progressive sensibility of a cosmopolitan who is unperturbed about diversity within the dynamics of culture (Beck, 2003).

Beck (2003) asserts that there are many types of cosmopolitanisms and that their sensibility lies beyond multiculturalism (which, to varying degrees, essentializes difference) – but in a common humanity, which is lived out in different places, ethnicities, religions and regimes. Silverstone (2006, p.14) understands this as 'a claim for an empirically grounded plurality as the condition of humanity in late modernity'. To move beyond the current 'condition of cosmopolitanism' (Roche, 2007) into a genuine and lived cosmopolitanism requires some facility for dialogue and the exchange of ideas and understanding. This is because a cosmopolitan individual lives within a 'doubling of identity and identification; the cosmopolitan ethic embodies a commitment, indeed obligation, to recognize not just the stranger as other, but the other in oneself' (Silverstone, 2006, p.14). Thus, communication entails both welcoming the other and understanding the other as being different but still forming part of one's own and each other's identity and condition. The media provide one resource for facilitating dialogue – or at least communication – however, the communication spaces of the mediapolis can only create the conditions for a progressive cosmopolitanism by welcoming the other and thereby genuinely intermingling minority and majority voices within media and communication spaces. Silverstone (2005a) suggests that consideration should be given to discerning how cultures in Europe can be negotiated through the media in ways that could, potentially, offer plural spaces for mediation.

This plurality of cultures within people who aspire to communicate across difference cultures creates situations of the counterpoint or the contrapuntal (Silverstone, 2006). This concept addresses the articulation of diversity within and between cultures. In the European context, for instance, there is diversity between and within a variety of cultures, languages and ethnicities. This diversity is also the context in which the European media environment exists. This media environment and its various media are active and influential in representing difference, and they are therefore a key institution in shaping the relationships that underpin and give form to diversity. In the media, these relations are realized through the power differential between dominant and subordinate media institutions; in the capacities and reach of the technologies and their platforms; in the social organization of audiences and producers, including their real and represented locations; and in patterns of inclusion and exclusion across and within nation states (Silverstone, 2005a, 2006).

The concept of contrapuntal culture includes the way diversity is articulated in the media. The characteristics of the media are therefore significant because they frame the character of communication in both form and content. Thus, for example, media institutions and characteristics of communication frame the possible ways in which the production of voices and responses can be created and represented, as well as enabling and determining levels of reciprocity and responsibility in communications (Silverstone, 2006). Sociologically speaking, Silverstone (2006) argues that contrapuntal moments show the presence of the other (the stranger) in time and space as a point of reference in relation the significance of the here, the now and the self. He suggests that the contrapuntal points to the necessary presence of a multiplicity of voices, as well as the mediapolis's own plurality in creating a genuine space where dialogue can take place to foster respect and hospitality among people in Europe (and globally).

To summarize, key aspects of the contrapuntal include the notion that any particular identity only exists within a range of opposites. The contrapuntal does not suggest that cultural difference and conflict can be ameliorated, but that there is an ongoing recognition and re-recognition of difference with which social actors engage in varying ways. Not all engagement, however, is open and hospitable to the 'other'; for example, in mass media communication the 'one to many' format is unequal and unjust, with freedom 'to be heard and to speak' denied to many (Silverstone, 2006). New interactive digital media can open up innovative networks of communication by various forms such as social networking, blogging and wikis, but these forms require new patterns of association to create dialogue and trust in communication. Nonetheless, the mediapolis's multiple communication formats of broadcast programs, websites, blogs and other social media are weaving multiplicity into communication that may inform civil society and the public sphere. However, this poses questions about how these media spaces are used by different people in Europe and beyond.

There is some tentative and fragile interlinking between social and symbolic worlds as nation-states gradually orientate to Europeanization through the expansion of the EU and the movements of migration throughout Europe. It is partly through the media and the process of mediation that the plurality of cultures and their representation becomes visible. Silverstone (2006) argues that analysts must to listen to the expressive score of different cultures, noting what is present and absent, and shifts in positions of dominance and subordination in order to understand this process. Mediation and culture are contrapuntal, and lived experiences such as migration express this through the movement and displacement of individuals, groups and populations, which are impelled by economic, political, religious or environmental changes (Wessels, 2008).

Silverstone's (2005a) study of mediation in the everyday lives of migrants and minority group producers and users of media explores the dynamics of mediation between 2001 and 2003. The research explores minorities' engagement with local, national and transnational media in EU nation-states. The team worked with 75 distinct groups among recent and established minorities with populations of over 1000 in the 15 EU member states (before enlargement in 2004) to explore their media and media practices (Silverstone, 2005a, p.91). Silverstone (2005a) thereby addresses the way in which the media interact within individual and institutional processes of communication. He traces the link between production and reception in the ways that minorities make sense of and make meaningful global, national and local events across the public and the private aspects of their everyday life.

Silverstone's (2005a) study shows that mediation is highly contextualized, and that minorities tend not to relate directly to the social and cultural content in the mainstream media of any 'host' country. Furthermore, they do not relate to many of the marketing strategies that are aimed at national audiences.

Instead, many minorities construct a separate media space out of national, local and transnational media, which they use and appropriate in complex and layered ways. Within this context, the local is of primary importance for minorities, as it provides the situated context for access, production and use. Thus, in cities, access to media and communication for minorities is through neighborhood phones, Internet or DVD hire shops, Internet cafés and local authority centers. These sites are important since they provide access to media and communication for those who may otherwise lack the resources to gain individual or private access. Although some such sites may generate specific user groups based on ethnicity due to their location within migration patterns, they nonetheless provide open and inclusive sites of communication that can be appropriated by locally placed communities (Silverstone, 2005a, pp.90–95). The study also found that cities act as sites where difference is negotiated, which in part is done through the provision of cultural and multicultural media outlets and projects, such as local print, radio and cable TV. This provides opportunities for engagement in locally available media production processes.

These culturally based media outlets tend to produce content that is centered on particular linguistic and cultural traditions for specific minority audiences. Although there are some independent local media projects, most local media production and consumption is linked to national initiatives, which are often part of multicultural policy agendas and include public service multiple ethnic and multicultural programming. Examples of these facilities include Couleur Locale (Belgium), Radio Multikulti (Germany), Colourful Radio (the Netherlands) and Sesam (Sweden). However, because these types of initiatives are often shaped by national initiatives, they may not fully recognize the presence of minorities or give voice to their concerns. They can limit access to production processes for minority groups and hence curtail opportunities for self-representation in mediating cultural expression by minority groups. Another aspect of this dynamic is the role of minority media, which, although often small in scope, undersupported and underrepresented in relation to the mainstream media, nonetheless provide important services. Examples include national local hybrids such as London Greek Radio, which offers information in Greek on people's rights and about UK social services for a national Greek audience in London; and the BBC Asian Network that provides some broadcasting in Bengali, Gujarati, Hindi, Punjabi and Mirpuri to UK audiences and listeners (Silverstone, 2005a).

A further media source interacting in the communications environment of migrants and minority groups is the presence of transnational satellite TV that transmits programming from various destinations, including the 'homelands', which migrants have left behind (Silverstone, 2006). This type of programming varies across cultures, but there are 30 Arabic satellite channels, 36 Turkish channels and increasing numbers of channels from Russia, Poland and the ex-Soviet states, as well as eight Hindu channels and 20

Spanish and Portuguese channels. However, these types of transnational media are limited to countries that are economically strong enough to support such media production, which therefore excludes migrants from nations with weaker economies. In this context of local, national and transnational media outlets, the Internet acts as a distinct form of communication for minority communities.

The Internet provides an information and communication medium for diasporic communities, which is low cost in comparison to other media (Silverstone, 2005a). It is also significant because its design enables user participation, leading to the rapid growth of online news and information sites produced by individuals and communities within diaspora networks and minority populations. Sites hosted by these networks therefore have the ethos and capacity to include the displaced as well as those left behind in the home societies. Some particular characteristics of digital technology support these types of producer-consumer-led new media projects – for example, the development of search engines that are specifically dedicated to Spanish or Latin American websites hosted in Belgium. Silverstone (2005a) and his research team found that these types of websites are culturally convergent and often bilingual. In these spaces of communication, various groups debate their concerns, with many contributors voicing oppositional perspectives of both the home and the host nations (Silverstone, 2006, pp.90–95). These sorts of spaces provide emerging frameworks for debating public and private issues, but they are not especially well linked to other public fora, which limits their contribution to a public sphere within Europe and beyond.

Proper distance in respecting difference

Silverstone (2006) critically assesses current media through the concept of 'proper distance', addressing issues of hospitality, responsibility and trust in the mediation of public and everyday life. This has been discussed in Chapter 9; however, it is reiterated and expanded upon to inform understanding of the role of the media in the negotiation of difference. 'Proper distance' means the degree of proximity required in mediated interrelationships to create and sustain a sense of 'other', which is sufficient for reciprocity and to exercise the duty of care, obligation, responsibility and understanding. If proper distance is achieved in mediated communication, it maintains a sense of other through both difference and, conversely, shared identity, thus proper distance is a prerequisite for, and part of, plurality (Silverstone, 2006). Silverstone draws on the work of Arendt (1958), who sees proximity as an important aspect of politics and Levinas (1969), who views proximity as an important dimension of morality. To this end, as quoted in the previous chapter, Silverstone (2006) argues that imaginative approaches are required to generate media spaces that can embrace both the epistemological (Arendt) and the ontological (Levinas) aspects of creating a space to express what is experienced (Arendt) and essential (Levinas). Furthermore, it requires a deep understanding and a duty of care for people to forge proper distance in their relationships with each other.

As discussed in Chapter 9, relationships and social knowledge among people are highly dependent on the media as a key communicator within late modern society. Silverstone argues that the current organization of the media fails to value and to practice proper distance, stating that the media 'trade in otherness, in the spectacular and the visible' (Silverstone, 2006, p.47) and so limit the possibility of connection and identification. Identity, in this context, is a commodity that is traded, which empties identity of its distinctiveness and connectiveness. It denies the validity of difference and the irreducibility of otherness in social relations, and this approach to representation highlights the failure of contemporary European media to hear different perspectives or address the complexities of social life, sustaining modernity's inability to engage with plurality and the rights of the stranger.

As discussed in the previous chapter, Silverstone (2006) argues that proper distance is an important aspect in media reporting. He points out that distance that is 'too close' or 'too far' cannot foster respect between people as it simply negates difference. For example, he points out that journalists embedded within the armies of occupying forces, the media intrusion into private life of public figures and exotic images in global advertising are all examples of incorporation and the denial or reduction of difference. These are instances of being 'too close' to foster respect of the other. Conversely, the way that Moslems, Iraqis and Palestinians are represented as beyond the pale of humanity is, in practice and in convention, a position that is 'too far' to create any understanding of the other. An example of distance that is neither 'too close nor too far' is found in the cult of celebrity, which destroys difference by exaggerating it (the ordinary made exceptional) and naturalizing it (the exceptional made ordinary) thus, through this dialectic negates the legitimacy of difference. Proper distance in mediation as 'both close and far' where the other is acknowledged, understood and respected needs, Silverstone argues, producers and audiences with imagination (Silverstone, 2006, pp.47–48).

In summary, an important aspect of imagining and achieving proper distance is the virtue of hospitality – showing that hospitality is the first virtue of the mediapolis (Silverstone, 2006). Hospitality means an obligation to welcome the stranger, the right to freedom of speech and an obligation to listen and to hear. Silverstone (2006) writes that it is universal, and cites Kant that

> the right to visit, to associate, belongs to all men by virtue of their common ownership of the earth's surface; for since the earth is a globe, they cannot scatter themselves infinitely, but must, finally, tolerate living in close proximity, because originally no one had a greater right to any region of earth than anyone else.
>
> (Silverstone, 2006, p.136 citing Kant, 1983, p.118)

In relation to hospitality in the media, Silverstone (2006) asserts that hospitality must be seen as a culture rather than one ethic in an array of media ethics. This is because hospitality is about a sense of ethos, one that is about 'home, the familiar place of dwelling... the manner in which we relate to ourselves and to others, as our own or as forgiveness... ethics is so thoroughly coextensive with the experience of hospitality' (Derrida cited in Silverstone, 2006, p.139).

Silverstone (2006) recognizes that Derrida's notion of ethics-as-hospitality is important because hospitality as an obligation rather than a right is a primary ethic in a cosmopolitan world. He argues that it is at the heart of our relationships with others and is constitutive of such relations:

The capacity, indeed the expectation, of welcoming the other on one's space, with or without any expectation of reciprocity, is a particular and irreducible component of what it means to be human. Hospitality is the mark of the interface we have with the stranger. It speaks of the long relationship between the sedentary and the nomad. It is inscribed into the cultures of most of the world religions as an ethic beyond the political, an ethic of humility and generosity, which bypasses differences of power and inequalities of wealth and status (Silverstone, 2006, p.139).

From Silverstone's (2006) perspective, hospitality is the ethos in which 'the other' not only speaks but where 'the stranger' should be heard. He also differentiates hospitality from tolerance or toleration in that it is not a relation of sufferance or patronage of the powerful. He supports the point made by Derrida cited earlier that tolerance is 'scrutinised hospitality, always under surveillance, parsimonious, and protective of its sovereignty' (Derrida in Borradori, 2003, p.128). Hospitality, in contrast, is unconditional, entirely innocent and devoid of judgment and discrimination. For Silverstone (2006), hospitality is uniform and universal, and is an obligation whatever anyone's position is in social or symbolic hierarchies. Here Silverstone (2006) links hospitality as a core component of justice in the work of the media, stating that, when it is absent, it is a sign of injustice in the lived – as well as – the mediated world. The culture of hospitality is therefore at the center of a plural and just mediated world that informs, and is constituted through, a proper distance between selves and others.

Conclusion

To assess the dynamics of difference, diversity and power, the processes through which these phenomena materialize and are negotiated must be understood. This chapter has shown that the social is both material and ideational, and that any contemporary analysis of power must be rooted in the relations of diverse societies, which are lived and experienced within what Westwood (2002) calls 'modalities of power'. The modalities of contemporary society are racial, gendered, class based and sexualized, and they involve spatial and visual power within the mobilities of a diverse society. These modalities have their own processes and interrelate to form new conditions of oppression, while also providing spaces for agency in which inherited prejudices and forms of domination can be resisted and new opportunities produced. The struggle for freedom and recognition is an ongoing social process in society, whereas oppression and domination are constructed historically. However, as Castells (2001) argues, freedom is hard fought for, and that fight is continuous. The struggle for recognition and for freedom shows how human agency seeks to overcome oppression, but it can also institutionalize new oppression of others through the social relations of power. Hence, the relations of power are made and remade through the dynamic of agency and institutions in historical time.

11
Conclusion

Introduction

Social change is a central topic of study in the social sciences, and sociology in particular. The focus on change is rooted in the early development of the discipline, which was formed in response to the social upheaval that arose with the advent of industrial capitalism in the West. Society continues to change as people make and remake social institutions, which interact with social structures and social values. A key part of the work of social scientists is identifying this social change and analyzing its significance for individuals, groups and institutions within society. This requires taking an historical perspective to consider what is changing, as well as a sociological perspective to address how change is occurring. Analysts can only extract the significance of change by understanding both the 'what' and the 'how' of change.

The chapter first recaps the approach taken to social change, which is to address social change through the idea of process. It then summarizes some of the key aspects in understanding social change before considering some of key dimensions of change. The chapter then identifies some of the main characteristics of social change in contemporary society.

Approaching social change as process

This book addresses the concept of social change and argues that it is necessary to consider process in order to understand change. The concept and the study of process are two tools that may be used to unlock what Berger and Luckmann (1967) call the 'awesome paradox' of the 'two sidedness of the social world' – the way that individuals experience society as a factlike system external to them and yet also as something that is made and remade through their personal actions. This paradox requires bringing a particular method to the study of social change, an historical approach that considers how actions become institutions over time and then, in turn, institutions are changed by actions. This sense of process provides a link between action and structure. As Abrams (1982) argues, people can only construct worlds on the basis of what their predecessors constructed for them. This study of process involves understanding the relationship between personal activity and experience on the one hand, and social organization on the other, as something that is continuously constructed in time. In order to explore social change, institutional factors and the way that individuals negotiate change within and across the dimensions of social life must be examined.

A common experience of change (as Lamartine said of the political and industrial revolutions of 1840 Europe) is that 'the world has jumbled its catalogue'. Faced with intellectual and social disruption, sociologists seek to understand the dynamics and processes of social change in which the relationship between the changes people want and the changes that actually occur are often very different, as well as being difficult to understand. The focus on process helps to address change in all its richness – working with grand transformations as well as changes to ordinary and everyday experience. Process involves the subjective, intersubjective and institutional experiences of change, which span the various dimensions of social life – economic, political, social and cultural.

In order to analyze the phenomena of change, it is necessary to ask what 'social change' means, how change can be recognized and what the significance of particular changes in social life are. On the one hand, change can occur in one or more dimensions, which may, or may not, interact with other dimensions. On the other hand, it can involve radical and structural changes in all dimensions, which fundamentally usher in a new type of society. The interaction and articulation of change within economic, political and cultural spheres generates a social dynamic through which life is experienced, engaged in and embraced or resisted.

To explore social change and its contemporary character, this book addresses the following questions:

1. How do we understand social change?
2. What are the key dimensions of change and how do they interact to produce new social conditions, new artifacts and new values and ideologies?
3. What are the main characteristics of social change in contemporary society and what is their significance?

Understanding social change

To answer the first question – how do we understand social change – this book notes that the focus on, and study of, process generates an understanding of the relationship between agency and structure in the dynamic of social change.

The book argues that the focus on institutional change, agency and the process of social change is useful because it seeks to understand change in terms of its sociocultural dynamics. This approach includes the consideration of broader structural change because the context of economics, politics and social organization is meaningful both within respective lifeworlds and structures and within ordinary social life where changes are interpreted. In order to understand these dynamics, there needs to be a framework of analysis that captures the richness of change, the dimensions of change, the way these dimensions interact and their interdependencies. The framework of analysis proposed in this book is based on a sociocultural dynamic that is made up of the social relations of production, the discourses within societies and the characteristics of participation within social life.

The idea of a sociocultural dynamic in social change acts as an organizing principle for understanding social change and situates change within three main areas and the relations between these areas. The first area is concerned with how goods and services are produced by people around the world – the relations of production at local, regional, national and global levels. This involves ascertaining who is producing what, where and how; what resources they are using; and what the power relations are within the social organization of production. The second area relates to the ways in which the economic, political and cultural dimensions of social life are narrated and interpreted – the ways that change is made sense of by those experiencing the change and those observing and commentating on the change. These types of perceptions are articulated in the discourses of particular societies, and these discourses are open to analysis. The third area addresses the forms of participation in society and the characteristics of participation – the way that humans engage with each other through the social institutions they develop, and how they engage with the structural arrangements of economic systems, political systems and cultural life in general. The forms and characteristics of participation create a culture of participation, which often materializes in a continuum between an inclusionary and exclusionary form. Participation is experienced, as well as structured, in different ways for different people, and this shaping of participation involves senses of identity and the recognition and validation of identity by those with the power to define who is included, to what degree and who is excluded. Participation also involves considering what resources people need in order to be able to participate – economic, political, social and cultural.

In order to understand and explore change, it is also necessary to identify the points and boundaries of change. This involves defining historical periods as a way of characterizing specific types of relations of production and consumption, forms of power, senses of individual selves and processes of identity, social values and cultural mores, as well as cultural forms and creativity within society. Although exact definitions of historical periods are often debated, they nonetheless act as sensitizing frameworks that aid in identifying change and characterizing the nature of change. Classic studies of social change of particular historical periods include Weber's assertion that bureaucracy was a dominant tendency within industrialization, which he related to the nature of legitimate authority and to the social bases of power, among other factors. Furthermore, the study of bureaucratization addresses the relationship between individuals and institutions, showing how agents create an 'iron cage' of bureaucracy through their rational action, which results in a pervasive sense of disenchantment. In much the same way, Marx's emphasis on the formation of classes and the structuring of class conflict was also a method of identifying the ways that people could organize themselves and act within a powerfully constructed social setting, and thus comprised an example of a study of the relationship of social action and social structure. The same can be said of Durkheim's exploration of the division of labor and the moral alienation termed 'anomie', which he believed people experienced in the rise of complex industrial society.

Similarly, theorists such as Bell (1973), Beck (1992), Lash and Urry (1993) and Castells (2001) focus on the change from industrial to postindustrial society and beyond, to information and networked society. They address the social, cultural, technological and environmental aspects of change. The changing organization of capital, postindustrialization, networked society and globalization involves transforming the processes of production and distribution, generating new products and new patterns of consumption that relate to the proliferation of lifestyles and lifestyle politics of late modern Western society in the Global North. However, globalization is experienced differently in the Global South, where many people struggle to survive materially due to poverty of resources as well as fighting for democratic recognition and personal freedoms. The global economy, based on an ICT infrastructure, has enabled some nation-states to strengthen their economic performance. This is seen in the 'tiger economies' of Singapore, Hong Kong, Taiwan and South Korea, where it has significantly reduced poverty in each respective nation-state, but this is not the case for all developing countries or for all the inhabitants of any nation-state.

This overview shows that social change is not a determined process, and not one that is evolutionary or convergent. Rather, social change involves the way that institutions and people's agency interact in the social relations of power within historically specific contexts – and it is from these interactions that the character of change is shaped.

Key dimensions of change

Some of the key dimensions of change include the rise of individualism, e-business, social media, informalization in everyday life, cultural fragmentation and new, as well as continuing, struggles for the recognition of difference in a diverse society.

Giddens (1991) asserts that, in late modernity, individuals are reflexive because the social relations and structures of individualism are less fixed and much more open to interpretation than ever before. Individuals in late modernity construct their own individuality through creating a changeable identity, and through networked individuals. Beck (1992) asserts that there is a paradox in individualism, which is that individuals are forced into – or feel they choose – a lifecourse that is liberated from personal and traditional obligations – and yet that very liberalized push to individualism can only be achieved through increased institutionalization of the individual. The individual in his or her individuated condition instead has to engage with the mechanics of the market, educational and other support institutions as well as consumer culture, in order to construct their unique individuality.

A distinctive development in contemporary society is rise of the e-economy, through which consumerism is enabled on a global scale via the Internet (Wessels, 2010). There is continuity in some aspects of consumerism such as shopping, which has merely moved some of its processes to online research and ordering systems. What has changed is the way that cultural content and information is being shared and developed by consumers themselves, which is blurring the boundaries between consumerism and the cultural and media industries. Within this culture of popular democratization, social media is facilitating ordinary people to create cultural content that other people may consume. This activity and its agency in individuals is an example of prosumerism, whereby production and consumption become merged, with consumers being producers as well (Wessels, 2013). The ability to consume is tightly linked with how they can participate in social life. The circulation of more goods and services globally raises concerns about environmental degradation (Beck, 1992). Lash and Wynne assert, in their introduction to Beck's 1992 work, that a global economy combined with high levels of consumerism, will have grave environmental consequences. The individualization process within the development of consumer society is thus combining to form a cultural fabric that exploits environmental resources. One the hand, consumerism provides people with a sense of choice and the ability to create lifestyles that are markers of identity in contemporary social life. On the other hand, consumerism incorporates people into a dominant market system. Furthermore, inequality in Western society is increasingly understood in terms of not being able to consume at a level that is designated 'appropriate'. Therefore, those without a disposable income or access to credit are unable to participate in a mainstream society shaped through consumerism.

Everyday life has also become more fluid, with people adapting to a flexible and networked economy, while seeking to enjoy their own leisure and cultural time. Within contemporary change and everyday life, there is a rise of what can be termed 'popular democratization', in which populism is dominant in public discourse but may not entail any substantial popular emancipation (Chaney, 2002). There is also a pervasive sense of cultural fragmentation. Chaney (2002) uses the term 'fragmentation' not to imply that culture is becoming less important, but that the authority of a dominant culture is increasingly being contested by a variety of perspectives. Together, these processes are seen as part of a wider process of 'informalization', in which many of the authority structures dominant in earlier phases of modernity become merged and blurred. A combination of a global e-economy, informalization and a prosumer ethic among people who are connected via ICT is creating a social life that is both virtual and situated. A key dynamic of contemporary change is that both material and ideational resources are interlinked in the development of a society that is organized on technological and economical networks, and at the level of networked individualism.

Power as sociality is embedded in the dimensions of the social change described above. If individuals or institutions cannot 'make a difference they cease to exist in that they cannot exercise some sort of power' (Giddens, 1984, p.14). Giddens states that 'power is not one thing but many, from the transactional level wherein power is constituted as transformative capacity, to the state and institutional level wherein domination is inscribed in institutions and the state' (cited by Westwood, 2002, p.17). This illustrates the point made by Abrams (1982) that social change is a process over time, in which agency and institutions are in an active dynamic, producing new sociality and social experience. Globalization and heightened levels of geographical mobility are producing societies that are more diverse, and in which power is unequally held. The experience of that diversity varies for different people, depending on their situations and identities (Wessels, 2013). The attainment of power is often based on racism, sexism and homophobia, and this is leading some progressive commentators (Roche, 2007) to actively change the discourse surrounding difference in order to challenge the power hierarchies and make society more open to diversity.

The first step in addressing diversity was multiculturalism, with its framework of tolerance, although, as Beck (2002, 2003) argues, multiculturalism to varying degrees essentializes difference. Difficulties with these types of discourse, as well as the ongoing social change, are therefore producing debates regarding cosmopolitanism. Beck (2003) argues that there are many types of cosmopolitanisms and that their sensibility lies beyond multiculturalism – in a sense of common humanity, which is lived out in different places, ethnicities, religions and regimes. Similarly, Silverstone (2006) posits that the condition of humanity in late modernity is one of an empirically grounded plurality. The negotiation of diversity in society is, however, complex, resting on entrenched historical and cultural positions and involving questioning the existing social relations of power (Touraine, 1981). As this book shows, these struggles can be seen in contemporary society among Latin American women in the Global South and in a supraregional institution, the European Union, in the Global North.

The main characteristics of social change in contemporary society

The main characteristics of social change in contemporary society are embedded within the key dimensions of social life as described above. This book shows how these changes materialize in the practices of everyday life, relations of production, modes of labor and reconfiguring class, consumerism and lifestyles, creative and cultural industries, changes in communication, changing experiences of difference and diversity, as well as formations of power. Each of these areas highlights a key aspect of change in contemporary life, as well as their respective historical antecedents.

These include the development of a networked global economy, flexible work practices and changing senses of time and space away from industrial time and place-bound routines to more fluid and mobile patterns of everyday life managed by networked individuals. These changes interact with new patterns of consumption and the construction of lifestyles and lifestyle choices, which act as status markers, and which express values, ideologies and politics. The ubiquity of consumption as a central dynamic in late modern culture is influencing the rise of the creative industries and is flattening cultural values, which might either involve a democratization of culture or, conversely, might undermine the cultural authority and social values embodied in definitions of taste.

These trends are indicative of changing class formations, in which industrial class relations are blurring in ways that produce a new dynamic of inclusion and exclusion, both at a global level and within nation-states, and which includes strata of displaced, dispossessed and disempowered people. Although this is resulting in more fluidity and mobility and an opening up of culture, power differentials nonetheless remain among people that have real material and ideational outcomes. There is little evidence to support the concept of an emerging diverse and cosmopolitan society. To open society up to a progressive diversity requires both an open and interactive communication space for dialogue and a political process in which the social relations of power can be addressed in an open and progressive way. However, no such communication system yet exists.

Conclusion

The main argument of this book is that the broad social characteristics of change are leading to a world that is more informational and mediated, and tightly related to the generating value within globalization to produce material resource and outcomes. This new materiality is being created in a more dynamic and mobile economy of things and people – one in which inequality, poverty and oppression are being reproduced in the social relations of informational capitalism. These inequalities, as well as new aspirations and cultural frameworks for developing a better life, are being negotiated, contested and shaped by individuals and groups as they challenge existing power relations. Existing institutions are being challenged and, as currently, there is ambiguity about the character of emerging institutions, which can support some of the new aspects of contemporary change.

This book concludes that contemporary society requires new institutions to shape and support social life and to act in normative terms to create a more fulfilling, fairer life for global citizens – these institutions will emerge and be shaped through human action. They will be located in interactions between the relations of production, societal discourse and the ways that people participate in social life. In short, institutions are embedded within sociocultural change as well as within economic and political change. Hence, as this book argues, there is a need to focus on process – the relations between human agency and institutions in social change – because those relations will shape the kind of society and world that humans create for our contemporaries as well as the world we leave, historically, for the next generation.

Notes

1 Introduction: Social Change and Its Historical and Contemporary Dynamics

1. Lievrouw and Livingstone (2006) argue that the term 'people' is an improvement on the term 'user' in social science and engineering because it evokes human interests, concerns, knowledge and rights. They suggest that it seems odd to talk about the civic potential of audiences, the rights of users or the creativity of consumers. In contrast, using the term 'people' captures their individuality and collectivity; the word is neutral about their abilities and interests but advances their needs and rights and takes plurality and diversity for granted. In this book, the term 'people' is used in relation to human agency, which refers to a person's individual to act and to have an effect by their actions; and in relation to the term 'social actor', which refers to institutional as well as individual identities.

2 Exploring Social Change

1. There are several approaches to action and agency, which stem from Weber, who stresses that action is defined in the terms of 'meaningfulness' and that sociological analysis must proceed by identifying the meanings that actions have for actors (1922, 1949). These can broadly be defined as 'hermeneutic' or 'positivist' approaches. 'Hermeneutic' action theories make 'meaningfulness' an absolute theoretical priority (Schutz, 1971), whereas 'positivist' approaches (Parsons, 1951) tend to be more interested in how social structure sets the goals and means available to actors. Social structure refers to the enduring, orderly and patterned relationships between elements of a society, although there is debate about what should count as an 'element'. Social structures are relationships of a general and regular kind between people (Radcliffe-Brown, 1952); roles as the elements (Nadel, 1957); and social institutions as organized patterns of behavior – all of which are proposed as the elements of social structures by a wide range of sociologists, particularly functionalists, who then define societies in terms of functional relations between institutions. Sociologists typically aim to use concepts of social structure to explain something; usually the explanation is a causal one.
2. Another approach that emerged in the focus on agency was 'ethnomethodology'. Garfinkel (1984) coined this term, which refers to methods of individuals in their particular context. His studies are not considered here because this book focuses on broader social and cultural change, rather than change that is achieved through the detailed actions of individuals.

3. Other theorists who have addressed this reformulation include Berger and Luckmann (1967), Berger and Pullberg (1966) and Bhaskar (1979).
4. Toennies (1957) coined the German term *gemeinschaft* to convey community found more commonly in preindustrial society and the term *gesellschaft* to convey society in terms of more instrumental patterns of association of industrial society.
5. Technological determinism refers to an approach that posits that technology is an independent factor that causes social change. Approaches differ from one another in various ways, but display a similar interest in the relationship between technology and society by focusing on the influence of technology upon social structure rather than the social constitution of technology. White's (1978) technological determinism is an extreme formulation, asserting that technology causes social development, whereas Marx (1976) takes into account economic factors as well as technology in the relations of production. Poster (1990) argues that the spread of information technologies is one element of 'the post-modern experience' that, through the spread of simulation, for example, contributes to altering social relations. These sociological approaches, therefore, use a study of technology to observe the constitution and organization of the structural arrangements of society, rather than concern for the constitution and organization of technology *per se* (Button, 1996).
6. The Enclosure Acts were a series of United Kingdom Acts of Parliament that enclosed open fields and common land in the country, creating legal property rights to land that was previously considered common. Between 1604 and 1914, over 5200 individual Enclosure Acts were put into place, enclosing 6.8 million acres of land (almost 11,000 square miles) ('Enclosing the Land', *www.parliament.uk*. Retrieved 12 December 2013).

3   Key Periods of Change

1. Part of the power dynamic lays in the fact that the centralizing authorities could only qualitatively improve and entrench their ascendancy and purchase the support of their nobles by campaigns of external raids, wars and other such military adventures. These could be against neighboring societies and states, or against Europe's various enemies and 'others', particularly in the Islamic world during the period of the Crusades (11th–13th centuries).
2. The exact period of the Industrial Revolution is debated between historians. However, to provide some guidance, the First Industrial Revolution began in the 18th century and merged into the Second Industrial Revolution around 1850, when technological and economic progress gained momentum with the development of steam-powered ships, railways and later in the 19th century with the internal combustion engine and electrical power generation. The Industrial Revolution began an era of per-capita economic growth in capitalist economies.
3. The Test Acts were a series of English penal laws that served as a religious test for public office and imposed various civil exclusions on Roman Catholics and Nonconformists. The principle was that only members of the Established Church were eligible for public employment, and there were severe penalties against recusants, whether they were Catholic or Nonconformist.
4. The axial principle refers to a central, defining or *energizing* principle that has the primary logic, around which all other principles are organized. (Bell, 1973, p.10).

5. Freeman (2000) addresses the relationship between technology, economic development and social policy, using ideas from Schumpeter (1939), who drew on Kondratieff to identify waves of innovation and cycles of economic growth. For example, the industrial revolution used mechanization processes with resources such as cotton and water power; the Victorian boom used steam engine railways and cheap coal and iron; the *belle epoque* era of heavy engineering (civil, chemical, electrical) used cheap steel; the Keynesian boom was based on mass production involving automobiles and durable goods; the production of weapons and petrochemicals using the key resource of cheap petroleum; and a question of the next boom based, perhaps, on flexible production and information technology for equipment, goods and services, founded on cheap microelectronics (Freeman in Wyatt, Henwood, Miller and Senker, 2000, p.158).

6. Technopole refers to a center of high-tech manufacturing and information-based quaternary industry.

7. Poster (1990) maintains a postmodern position within his idea of the 'influences' of technologies on social relations. The key elements of postmodernism as an intellectual and social phenomenon are the rejection of: modernist thought, values and practices; claims to identify 'truth' on grounds that there are only versions of 'truth'; the search for authenticity since everything is inauthentic; quests to identify meaning because there are an infinity of meanings; and the celebration of differences, an emphasis on pleasure, a delight in the superficial, in appearances, in diversity, in parody, irony and pastiche (in Webster, 1995, p.175).

4 Exploring the Dimensions of Change

1. The development of the rights of the individual has a long history, but it was first clearly articulated in the Greek city states during the Classical Period. These rights – which were democratic rights – were, however, only granted to men and those who owned property. It was during the early modern period within political philosophy and in Western nation-state building that individuals' political and social rights were assigned a common currency and legitimacy. This was further extended in the creation of the United States, whose constitution formally encodes the rights of the individual. Legal, political and social rights institutionalized a modern understanding of the individual.

2. Beck (1992) draws on Elias (1969, 1982, 2000,) to show that the process of individualization form part of the civilization process.

3. The period after the Second World War is a significant period in the move towards consumer society as opposed to some consumer activity within a market economy and society. The Marshall Plan helped to rebuild Europe and brought an economic boom that lasted for 25 years. There was a great deal of innovation in science and technology during this period, as well as in domestic household technologies, media technology, automobile and other consumer services such as package holidays. This economic boom also provided a wage-based resource for working-class people that enabled them to buy goods that had not been available, or affordable, to their parents. The key period of this economic boom and the innovation of consumer products was the 1950s.

4. In relation to sociological understanding of power, the works of Hobbes (1588–1679), Locke (1632–1704) and Machiavelli (1469–1527) are seen as precursors to the modern period (Westwood, 2002). These writings of these men shows how they were attempting to address the exercise of power. They sought to do this by exploring the relations between people and the state, questions of governance and moral questions that relate to the exercise of power, responsibility and freedom (Westwood, 2002).

5 Everyday Life and Social Change

1. Haddon (2004, p.1) notes that the concept of everyday life has an intellectual heritage stemming from the work of Lukacs, Lefebrve and de Certeau in Europe and from the work of the Chicago School, Goffman and Garfinkel in the United States.
2. Scholars working in Central Europe and Germany during the 1930s and early 1940s formed a School at the University of Frankfurt, with key proponents including Adorno, Horkheimer and Marcuse. They developed their early work in Germany before moving to New York. The defining feature of their work was 'Critical Theory' and they drew on the Marxist theory of alienation, theories of ideology including that of Gramsci and Freudian psychoanalysis. One of their main areas of study was popular culture and the culture industry. Culture was understood as being pervasive because it generated a framework of wants, desires and sense making that inculcated populations into the dominant relations of capitalism. Thus, political dominance and incorporation of the masses were achieved through the new means of mass communication and mass culture.
3. Simmel notes that social forms are located in historical time. In *Metropolis and Mental Life* (1950), he discussed the different experiences of living a small-town life in Antiquity and the Middle Ages, as compared to modern urban city life.
4. Goffman (1959) addresses the way in which individuals in everyday life present themselves and their activities to others. This highlights the ways that individuals seek to construct and manage the impressions others form of them – this is called impression management. Parts of the actual practice of impression management are *front* and *back regions*. Front is defined as 'that part of the individuals' performance which regularly functions in a general and fixed fashion to define the situation for those who observe the performance' (Goffman, 1959, p.22). The 'back region' refers to places that are closed and hidden from audiences. Through these concepts, and in their observation, Goffman shows how individuals manage themselves and their situations in the drama of everyday life.
5. Hochschild (1983, 1989, 1997) developed the work of the SI school and Goffman further by addressing the role and management of emotions in daily life. She sought to research emotions seriously and covered a whole range of emotions including grief, depression, frustration, anger, fear, contempt, guilt, anguish, envy, jealousy, embarrassment, shame, anxiety about love, compassion, nostalgia, joy, gratitude, pride and ambivalence. She develops this in two related ways: in terms of emotional labor in occupations such as flight attendants and bill collectors and the emotional aspects of social change in family and work patterns.

6. The first age of the Internet dates from its inception to its commercialization around 1995. The ethos of this time was one of excitement about its 'newness', which was seen in both positive and negative terms.

7. This marks a move away from a determinist position looking at the use of the Internet that posits that the Internet determines behaviors. Rather, Wellman and Haythornthwaite (2002) and their contributors start to explore the way in which the use of the Internet is integrated into action and behavior. They develop this position from research in Computer Mediated Communication (CMC) that works with the idea that there are differences between computer-mediated and face-to-face communication, thus working with a distinction between online and offline communication. Although there are differences in communication between these forms, Wellman and Haythornthwaite (2002) argue that the research done within CMC has perpetuated a dichotomized view of human behavior, which needed to be questioned. Furthermore, such either/or dichotomies pit one form of CMC against another – for example, synchronous versus asynchronous communication (e.g. chat versus email), text versus graphics, as well as one category of human endeavor against another, such as computer use at work versus at home, online content for adults versus children and computer and Internet users versus nonusers. Wellman and Haythornthwaite (2002), therefore, argue for an integrative approach that links online and offline together.

8. Bauman's book *Liquid modernity* (2000) uses the notion of fluid and light as opposed to the solid and heavy life to explore contemporary transformations. Bauman explore five areas of human experience in his book: emancipation, individuality, time/space, work and community.

6 Work, Production and Social Change

1. This has mainly been in the formal economy, although there is research about work in the informal economy (Williams, 2004).

2. The 1833 Factory Act was the first step to improving and beginning to regulate the working conditions of children (National Archives). This act was one of the many that comprised the Factory and Workshop Acts from 1878 to 1895, which includes the Factory and Workshop Act 1878, the Factory and Workshop Act 1883, the Cotton Cloth Factories Act 1889, the Factory and Workshop Act 1891 and the Factory and Workshop Act 1895. These acts built upon the Factories Act 1802 (also called the 'Health and Morals of Apprentices Act'), which was a UK Act of the Parliament which regulated factory conditions, especially in regard to child workers in cotton and woolen mills. It was the culmination of a movement originating in the 18th century, where reformers had tried to push several acts through Parliament to improve the health of workers and apprentices. There is debate, however, in how much power Parliament had over the manufacturers, but nonetheless, it did at least start to raise awareness of the poor working conditions and it did mitigate some of the worst abuses of workers in factories.

3. In 1926, the Trade Union Congress (TUC) called a general strike to defend reasonable pay and conditions for coal miners. After a nine-day industrial dispute, two

unions took the TUC to court to prevent them being called out on strike. The subsequent court decision, the Astbury Judgement, ruled the general strike illegal. The ruling forced the TUC to capitulate as it resulted in the TUC being directly liable for huge fines from employers, and simultaneously gave the government the ability to confiscate all union funds. Ultimately, many miners returned to work, and were forced to accept longer hours and lower pay.

4. A truck system is an arrangement in which employees are paid in commodities or some currency substitute rather than with money.

5. A cottage system is where goods are manufactured by people working individually in their own homes.

6. Taylorism or 'scientific management' is a theory of management that analyzes and synthesizes workflow processes to improve labor productivity. Taylor (1905, 1911) believed that decisions based upon tradition and rules of thumb should be replaced by precise procedures, which are developed after careful study of an individual at work. Taylorism pushes the division of labor to its logical extreme, with a consequent deskilling of the worker and dehumanization of the workplace.

7. Gramsci (1971) used the term 'Fordism' to describe a form of production characterized by an assembly line (conveyor belt factory system) and standardized outputs linked to the stimulation of demand brought about by low prices, advertising and credit. Fordism, exemplified by the mass-production systems based on the principles of Taylorism used by the car maker, Henry Ford (1863–1947), gave workers high wages in return for intensive work.

7 Social Change and Consumerism

1. McCracken (1988) defines 'patina' in relation to the way goods are given value. Patina refers to goods that favor established heritage and 'old money', seeking to prove that wealth stretches across generations. Because patina goods are so bespoke and old, it is difficult for other classes to emulate them.

8 The Creative and Cultural Industries

1. Leading members of the school include Adorno (1947), Adorno and Horkheimer (1973), Benjamin (1970) and Marcuse (1964). Habermas adapted this tradition in 1973 and 1989; and the most recent work is Steinert (2003).

2. For example: Hobson (1982); Ang (1985); Radway (1987); Scannell et al. (1992); Morley (1980, 1986); Silverstone (1990); and Silverstone, Morley, Dahlberg and Livingstone (1989).

3. The term 'affordances' is used in the studies of science and technology and refers to the fact that a technology can be adapted and used in a variety of ways. This means that the way technology is developed into products and services depends on how it can be adapted and used in relation to the type of service or product under development.

9 Changes in Communication

1. The Internet is part of the broader category 'Information and Communication Technology' (ICT). Dutton (2001) defines ICT as: 'all kinds of electronic systems used for broadcasting, telecommunications and computer-mediated communication' (2001, p.7). He also provides some examples of ICT: 'personal computers, video games, interactive TV, cell phones, the Internet [and] electronic payment systems' (Dutton, 2001, p.3).
2. A community of interest is a community of people who share a common interest or passion. These people exchange ideas and thoughts about the given passion, but may know (or care) little about each other outside of this area.

10 Diversity, Difference and Contesting Power

1. *Marianismo* originates in Latin American folk culture, and it includes ideas of feminine passivity and sexual purity. There is power in *marianismo* that stems from the female ability to produce life.
2. Democracy refers to a polity of multiple distinct people. *Demoi* is the plural form, which refers to a populace of people.

Bibliography

Abrams, P. (1982), *Historical Sociology* (Ithaca: Cornell University Press).

Ackoff, R. (1969), 'Management Misinformation Systems', *Management Science*, (14/4), 147–156.

Adams, J. (2000), 'Hypermobility', *Prospect*, March, Retrieved from http://www.prospect-magazine.co.uk/highlights/hypermobility/index.html.

Adorno, T. (1947), 'Culture Industry Reconsidered', in J.M. Bernstein (ed.) (1991), *The Culture Industry: Selected Essays on Mass Culture* (London: Routledge), pp.85–92.

Adorno, T. and Horkheimer, M. (1973), *Dialectic of Enlightenment* (London: The Penguin Press).

Aldrich, H.E. (1972), 'Technology and Organisation Structure: A Re-examination of the Findings of the Aston Group', *Administrative Science Quarterly*, 17, 26–43.

Allen, I.E. and Seaman, J. (2003), 'Sizing the Opportunity: The Quality and Extent of Online Education in the United States, 2002 and 2003', The Sloan Consortium, Retrieved from http://www.sloan-c.org/resources/sizing_opportunity.pdf.

Alvarez, S. (1990), *Engendering Democracy in Brazil* (Princeton, NJ: Princeton University Press).

Anderson, J.Q. (2005), *Imagining the Internet: Personalities, Predictions, Perspectives* (Maryland: Rowman & Littlefield).

Anderson, J.Q. and Tracey, K. (2002), 'Digital Living: The Impact (or otherwise) of the Internet on Everyday British Life', in C. Haythornswaite and B. Wellamn (eds.), *The Internet and Everyday Life* (Malden, MA: Blackwell Publishing), pp.139–163.

Ang, I. (1985), *Watching 'Dallas': Soap Operas and the Melodramatic Imagination* (London: Methuen).

Archer, M. (1992), 'Morphogensis versus Structure and Action', *British Journal of Sociology*, 33:4, 56–78.

Arendt, H. (1958), *The Human Condition* (Chicago: Chicago University Press).

Arendt, H. (1969), *On Violence* (London: New Left Books).

Atkinson, P. and Housley, W. (2003), *Interactionism* (London: Sage).

Attewell, P. (1987), 'Big Brother and the Sweatshop: Computer Surveillance in the Automated Office', *Sociological Theory*, 5, 87–100.

Attewell, P. and Rule, J. (1984), 'Computing and Organisations: What we Know and What we don't Know', *Communications of the ACM*, 27:12, 1184–1191.

Baggulay, P. (1994), 'Prisoners of the Beveridge Dream? The Political Mobilisation of the Poor Against Contemporary Welfare Regimes', in R. Burrows and B. Loader (eds.), *Towards a Post-Fordist Welfare State?* (London: Routledge).

Bakardjieva, M. and Feenburg, A. (2004), *Virtual Community: No 'killer implication'* (London: Sage Publications).

Balakrishnan, R. (ed.) (2002), *The Hidden Assembly Line – Gender Dynamics of Subcontracted Work in a Global Economy* (West Hartford: Kumaria Press).

Banks, J.A. and McGee, C.A. (1989), *Multicultural Education* (Needham Heights, MA: Allyn & Bacon).

Barker, J. and Downing, H. (1985), 'Word Processing and the Transformation of Patriarchal Relations of Control in the Office', in D. MacKenzie and J. Wajcman (eds.), *The Social Shaping of Technology* (Milton Keynes: Open University Press), pp.147–165.

Barley, S. (1986), 'Technology as an Occasion for Structuring: Evidence from Observation of CT Scanners and the Social Order of Radiology Departments', *Administrative Science Quarterly*, 31, 78–108.

Barley, S. (1990), 'The Alignment of Technology and Structure through Roles and Networks', *Administrative Science Quarterly*, 35, 61–103.

Barnes, J.A. (1954), *Class and Committees in a Norwegian Island Parish* (London School of Economics: University of London).

Barney, D. (2004), *The Network Society* (Cambridge: Polity Press).

Barth, F. (1966), *Models of Social Organisation*, Occasional Paper 23 (London: Royal Institute of Great Britain and Ireland).

Bassett, C. (1997), 'Virtually Gendered: Life in an On-line World', in K. Gelder and S. Thornton (eds.), *The Subcultures Reader* (London: Routledge).

Baudelaire, C. (1964), *The Painter of Modern Life and Other Essays*, J. Mayne (ed.) (London: Phaidon Press), pp.1–41.

Baudelaire, C. (1994), *Simulations and Simulatra* (Michigan: Michigan University Press).

Baudrillard, J. (1981), *Simulacra and Simulations* (Michigan: Michigan University Press).

Baudrillard, J. (1983), *Simulations* (New York: Semiotext(e)).

Bauman, R. (1977), *Verbal Art as Performance* (Massachusetts: Newbury House Publishers).

Bauman, Z. (1998), *Globalization: The Human Consequences* (Cambridge: Polity Press).

Bauman, Z. (2000), *Liquid Modernity* (Cambridge: Polity Press).

Bauman, Z. (2007), *Consuming Life* (Cambridge: Polity).

Baym, N. (1998), 'The Emergence of an On-line Community', in S. Jones (ed.), *Cybersociety 2.0: Revisiting Computer-mediated Communication and Community* (London: Sage), pp.35–68.

Beck, U. (1992), *Risk Society: Towards New Modernity* (London: Sage).

Beck, U. (2002), 'The Cosmopolitan Society and its Enemies', *Theory, Culture & Society*, 19:1–2, 17–45.

Beck, U. (2003), 'Towards a New Critical Theory with a Cosmopolitan Intent', *Constellations*, 10:4, 453–468.

Becker, H.S. (1953), 'Becoming a Marihuana User', *The American Journal of Sociology*, 59:33, 235–242.

Beechey, V. (1982), 'The Sexual Division of Labour and the Labour Process', in S. Wood (ed.), *The Degradation of Work?: Skill, Deskilling and the Labour Process* (London: Hutchinson), pp.54–73.

Bell, D. (1973), *The Coming of the Post-Industrial Society* (New York: Basic Books).

Bell, D. (2001), *An Introduction to Cybercultures* (London: Routledge).

Bell, D. and Kennedy, B. (2000), *The Cybercultures Reader* (London: Routledge).

Bellamy, C. and Taylor, J.A. (1998), *Governing in the Information Age* (Buckingham: Open University Press).

Benjamin, W. (1970), *Illuminations* (London: Cape).

Benson, D. (1990), 'Science, Science Policy and Ethics', in A. Elzinga (ed.), *In Science We Trust?* (Lund: Lund University Press).

Berger, P.L. and Luckmann, T. (1967), *The Social Construction of Reality* (London: The Penguin Press).

Berger, P.L. and Pullberg, S. (1966), 'Reification and the Sociological Critique of Consciousness', *New Left Review*, 35:2, 56–73.

Berker, T., Hartmann, M., Punie, Y. and Ward, K. (eds.) (2005), *Domestication of Media and Technologies* (Maidenhead: Open University Press).

Berker, T. with Hartmann, M., Punie, Y. and Ward, K. (2005), 'Introduction' in Berker, T., Hartmann, M., Punie, Y. and Ward, K. (eds) *Domestication of Media and Technologies* (Maidenhead: Open University Press), pp.1–16.

Berman, M. (1982), *All that Is Solid Melts Into Air: The Experience of Modernity* (New York: Penguin Books).

Berners-Lee, T. (1999), *Weaving the Web: The Past, Present and Future of the World Wide Web by its Inventor* (San Francisco: Harper Collins).

Bernstein, R.J. (1978), *The Restructuring of Social and Political Theory* (Philadelphia, PA: University of Pennsylvania).

Bhambra, G.K. (2007), *Rethinking Modernity: Postcolonialism and the Sociological Imagination* (Palgrave: Basingstoke).

Bhasker, R. (1979), *The Possibility of Naturalism* (Brighton: Harvester Press).

Bijker, W.E. (1987), 'The Social Construction of Bakelite: Toward a Theory of Invention', in W.E. Bijker, T.P. Hughes and T. Pinch (eds.), *The Social Construction of Technology Systems* (Cambridge, MA: MIT Press), pp.159–187.

Bijker, W.E., Hughes, T.P. and Pinch, T. (eds.) (1987), *The Social Construction of Technology Systems* (Cambridge, MA: MIT Press).

Bingham, A. (2007), 'Drinking in the Last Chance Saloon: The British Press and the Crisis of Self Regulation 1989–95', *Media History* 13:1, 80–94.

Biresse, A. (2005), *Reality TV: Realism and Revelation* (New York: Columbia University Press).

Biressi, A. and Nunn, H. (2005), *Reality TV: Realism and Revelation* (New York: Columbia Press).

Bittner, E. (1967), 'Police Discretion in the Emergency Apprehension of Mentally-ill Persons', *Social Problems*, 14, 699–715.

Blake, M.L. and Moonstan, C. (1981), 'Women and Transnational Corporations: The Electronics Industry in Thailand', East West Centre, Honolulu.

Blau, P., McHugh-Falbe, W. and Phelps, T. (1996), 'Technology and Organisation in Manufacturing', *Administrative Science Quarterly*, 21, 20–40.

Bloch, M. (1989), *Feudal Society*, vol. 1 (London: Routledge).

Blumer, H. (1969), *Symbolic Interactionism; Perspective and Method* (Englewood Cliffs, NJ: Prentice-Hall).

Blumler, J.G. and Gurevitch, M. (1995), *The Crisis of Public Communication* (London: Routledge).

Boden, M.A. (ed.) (1994), *Dimensions of Creativity* (Cambridge, MA: MIT Press).

Bolter, J.D. and Grusin, R. (1999), *Remediation: Understanding New Media* (Cambridge, MA: MIT Press).

Bontcheva, K., Gorrell, G. and Wessels, B. (2013), 'Social Media and Information Overload: Survey Results', Cornell University Library, arXiv:1306.0813 [cs.SI].

Born, G. (1993), 'Against Negation, for a Politics of Cultural Production: Adorno, Aesthetics, the Social', *Screen*, 3, 223–242.

Borradori, G. (2003), *Philosophy in the Time of Terror: Dialogues with Jurgen Habermas and Jacques Derrida* (Chicago: University of Chicago Press).

Bott, E. (1957), *Family and Social Network: Role Norms and External Relationships in Ordinary Urban Families* (London: Tavistock).

Bourdieu, P. (1973), 'Cultural Reproduction and Social Reproduction', in R. Brown (ed.), *Knowledge, Education and Cultural Change* (London: Tavistock), pp.71–112.

Bourdieu, P. (1977), *Outline of a Theory of Practice*, trans. R. Nice (Cambridge: Cambridge University Press).

Bourdieu, P. (1984), *Distinction: A Social Critique of the Judgement of Taste* (London: Routledge & Kegan Paul).

Bourdieu, P. (1996), *The Rules of Art* (Cambridge: Polity Press).

Bowles, K. (2000), 'No End of Story, Ever', in G. Turner and S. Cunningham (eds.), *The Australia TV Book* (New South Wales: Allen and Unwin).

Boyd, D. (2014), *Its Complicated: The Social Life of Networked Teens* (New Haven: Yale University Press).

Boyd, D. and Ellison, N. (2007), 'Social Network Sites: Definition, History and Scholarship', *Journal of Computer-Mediated Communication*, 13:1, article 18, Retrieved from http://jcmc.indiana.edu/vol13/issue1/boyd.ellison.html.

Boyne, R. and Rattansi, A. (eds.) (1999), *Postmodernism and Society* (London: MacMillan).

Branwyn, G. (2000), 'Compu-Sex: Erotica for Cybernauts', in D. Bell and B.M. Kennedy (eds.), *The Cybercultures Reader* (London: Routledge).

Braverman, H. (1974), *Labor and Monopoly Capital: The Degradation of Work in the Twentieth Century* (New York: Monthly Review Press).

Bromberg, H. (1996), 'Are MUDs Communities? Identity, Belonging and Consciousness in Virtual Worlds', in R. Shields (ed.), *Cultures of the Internet* (London: Sage).

Bromley, R. (2000), 'The Theme that Dare Not Speak its Name: Class in Recent British Film', in S. Munt (ed.), *Cultural Studies and the Working Class* (London: Cassell).

Brown, R. (1978), 'Work', in P. Abrams (ed.), *Work, Urbanism and Inequality* (London: Weidenfeld & Nicholson).

Brown, R. (1988), 'The Employment Relationship in Sociological Theory', in D. Gallie (ed.), *Employment in Britain* (Oxford: Blackwell).

Brown, R.H. (1977), *A Poetic for Sociology* (London: Cambridge University Press).

Brown, S. (1995), *Postmodern Marketing* (London: Routledge).

Bryant, C. and Jary, D. (eds.) (1991), *Giddens' Theory of Structuration: A Critical Appreciation* (London: Routledge).

Buchner, P. (1990), Das Telefon im Alltag von Kindern', in *Forschungsgruppe Telefonkomunikation* (eds.), *Telefon and Gesellschaft*, 2 (Berlin: Volker Speiss).

Burawoy, M. (1979), *Manufacturing Consent: Changes in the Labor Process under Monopoly Capitalism* (Chicago: University of Chicago Press).

Burawoy, M. (1985), *The Politics of Production: Factory Regimes under Capitalism and Socialism* (London: Verso).

Burawoy, M. (2009), *The Extended Case Method: Four Countries, Four Decades, Four Great Transformations, and One Theoretical Tradition* (California: University of California Press).

Burgess, R. (1991), *In the Field: An Introduction to Field Research* (London: Routledge).

Burke, K. (1945), *A Grammar of Motive* (New York: Prentice Hall).

Burke, K. (1950), *A Rhetoric of Motives* (New York: Prentice Hall).

Burke, K. (1957), *The Philosophy of Literary Form: Studies in Symbolic Action* (New York: Vintage Books).

Burke, K. (1977), 'Bodies that Learn Language', Lecture at University of California, San Diego.

Burke, K. (1984), *Attitudes Toward History* (Berkeley and Los Angeles: University of California Press).

Burke, K. (1989), *On Symbols and Society* (Chicago: University of Chicago Press).

Burke, P., Burke, J.S., Timothy, P.J., Owens, J., Richard, T., Serpe, R.T. and Thoits, P.A. (eds.) (2003), *Advances in Identity Theory and Research* (New York: Kluwer Academic/Plenum).

Burke, P.J., Owens, T.J., Serpe, R.T. and Thoits, P.A. (2003), *Advances in Identity Theory and Research* (New York: Kluwer Academic Publishers).

Burrell, G. and Morgan, G. (1979), *Sociological Paradigms and Organisational Analysis* (London: Heinemann).

Burrow, J.W. (1966), *Evolution and Society: A Study in Victorian Social Theory* (Cambridge: Cambridge University Press).

Burrows, R. (1997), 'Cyberpunk as Social Theory: William Gibson and the Sociological Imagination', in S. Westwood and J. Williams (eds.), *Imagining Cities: Scripts, Signs, Memory* (London: Routledge).

Burrows, R. and Loader, B. (eds.) (1994), *Towards a Post-Fordist Welfare State?* (London: Routledge).

Butler, J. (1990), *Gender Trouble. Feminism and the Subversion of Identity* (New York: Routledge).

Butler, J. (1993), *Bodies that Matter. On the Discursive Limits of 'Sex'* (New York: Routledge).

Button, G. (ed.) (1996), *Technology in Working Order. Studies of Work, Interaction, and Technology* (London, New York: Routledge).

Byrne, D. (1999), *Social Exclusion* (Buckingham: Open University Press).

Byrne, S., Katz, S.J., Lee, T., Linz, D. and McIlrath, M. (2013), 'Peers, Predators, and Porn: Predicting Parental Underestimation of their Children's Risky Online Experiences', *Journal of Computer-Mediated Communication*, doi:10.1111/jcc4. 12040.

Calhoun, C. (ed.) (1992), *Habermas and the Public Sphere* (Cambridge MA: The MIT Press).

Callon, M. (1996), 'Some Elements of a Sociology of Translation', in J. Law (ed.), *Power, Action and Belief* (London: Routledge & Kegan Paul), pp.196–233.

Campbell, C. (1987), *The Romantic Ethic and the Spirit of Modern Consumerism* (Oxford: Blackwells Publishers).

Cardosa, J. and Khoo, K.J. (1978), 'Workers in Electronics Runways: The Case of Malaysia', IDS, University of Sussex.

Carey, J. (1993), 'Everything that Rises must Diverge: Notes on Communications, Technology and the Symbolic Construction of the Social', in P. Gaunt (ed.), *Beyond Agendas* (Westport, CT: Greenwood), pp.171–181.

Carnoy, M. (2000), 'Sustaining the New Economy: Work, Family and Community in the Information Age', in M. Castells (ed.), *The Internet Galaxy* (Cambridge: Harvard University Press).

Castells, M. (1996), *The Rise of the Network Society* (Oxford: Blackwell).

Castells, M. (2001), *The Internet Galaxy: Reflections on the Internet, Business and Society* (Oxford: Oxford University Press).

Castells, M. (2009), *Communication Power* (Oxford: Oxford University Press).

Castells, M. and Cardoso, G. (eds.) (2005), *The Network Society: From Knowledge to Policy* (Washington, DC: Johns Hopkins Center for Transatlantic Relations).

Cerny, P.G. (1997), 'Paradoxes of the Competition State: The Dynamics of Political Globalization', *Government and Opposition*, 32:2, 251–274.

Chaney, D. (1983), 'The Department Store as Cultural Form', *Theory, Culture and Society*, 1:3, 64–87.

Chaney, D. (1990), 'Subtopia in Gateshead: The MetroCentre as Cultural Form', *Theory, Culture and Society*, 7:4, 49–68.

Chaney, D. (1994), *The Cultural Turn* (London: Routledge).

Chaney, D. (1996), *Lifestyles* (London: Routledge).

Chaney, D. (2002), *Cultural Change and Everyday Life* (Basingstoke: Palgrave).

Chapple, E.D. (1953), 'Applied Anthropology in Industry', in A.L. Kroeber (ed.), *Anthropology Today* (Chicago: Chicago University Press), pp.69–94.

Cheung, C. (2000), 'A Home on the Web: Presentations of Self on Personal Home-Pages', in D. Gauntlett (ed.), *Web. Studies: Rewiring Media Studies for the Digital Age* (London: Arnold).

Child, J. (1972), 'Organisational Structure, Environment and Performance: The Role of Strategic Choice', *Sociology*, 6:1, 1–22.

Clerc, S. (2000), 'Estrogen Brigades and "Big Tits" Threads: Media Fandom On-Line and Off', in D. Bell and B.M. Kennedy (eds.), *The Cybercultures Reader* (London: Routledge).

Clifford, J. (1984), *The Predicament of Culture* (Cambridge, MA: Harvard University Press).

Clifford, J. and Marcus, G. (1986), *Writing Culture, the Poetics of Ethnography* (Berkeley: University of California Press).

Cockburn, C. (1983), *Brothers: Male Dominance and Technological Change* (London: Pluto).

Cockburn, C. (1985), 'Caught in the Wheels: The Higher Cost of Being a Female Cog in the Male Machinery of Engineering', in D. MacKenzie and J. Wajcman (eds.), *The Social Shaping of Technology* (Milton Keynes: Open University Press), pp.55–65.

Cohen, R. and Rai, S. (2002), *Global Social Movements* (London: Athlone Press).

Coleman, S.J., Taylor, J. and Van der Dunk, W. (eds.) (1999), *Parliament in the Age of the Internet* (Oxford: Oxford University Press).

Collins, P.H. (1998), *Fighting Words: Black Women in the Search for Justice* (Minneapolis: University of Minneapolis Press).

Collins, P.H. (2000), 'Gender, Black Feminism and Black Political Economy', *Annals of the American Academy of Political and Social Science*, 568, 41–53.

Collinson, H. (ed.) (1990), *Women and Revolution in Nicaragua* (London: Zed).

Consalvo, M. and Haythornthwaite, C. (eds.) (2006), *AoIR Internet Annual, Volume 4* (New York: Peter Lang).

Cooley, M. (1980), 'Computerization: Taylor's Latest Disguise', *Economic and Industrial Democracy*, 1, 523–539.

Corner, J. (2000), ' "Influence": The Contested Core of Media Research', in J. Curran and M. Gurevitch (ed.), *Mass Media and Society* (London: Hodder Arnold), pp.376–397.

Cornford, J. and Pollock, N. (2003), *Putting the University Online: Information, Technology and Organizational Change* (Buckingham: Open University Press).

Corrigan, P. (1997), *The Sociology of Consumption* (London: Sage).

Cowan, R.S. (1983), *More Work for Mothers: The Ironies of Household Technologies*: (New York: Basic Books).

Critcher, S., Bramham, P. and Tomlinson, A. (1995), *Sociology of Leisure: A Reader* (London: E&FN Spon).

Crompton, R. (1993), *Class and Stratification: An Introduction to Current Debates* (Cambridge: Polity Press).

Crook, S. (1998), 'Minotaurs and Other Monsters: "Everyday Life" in Recent Social Theory', *Sociology*, 32:3, 523–540.

Crouch, C. (2012), *Post Democracy* (Cambridge: Polity Press).

Cunningham, J. and Roberts, P. (2006), *Inside Her Pretty Little Head: A New Theory of Female Motivation and What it Means for Marketing* (London: Marshall Cavendish).

Dahl, R. (1973), *Modern Political Analysis* (New Jersey: Prentice Hall).

Dahlgren, P. (2005), 'The Internet, Public Spheres, and Political Communication: Dispersion and Deliberation', *Political Communication*, vol. 22 (London: Routledge), pp.147–162.

Danet, B. and Herring, S.C. (eds.) (2007), *The Multilingual Internet: Language, Culture, and Communication Online*, co-edited by Brenda Danet and Susan C. Herring (Oxford: Oxford University Press).

Davis, L.E. and Taylor, J.C. (1986), 'Technology, Organisation and Job Structure', in R. Dubin (ed.), *Handbook of Work, Organisation, and Society* (Chicago, IL: Rand McNally), pp.379–419.

Davis, M. (1990), *City of Quartz: Excavating the Future in Los Angeles* (London: Verso).

Deakin, R. (1984), *Women and Computing: The Golden Opportunity* (London: MacMillan Press).

De Certeau, M. (1984), *The Practice of Everyday Life* (London: University of California Press).

Delanty, G. (1995), *Inventing Europe: Idea, Identity, Reality* (Basingstoke: MacMillan).

Delanty, G. (2007), 'Modernity', in G. Ritzer (ed.), *Blackwell Encyclopedia of Sociology* (Malden, MA: Blackwell Publishing).

De Lauritis, T. (1987), *Technologies of Gender* (London: MacMillan).

Derrida, J. (1978), *Writing and Difference* (Chicago: Chicago University Press).

Derrida, J. (2003), cited in Borradori, G. (2003), *Philosophy in the Time of Terror: Dialogues with Jurgen Habermas and Jacques Derrida* (Chicago: University of Chicago Press), p.128.

de Swaan, A. (1991), 'Notes on the Emerging Global Language System – Regional, National and Supranational', *Media, Culture and Society*, 13:3, 309–323.

Dewey, J. (1939), *Intelligence and the Modern World* (New York: Modern Library).

Dilthey, W. (1914–1936), *Gesammelte Schriften*, vols 1–12 (Stuugart: Teubner).

Dilthey, W. (1957), *Dilthey's Philosophy of Existence*, trans. W. Kluback (New York: Bookman).

Disney, R., Gosling, A. and Machin, S. (1995), 'What Has Happened to Union Recognition in Britain?' *Economica*, 63, 1–18.

Douglas, D.A. (1992), *Working Knowledge: Skill and Community in a Small Shop* (Chicago: University of Chicago Press).

Driver, F. (1985), 'Power, Space and the Body: A Critical Assessment of Foucault's Discipline and Punish', *Environment and Planning: Society and Space*, 3, 425–446.

Drucker, P. (1969), *The Age of Discontinuity; Guidelines to Our Changing Society* (New York: Harper and Row).

Duncan, G. (1989), *Democracy and the Capitalist State* (Cambridge: Cambridge University Press).

Durkheim, E. (1982), *The Rules of Sociological Method* (New York: Free Press).

Durkheim, E. (1984), *Division of Labour in Society* (New York: Free Press).

Durkheim, E. (1997), [1893], *The Division of Labor in Society* (New York: Free Press).

Dutton, W.H. (2001), *Society on the Line: Informational Politics in the Digital Age* (Oxford: Oxford University Press).

Edelman, M. (1964), *The Symbolic Uses of Politics* (Urbana, IL: University of Illinois Press).

Edelman, M. (1971), *Politics as Symbolic Action* (Chicago: Markham Publishing Co).

Edwards, P. (1996), *The Closed World: Computers and the Politics of Discourse in Cold War America* (Cambridge, MA: MIT Press).

Edwards, R. (1979), *Contested Terrain: The Transformation of the Workplace in the Twentieth Century* (New York: Basic Books).

Elias, N. (1969), *The Civilizing Process, Vol. I. The History of Manners* (Oxford: Blackwell).

Elias, N. (1978), *The Civilising Process: The History of Manners* (Oxford: Basil Blackwell Publisher Ltd.).

Elias, N. (1982), *The Civilizing Process, Vol. II. State Formation and Civilization* (Oxford: Blackwell).

Elias, N. (2000), *The Civilizing Process: Sociogenetic and Psychogenetic Investigations*. Revised edition (Oxford: Blackwell).

Ellison, N. (1997), 'Towards a New Social Politics: Citizenship and Reflexivity on Late Modernity', *Sociology*, 31:4, 697–717.

Engels, F. (1887), *Condition of the Working Class in England* (Leipzig: Otto Wigand).

Entrikin, N. (1992), 'The Geographical Moment', *Contemporary Sociology*, 21:3, 23–46.

Esping Andersen, G. (1990), *The Three Worlds of Welfare Capitalism*, Cambridge: Polity Press.

European Commission. Office. Europe and the Global Information Society: Recommendations to the European Council. ISPO. Brussels, Belgium (26 May 1994), www.ispo.cec.be/infosoc/backg/bangeman.html.

Featherstone, M. (1991), *Consumer Culture and Postmodernism* (London: Sage).

Featherstone, M. and Burrows, R. (eds.) (1995), *Cyberspace, Cyberbodies, Cyberpunk: Cultures of Technological Embodiment* (London: Sage).

Fellner, W. (1951), 'The Influence of Market Structure Upon Technical Progress', *Quarterly Journal of Economics*, 65, 556–577.

Fernie, S. and Metcalf, D. (eds.) (2005), 'Trade Unions: Resurgence or Demise?' *The Future of Trade Unions in Britain* (London: Routledge).

Flew, T. (2002), *New Media – An Introduction* (Oxford: Oxford University Press).

Florida, R. (2002), *The Rise of the Creative Class* (New York: Basic Books).

Florida, R. (2011), *The Rise of the Creative Class revisited* (New York: Basic Books).

Foot, K. and Schneider, S.M. (2006), *Web Campaigning (Acting with Technology)* (Cambridge, MA: MIT Press).

Foucault, M. (1964), *Madness and Civilization: A History of Insanity in the Age of Reason* (New York: Pantheon Books).

Foucault, M. (1970), *The Order of Things* (New York: Random House).

Foucault, M. (1972), *The Archaeology of Knowledge* (London: Routledge).

Foucault, M. (1977), *Discipline and Punish* (London: Allan Lane).

Foucault, M. (1980), *Power/Knowledge. Selected Interviews and Other Writings* (London: Harvester Press).

Fox, S. (2005), *Digital Divisions: There are Clear Differences among those with Broadband Connections, Dial-up Connections, and No Connections at all to the Internet* (http://www.pewinternet.org/ Pew Internet & American Life Project).

Fraser, N. and Nicolson, L. (1988), 'Social Criticism without Philosophy: An Encounter between Feminism and Postmodernism', *Theory, Culture and Society*, 2:3, 373–394.

Freeman, C. (1992a), 'The Human Use of Human Beings and Technical Change', in C. Freeman (ed.), *The Economics of Hope: Essays on Technical Change, Economic Growth and the Environment* (London: Pinter Publishers), pp.175–189.

Freeman, C. (1992b), 'Technology, Progress and the Quality of Life', in C. Freeman (ed.), *The Economics of Hope: Essays on Technical Change, Economic Growth and the Environment* (London: Pinter), pp.212–230.

Freeman, C. (1994), 'The Economics of Technical Change, Critical Survey', *Cambridge Journal of Economics*, 18, 463–514.

Freeman, C. (2000), 'Social Inequality, Technology and Economic Growth', in S. Wyatt, F. Henwood, N. Miller, and P. Senker. (eds.), *Technology and In/equality: Questioning the Information Society* (London: Routledge), pp.149–171.

Freeman, C. and Soete, L. (1997), *The Economics of Industrial Innovation* (Cambridge, MA: MIT Press).

Frenier, C. (1997), *Business and the Feminine Principle: The Untapped Resource* (Cambridge, MA: Newton).

Friedland, R. (1992), 'Space, Place and Modernity', *Contemporary Sociology*, 21:3, 74–89.

Friedman, A. and Cornford, D.S. (1989), *Computer Systems Development* (New York: Wiley).

Friedman, J. (1994), 'The Iron Cage of Creativity: An Exploration', in J. Liep (ed.), *Locating Cultural Creativity* (London: Pluto Press), pp.46–61.

Fuchs, C. (2007), 'The Notions of Class and Knowledge Labor in Informational Capitalism', Paper presented at the annual meeting of the American Sociological Association, TBA, New York, New York City, Online.

Fuchs, C. (2008), *Internet and Society: Social Theory in the Information Age* (New York: Routledge).

Fuentes, A. and Ehrenreich, B. (1983), *Women in a Global Factory* (New York/Boston, Institute for Global Communications, South End Press).

Galpin, S. and Sims, D. (1999), 'Narrative and Identity in Flexible Working and Teleworking Organisations', in P. Jackson (ed.), *Virtual Working: Social and Organisational Dynamics* (London: Routledge), pp.76–94.

Garfinkel, H. (1984), *Studies in Ethnomethodology* (New York: Prentice-Hall).

Garnham, N. (1990), *Capitalism and Communication* (London: Sage).

Garnham, N. (2005), *Political Economy of the Information Society* (London: Taylor and Francis).

Gauntlett, D. (ed.) (2000), *Web. Studies: Rewiring Media Studies for the Digital Age* (London: Arnold).

Gay, G., Stephanone, M., Grace-Martin, M. and Hembrooke, H. (2000), 'The Effects of Wireless Computing in Collaborative Learning Environments', *The International Journal of Human-Computer Interaction*, 13:2, 257–276.

Geertz, C. (1964), 'Ideology as a Cultural System', in D. Apter (ed.), *Ideology and Discontent* (Glencoe, IL: Free Press), pp.34–51.

Geertz, C. (1965), *The Social History of an Indonesian Town* (Cambridge, MA: MIT Press).

Geertz, C. (1973), *The Interpretation of Cultures* (New York: Basic Books).

Geertz, C. (1975), *Kinship in Bali* (Chicago and London: University of Chicago Press).

Geertz, C. (1976a), 'Art as a Cultural System', *Man*, 91, 1473–1499.

Geertz, C. (1976b), 'From the Native's Point of View: On the Nature of Anthropological Understanding', in K. Basso (ed.), *Meaning of Anthropology* (Albuquerque: University of Mexico Press).

Georgiou, M. (2005a), 'Mapping Diasporic Media Cultures: A Transnational Cultural Approach to Exclusion', in R. Silverstone (ed.), *Media, Technology and Everyday Life in Europe: From Information to Communication* (Farnham: Ashgate), pp.33–53.

Georgiou, M. (2005b), 'Mapping Diasporic Media Cultures: A Transnational Cultural Approach to Exclusion', in R. Silverstone (ed.), *Media, Technology and Everyday Life in Europe: From Information to Communication* (Ashagate: Aladershot).

Gerhards, J. (1993), 'Westereuropaische Integration und die Schwierigkeiten der Entstehung einer europaischen Offentlichkeit', *Zeitschrift fur Soziologie*, 22, 86–110.

Gerth, H.H. and Wright Mills, C. (eds.) (1948), *From Max Weber: Essays in Sociology* (London: Routledge).

Gibbons, T. and Humphreys, P. (2011), *Audiovisual Regulation Under Pressure: Comparative Cases from North America and Europe* (London: Routledge).

Gibson, J., Chapman, C. and Hardy, C. (2003), *ADR in Employment Law* (London: Cavendish).

Gibson, W. (1984), *Neuromancer* (London: Grafton).

Gibson, W. (1991), 'Academy Leader', in M. Benedikt (ed.), *Cyberspace: First Steps* (Cambridge, MA: MIT Press).

Giddens, A. (1979), *Central Problems in Social Theory, Action, Structure and Contradiction in Social Analysis* (Berkeley: University of California Press).

Giddens, A. (1984), *The Constitution of Society: Outline of the Theory of Structure* (Berkeley: University of California Press).

Giddens, A. (1990), *The Consequences of Modernity* (Stanford: Stanford University Press).

Giddens, A. (1991), *On Modernity and Self-Identity: Self and Society in the Late Modern Age* (Cambridge: Polity Press).

Gilbert, N., Burrows, R. and Pollert, A (1992), *Fordism and Flexibility: Divisions and Change* (Basingstoke: MacMillan).

Gilfillan, S.C. (1935), *The Sociology of Invention: An Essay in the Social Causes of Technic Invention and some of its Social Results* (Chicago: Follet).

Goddard, J.B. (1992), New Technology and the Geography of the UK Information Economy in Robins, *Networks of Transactions* in the Times Higher Education Supplement.

Goddard, J.B. (1994), 'ICTs, Space and Place: Theoretical and Policy Challenges', in R. Mansell (ed.), *Management of Information and Communications Technologies: Emerging Patterns of Control* (London: ASLIB).

Goddard, J. and Richardson, R. (1996), 'Why Geography will Still Matter: What Jobs Go Where?' in L. Dutton and M. Peltu (eds.), *Information and Communication Technologies: Visions and Realities* (Oxford: Oxford University Press).

Goffman, E. (1959), *The Presentation of Self in Everyday Life* (Garden City, New York: Doubleday Anchor).

Goffman, E. (1961), *Asylums: Essays on the Social Situation of Mental Patients and Other Inmates* (New York: Anchor Books).

Goffman, E. (1974), *Frame Analysis: An Essay on the Organisation of Experience* (Cambridge, MA: Harvard University Press).

Goffman, E. (1979), *Gender Advertisements* (New York: Harper & Rowe).

Gonzales, L. (1988), *Women Organising for Change: Confronting the Crisis in Latin America* (Rome/Santiago: Isis International in coordination with DAWN).

Gonzalez, J. (2000), 'The Appended Subject: Race and Identity as Digital Assemblage', in B. Kolko, L. Nakamura and G. Rodman (eds.), *Race in Cyberspace* (London: Routledge).

Gould, A. (1993), *Capitalist Welfare Systems: A Comparison of Japan, Britain and Sweden* (London: Longman).

Gouldner, A.W. (1979), *The Future of Intellectuals and the Rise of the New Class: A Frame of Reference, Theses, Conjectures, Arguments, and an Historical Perspective on the Role of Intellectuals and Intelligentsia in the International Class Contest of the Modern Era* (London: Macmillan).

Graham, S. (ed.) (2004), *CyberCities Reader* (London: Routledge).

Graham, S. and Marvin, S. (1996), *Telecommunications and the City, Electronic Spaces, Urban Places* (London: Routledge).

Graham, S. and Marvin, S. (2001), *Splintering Urbanism, Networked Infrastructures, Technological Mobilities and the Urban Condition* (London: Routledge).

Gramsci, A. (1971), *Selections from the Prison Notebooks* (London, New York: Academic Press).

Green, S. (1980), 'Silicon Valley's Women Workers: A Theoretical Analysis of Sex Segregation in the Electronics Industry Labour Market', East West Centre, Honolulu.

Griliches, Z. (1958), 'Hybrid Corn: An Exploration in the Economics of Technical Change', *Econometrica*, 25, 501–522.

Grint, K. (2005), *The Sociology of Work* (Cambridge: Polity Press).

Gronow, J. (1997), *The Sociology of Taste* (London: Routledge).

Grossberg, L. (1986), 'On Postmodernism and Articulation: An Interview with Stuart Hall', *Journal of Communication Inquiry*, 10:2, 37–60.

Grossman, R. (1979), 'Women's Place in the Integrated Circuit', *South East Asia Chronicle* (joint issue with *Pacific Research*), 9:5, 16–25.

Groze-PecLum, M-L. (1990), 'Gibt es den europaischen Zuschauer?' *Zeitschrift fur Kulturaustausch*, 2:40, 185–194.

Grundmann, R. (1999), 'The European Public Sphere and the Deficit of Democracy', in D. Smith and S. Wright (eds.), *Whose Europe? The Turn Towards Democracy*, New Jersey: Wiley, pp.125–146.

Grusky, D.B. (ed.) (1994), *Social Stratification: Class, Race, and Gender in Sociological Perspective* (Boulder, CO, Oxford: Westview).

Gurak, L.J. (2001), 'The Promise and the Peril of Social Action in Cyberspace: *Ethos*, Delivery and the Protests over MarketPlace and the Clipper Chip', in M.A. Smith and P. Kollock (eds.), *Communities in Cyberspace* (London: Routledge), pp.243–263.

Gusfield, J.R. (ed.) (1989), 'Introduction', in K. Burke (ed.), *On Symbols and Society* (Chicago: University of Chicago Press), pp.1–49.

Guthrie, K. and Dutton, L. (1991), *An Ecology of Games: The Political Construction of Santa Monica's Public Electronic Network: Informatization and the Public Sector* (London: Sage Publications).

Gutman, H.G. (1988), 'Work, Culture and Society in Industrailizing America', in R.E. Pahl (ed.), *On Work: Historical, Comparative and Theoretical Approaches* (Oxford: Basil Blackwell), pp.125–137.

Habermas, J. (1973), *Legitimation Crisis* (London: Heinemann Educational Books).

Habermas, J. (1989), *The Structural Transformation of the Public Sphere: An Inquiry into a Category of Bourgeois Society*, trans. T. Burger (Cambridge: Polity Press).

Hacker, S. (1990), *Doing it the Hard Way: Investigations of Gender and Technology* (Winchester, MA: Unwin Hyman).

Haddon, L. (1993), 'Interactive Games', in P. Hayward and T. Wollen (eds.), *Future Visions: New Technologies of the Screen* (London: BFI).

Haddon, L. (1998), 'The Experience of Teleworking: A View from the Home', in P. Jackson and J. Van de Wielen (eds.), *Teleworking: International Perspectives. From Telecommuting to the Virtual Organisation* (London: Routledge).

Haddon, L. (2000), 'Social Exclusion and Information and Communication Technologies: Lessons from Studies of Single Parents and the Young Elderly', *New Media and Society*, 2:4, 387–406.

Haddon, L. (2004), *Information and Communication Technologies and Everyday Life* (Oxford: Berg).

Haddon, L. (May 2008), 'Mobile Access to Social Networking Sites: A UK Survey', Retrieved from http.//members.aol.com/leshaddon/Index.html.

Haddon, L. and Silverstone, R. (1992), 'Information and Communication Technologies in the Home: The Case of Teleworking', Working Paper 17, Falmer, CICT, SPRU, University of Sussex.

Haddon, L. and Silverstone, R. (1993), *Teleworking in the 1990s: A View from the Home*, SPRU/CICT Report Series, No. 10 (Falmer: University of Sussex).

Haddon, L. and Silverstone, R. (1994), 'The Careers of Information and Communication Technologies in the Home', in K. Bjerk and K. Borreby (eds.), *Proceeding of the International Working Conference on Home Orientated Informatics, Telematics and Automation, Copenhagen 27th June–1st July* (Copenhagen: University of Copenhagen).

Haddon, L. and Skinner, D. (1991), 'The Enigma of the Micro: Lessons from the British Home Computer Boom', *Social Science Computer Review*, 9, 3: 435–449.

Hall, S. (1973), 'Encoding and Decoding in the Television Discourse', CCCS stencilled paper no.7, Birmingham Centre for Contemporary Cultural Studies.

Hall, S. (1981), 'Notes on Deconstructing the "popular"', in R. Samuel (ed.), *People's History and Socialist Theory* (London: Routledge & Kegan Paul).

Hall, S. (1987), *'Minimal selves'* in *ICA Document 6* (London: Institute of Contemporary Arts).

Hampton, K.N. and Wellman, B. (2002), 'The Not So Global Village', in C. Haythornwaite and B. Wellman (eds.), *The Internet and Everyday Life* (Malden, MA: Blackwell Publishing).

Haraway, D. (1991), *Simians, Cyborgs and Women: The Reinvention of Nature* (London: Free Association Books).

Harper, D. (2002), 'Talking about Pictures: A Case of Photo-elicitation' *Visual Studies* 17:1, 3–26.

Harrison, J. and Wessels, B. (2005), 'A New Public Service Communication Environment? Public Service Broadcasting Values in the Reconfiguring Media', *New Media and Society*, 7:6, 834–853.

Harrison, J. and Wessels, B. (eds.) (2009), *Mediating Europe: New Media, Mass Communications and the European Public Sphere* (Oxford: Berghahn).

Hartley, J. (2005), 'Creative Industries', in J. Hartley (ed.), *Creative Industries* (Malden, MA: Blackwell), pp.1–40.

Hartmann, H.I., Kraut, E. and Tilly, L.A. (1986), *Computer Chips and Paper Clips: Effects of Technical Change* (Washington, DC: National Academy Press).

Hartmann, M. (2004), *Technologies and Utopias: The Cyberflaneur and the Experience of 'being online'* (Munchen: Verlag Reinhard Fischer).

Harvey, D. (1989), *The Condition of Postmodernity* (Oxford: Blackwell).

Hayles, N.K. (1999), *How We Became Posthuman: Virtual Bodies in Cybernetics, Literature, and Informatics* (Chicago: University of Chicago Press).

Haythornthwaite, C. (2006), 'The Social Informatics of Elearning'. Paper presented at the Information, Communication & Society (ICS) 10th Anniversary International Symposium, York, England, 20–22 September 2006.

Haythornthwaite, C. (2011), 'Participation Models in Networks, Crowds and Communities', University of Sheffield (UK) seminar, 12 December.

Heim, M. (1998), Virtual Realism (New York: Oxford University press).

Heritage, J.C. (1984), *Garfinkel and Ethnomethology* (Cambridge: Polity).

Herman-Kinney, N., Reynolds, J. and Larry, T. (2003), *Handbook of Symbolic Interactionism* (New York: AltaMira).

Hesmondhalgh, D. (2007), *The Cultural Industries* (London: Sage).

Hetherington, K. (1998), *Expressions of Identity: Space, Performance, Politics* (London: Sage).

Hill, D. (1994), *Citizens and Cities: Urban Policy in the 1990s* (New York: Harvester Wheatsheaf).

Hills, M. (2001), 'Virtually Out There: Strategies, Tactics and Affective Spaces in On-line Fandom', in S. Munt (ed.), *Technospaces: Inside New Media* (London: Contiuum), pp.147–160.

Hine, C. (2000), *Virtual Ethnography* (London: Routledge).

Hirsch, E. and Silverstone, R. (1992), *Consuming Technologies: Media and Information in Domestic Spaces* (London: Routledge).

Hirsch, W.Z. (1952), 'Manufacturing Progress Functions', *Review of Economics and Statistics*, 34:2, 143–155.

Hirschheim, R., Klein, H., and Newman, M. (1987), 'A Social Action Perspective of Information Systems Development'. *Proceedings of the Eighth ICIS Conference*, Pittsburgh, PA, December 6–8th. Edited by J. DeGross and C. Kriebel, 45–56.

Hobsbawn, E.J. (1971), *Labouring Men: Studies in the History of Labour* (London: Weidenfeld and Nicolson).

Hobson, D. (1982), *'Crossroads': The Drama of the Soap Opera* (London: Methuen).

Hochschild, A.R. (1983), *The Managed Heart: Communication of Human Feeling* (Berkeley: University of California Press).

Hochschild, A.R. (1989), *The Second Shift* (New York: Avon Books).

Hochschild, A.R. (1997), *The Time Bind: When Work Becomes Home and Home Becomes Work* (New York: Metropolitan Books).

Hoggett, P. (1987), 'A Farewell to Mass Production? Decentralisation as an Emergent Private and Public Sector Paradigm', in P. Hoggett and R. Hambleton (eds.), *Decentralisation and Democracy*, Occasional Paper 28, School of Advanced Urban Studies, University of Bristol.

Hoggett, P. (1990), 'Modernisation, Political Strategy and the Welfare State', *Studies in Decentralisation and Quasi-Markets* 2, School for Advanced Urban Studies: University of Bristol.

Hoggett, P. (1991), 'Long Waves and Forms of Capitalism', *New Intervention*, 2, 27–42.

Hoggett, P. (1994), 'The Politics of Modernisation of the UK Welfare State', in R. Burrows and B. Loader (eds.), *Towards a Post-Fordist Welfare State?* (London: Routledge).

Horrigan, J.B. (2006), 'Home Broadband Adoption 2008: Home Broadband Adoption is Going Mainstream and that Means User-generated Content is Coming from All Kinds of Internet Users', *Pew Internet & American Life Project*, 202-415-4500, Retrieved from http://www.pewinternet.org/.

Howkins, J. (2001), *The Creative Economy: How People Make Money from Ideas* (London: Penguin).

Hughes, G. (ed.) (1998), *Imagining Welfare Futures* (London: Routledge).

Hughes, J.A. (1990), *The Philosophy of Social Research* (London: Longman).

Hughes, J.P. (1985), 'Edison and the Electric Light', in D. MacKenzie and J. Wajcman (eds.), *The Social Shaping of Technology* (Milton Keynes: Open University Press), pp.39–52.

Hutton, W. and Giddens, A. (2001), *On the Edge: Living with Global Capitalism* (London: Vintage).

Huws, U. (1982), *Your Job in the Eighties* (London: Pluto).

Huws, U. (2006), The transformation of work in a global knowledge economy: Towards a conceptual framework Workpackage 3: Theories and concepts (Work organisation and restructuring in the knowledge society: Project number: CIT3-CT-2005-006193).

Huws, U., Korte, W.B. and Robinson, S. (1990), *Telework: Towards the Elusive Office* (Chichester: John Wiley).

INIT (Instituto Nacional de Estudios Sobre el Trabajo) (1975), Incorporacion de la mano de obra feminine a la industria maquiladora de exportacion.

Innis, H. (1951), *The Bias of Communication* (Toronto: University of Toronto Press).

Innis, H. (1952a), *The Strategy of Culture* (Toronto: University of Toronto Press).

Innis, H. (1952b), *Changing Concepts of Time* (Toronto: University of TorontoPress). (New Edition, 2004).

International Telecommunications Union (ITU) (2012), http://www.itu.int/en/ITUD/Statistics/Pages/stat/default.aspx.

Jackson, P. (ed.) (1999), *Virtual Working: Social and Organisational Dynamics* (London: Routledge).

Jamieson, L. (2010), 'Changing Intimacy in the Twentieth Century: Seeking and Forming Couple Relationship', in L. Abrams and C. Brown (eds.), *A History of Everyday Life in Twentieth Century Scotland* (Edinburgh: Edinburgh University Press), pp.76–102.

Jamieson, L., Lewis, R. and Simpson, R. (eds.) (2011), *Researching Families and Relationships: Reflections on Process* (London: Palgrave MacMillan).

Jankowski, N.W. and van Selm, M. (2000), 'The Promise and Practice of Public Debate in Cyberspace', in K. Hacker and J. van Dijk (eds.), *Digital Democracy: Issues of Theory and Practice* (London: Sage), pp.149–165.

Jennings, H. (1985), *Pandaemonium, 1660–1886: Coming of the Machine by Contemporary Observers* (London: Picador Books).

Jessop, B. (1994), 'The Transition to Post-Fordism and the Schumpeterian Workfare State', in R. Burrows and B. Loader (eds.), *Towards a Post-Fordist Welfare State?* (London: Routledge).

Jewkes, J., Sawers, D. and Stillerman, R. (1958), *The Sources of Invention* (London: Macmillan).

Johnson, R. (1979), cited in Chaney, D. (1994), *The Cultural Turn* (London: Routledge).

Jones, S. (1995a), *CyberSociety: Computer-mediated Communication and Community* (Thousand Oaks: Sage).

Jones, S. (1995b), 'Understanding Community in the Information Age', in S. Jones (ed.), *Cybersociety: Computer-mediated Communication and Community* (London: Sage).

Jonscher, C. (1983), 'Information Resources and Economic Productivity', *Information Economics and Policy*, 1:1, 13–35.

Kaloski, A. (1999), 'Bisexuals Making Out with Cyborgs: Politics, Pleasure, Confusion', in M. Storr (ed.), *Bisexuality: A Critical Reader* (London: Routledge).

Kant, I. (1983), *Perpetual Peace and Other Essays* (Indianapolis: Hackett).

Karvonen, E. (2009), 'Entertainmentization of the European Public Sphere and Politics', in J. Harrison and B. Wessels (eds.), *Mediating Europe: New Media, Mass Communications and the European Public Sphere* (Oxford: Berghahn).

Kasworm, C. (1993), 'Adult Higher Education from an International Perspective', *Higher Education*, 25, 411–423.

Kasworm, C. (2007), 'Lifelong Learning – The Perspective of Higher Education Serving Adult Learners', Paper presented at the World Conference on Lifelong Learning Chongwon, Korea.

Kasworm, C. (2011), 'The Influence of the Knowledge Society: Trends in Adult Higher Education', *The Journal of Continuing Higher Education*, 59, 104–107.

Katz, J.E., Rice, R.E. and Aspden, P. (2001), 'The Internet, 1995–2000: Access, Civic Involvement, and Social Interaction', *American Behavioral Scientist*, 45:3, 405–419.

Keene, J., Ferguson, B. and Mason, J. (1998), 'The Internet, Other "nets" and Healthcare', in B. Loader (ed.), *Cyberspace Divide: Equality, Agency and Policy in the Information Society* (London: Routledge), pp.217–235.

Kellner, D. (1995), *Media Culture: Cultural Studies, Identity and Politics between the Modern and Postmodern* (London: Routledge).

Kelly, K. (2009), 'The New Socialism: Global Collectivist Society is Coming Online', *Wired Magazine*, 17 June.

Kendall, L. (1996), 'MUDder? I Hardly Know 'er! Adventures of a Feminist MUDder', in L. Cherney and E. Reba Weise (eds.), *Wired Women: Gender and New Realities in Cyberspace* (Seattle: Seal Press).

Kluver, R., Jankowski, N., Foot, K. and Schneider, S.M. (eds.) (2007), *The Internet and National Elections: A Comparative Study of Web Campaigning* (London: Routledge).

Kneale, J. (1999), 'The Virtual Realities of Technology and Fiction: Reading William Gibson's Cyberspace', in M. Crang, P. Crang and J. May (eds.), *Virtual Geographies: Bodies, Space and Relations* (London: Routledge).

Knights, D. and Wimott, H. (eds.) (1988), *New Technology and the Labour Process* (London: Macmillan Press Ltd.).

Knights, D., Wimott, H. and Collinson, D. (1985), *Job Redesign: Critical Perspectives on the Labour Process* (Aldershot: Gower).

Knorr-Cetina, K.D. and Mulkay, M. (eds.) (1983), *Science Observed: Perspectives on the Social Study of Science* (London: Sage).

Kolko, B., Nakamura, L. and Rodman, G. (eds.) (2000), 'Race in Cyberspace: An Introduction', in B. Kolko L. Nakamura and G. Rodman (eds.), *Race in Cyberspace* (London: Routledge).

Kolko, B.E., Nakamura, L. and Rodman, G.B. (eds.) (2000), *Race in Cyberspace* (London: Routledge).

Kolloch, P. (2001), 'The Economies of Online Cooperation: Gifts and Public Goods in Cyberspace', in M.A. Smith and P. Kollock (eds.), *Communities in Cyberspace* (London: Routledge), pp.220–242.

Kroeber, A.L. and Kluckhohn, C. (1952), *Culture: A Critical Review of Concepts and Definitions*. Harvard University Peabody Museum of American Archeology and Ethnology Papers 47 (Harvard: Harvard University).

Kroker, A. and Kroker, M. (2000), 'Code Warriors: Bunkering In and Dumbing Down', in D. Bell and B. Kennedy (eds.), *The Cybercultures Reader* (London: Routledge), pp.350–359.

Kuhn, A. (ed.) (1990), *Alien Zone: Cultural Theory and Contemporary Science Fiction Cinema* (London: Verso).

Kurazman-Morawetz, I. and Ronneling, A. (2007), 'Legal Exclusion and Social Exclusion: "Legal" and "Illegal" Migrants', in H. Stenert and A. Pilgram (eds.),

Welfare Policy from Below Struggles Against Social Exclusion in Europe (Aldershot: Ashgate).

Laclau, E. (ed.) (1994), *The Making of Political Identities* (London: Verso).

Laclau, E. and Mouffe, C. (1985), *Hegemony and Socialist Strategy: Towards a Radical Democratic Politics* (London: Verso).

Lakoff, G. and Johnson, M. (1980), *Metaphors We Live By* (Chicago: University of Chicago Press).

Lange, P. (2007), 'Publicly Private and Privately Public: Social Networking on YouTube', *Journal of Computer-Mediated Communication*, 13:1, article 18, Retrieved from http://jcmc.indiana.edu/vol13/issue1/lange.html.

Langer, S. (1964), *Philosophical Sketches* (New York: Mentor Books).

Lash, S. (1999), *Another Modernity: A Different Rationality* (Oxford: Blackwell Publishers).

Lash, S., Szerszynski, B. and Wynne, B. (1996), *Risk, Environment and Modernity: Towards a New Ecology* (London: Sage).

Lash, S. and Urry, J. (1987), *The End of Organized Capitalism* (Cambridge: Polity).

Lash, S. and Urry, J. (1993), *Economies of Signs and Spaces* (London: Sage).

Lash, S. and Wynne, B. (1992), 'Introduction', in U. Beck (ed.), *Risk Society: Towards New Modernity* (London: Sage).

Laudon, K.C. (1986), *Dossier Society: Value Choices in the Design of National Information Systems* (New York: Columbia University Press).

Layder, D. (1981), *Structure, Interaction and Social Theory* (London: Routledge and Kegan Paul).

Lazarsfeld, P.F. and Merton, R.K. (1948), 'Mass Communication, Popular Taste and Organised Social Action', in L. Bryson (ed.), *The Communication of Ideas* (New York: Harper & Bross), pp.76–93.

Leach, E. (1976), *Culture and Communication* (Cambridge: Cambridge University Press).

Leadbetter, C. (2000), *Living on Thin Air* (London: Pengiun).

Lee, D. and Newby, H. (1983), *The Problem of Sociology: An Introduction to the Discipline* (London: Routledge).

Lefebvre, H. (1984), *Everyday Life in the Modern World* (New Brunswick: Transaction Publishers).

Lefebvre, H. (1991), *Critique of Everyday Life* (London: Verso).

Leveson, J. (2012), *The Leveson Inquiry: Culture, Practice and Ethics of the Press* (London: The Stationary Office Ltd).

Levinas, E. (1969), *Totality and Infinity: An Essay on Exteriority* (Pittsburgh: Duquesne University Press).

Levi-Strauss, C. (1966), *The Savage Mind* (Chicago: University of Chicago Press).

Lewis, P., Newburn, T., Taylor, M., Mcgillivray, C., Greenhill, A., Frayman, H. and Proctor, R. (2011), *Reading the Riots* (London: LSE & Guardian).

Liep, J. (ed.) (2001), *Locating Cultural Creativity* (London: Pluto Press).

Lievrouw, L. and Livingstone, S. (2006), *The Handbook of New Media*, student edition/2nd (London: Sage).

Lim, L. (1978), *Women Workers in Multinational Corporations in Developing Countries. 'The case of the electronics industry in Malaysia and Singapore'*, Women's Studies Program occasional papers no. 9 (Michigan: University of Michigan).

Lipsig-Mummé, c. (1991), 'Future Conditional – Wars of Position in the Quebec', *Studies in Political Economy,* no 36, 73–108.

Littlejohn, J. (1963), *Westrigg* (London: Routledge and Kegan Paul).

Livingstone, S. (2002), *Young People and New Media* (London: Sage Publications).

Livingstone, S. (ed.) (2005), *Audiences and Publics: When Cultural Engagement Matters for the Public Sphere* (Bristol: Intellect).

Lofgren, O. (1994), 'Celebrating Creativity: On the Slanting of the Concept', in J. Liep (ed.), *Locating Cultural Creativity* (London: Pluto Press).

Lury, C. (2011), *Consumer Culture* (Cambridge: Polity Press).

Lyon, D. (1988), *The Information Society: Issue and Illusions* (Cambridge: Polity).

Lyon, D. (2001a), *The Information Society: Issues and Illusions* (Cambridge: Polity Press).

Lyon, D. (2001b), *Surveillance Society* (Buckingham: Open University Press).

Lyotard, J.F. (1984), *The Postmodern Condition: A Report on Knowledge* (Manchester: Manchester University Press).

Machlup, F. (1962), *The Production and Distribution of Knowledge in the United States* (Princeton: Princeton University Press).

MacKenzie, D. and Wajcman, J. (eds.) (2002), *The Social Shaping of Technology,* 2nd Edition (Maidenhead, Philadelphia: Open University Press).

Madanipour, A. (1998), *Social Exclusion in European Cities* (London: Jessica Kingsley).

Maine, H.S. (1861), *Ancient Law: Its Connection with the Early History of Society, and its Relation to Modern Ideas* (London: John Murray).

Manceron, V. (1997), Get Connected: Social Uses of the Telephone and Modes of Interaction in a Peer Group of Young Parisians in *The Future European Telecommunications User, Home and Work Group: Blurring Boundaries: When are Information and Communication Technologies Coming Home?* COST248 Report (Farsta: Telia).

Manning, P.K. (1977), *Police Work: The Social Organisation of Policing* (Cambridge, MA: MIT Press).

Mansell, R. and Silverstone, R. (1996), *Communication by Design. The Politics of Information and Communication Technologies* (Oxford: Oxford University Press). (Reprinted in 1997).

Mansell, R. and Steinmuller, W.E. (2000), *Mobilizing the Information Society: Strategies for Growth and Opportunity* (Oxford: Oxford University Press).

Marcuse, H. (1964), *One Dimensional Man: Studies in the Ideology of Advanced Industrial Society* (London: Routledge and Kegan Paul).

Marks, D. (1999), *Disability: Controversial Debates and Psychosocial Perspectives* (London: Routledge).

Markus, M.L. (1983), 'Power, Politics and MIS Implementation', *Communications of ACM,* 26, 430–444.

Marshall, T.H. (1950), *Citizenship and Social Class and Other Essays* (Cambridge: Cambridge University Press).

Marshall, T.H. (1977), *Class, Citizenship and Social Development* (Chicago: University of Chicago Press).

Martin, P.J. and Dennis, A. (eds.) (2010), *Human Agents and Social Structures* (Manchester: Manchester University Press).

Marx, K. (1976), *Capital: A Critique of Political Economy, 1* (Harmondsworth: Penguin).

Marx, K. and Engels, F. (1974), *The German Ideology* (New York: International Books).

Mauss, M. (1990), *The Gift: Forms and Functions of Exchange in Archaic Societies.* (London: Routledge).

McCracken, G. (1988), *Culture and Consumption. New Approaches to the Symbolic Character of Consumer Goods and Activities* (Bloomington: Indiana University Press).

McGuigan, J. (1992), *Cultural Populism* (London: Routledge).

McKendrick, N., Brewer, J. and Plumb, J.H. (1982), *The Birth of Consumer Society. The Commercialisation of Eighteenth-century England* (London: Europa Publications).

McLaughlin, J., Rosen, P., Skinner, D. and Webster, A. (1999), *Valuing Technology: Organizations, Culture and Change* (London: Routledge).

McLoughlin, I. (1999), *Creative Technological Change: The Shaping of Technologies and Organisations* (London: Routledge).

McQuail, D. (1983), *Mass Communication Theory: An Introduction* (London: Sage).

McRae, S. (1996), 'Coming Apart at the Scenes: Sex, Text and Virtual Body', in L. Cerney and E.B. Weise (eds.), *Wired Women* (Washington: Seal).

McRobbie, A. (1998), *British Fashion Design* (London: Routledge).

Meikle, G. (2002), *Future Active: Media Activism and the Internet* (London: Routledge).

Miliband, R. (1983), *Class Power and State Power* (London: Verso).

Millar, J. (1998), 'International Software Trade: Managing Knowledge Sharing Between Developing Country Producers and their Clients', mimeo, SPRUI, University of Sussex Press.

Millar, J. and Jagger, N. (2001), *Women in ITEC: Courses and Careers* (London: DfES Publications).

Miller, D. (1987), *Material Culture and Mass Consumption* (Oxford: Basil Blackwell).

Miller, D. (1994), *Modernity: An Ethnographic Approach, Dualism and Mass Consumption in Trinidad* (Oxford: Berg).

Miller, D. and Slater, D. (2000), *The Internet: An Ethnographic Approach* (Oxford: Berg).

Mills, C. Wright (1959), *The Sociological Imagination* (Harmondsworth: Penguin Books).

Mitter, S. (1986), *Women in the Global Economy* (London: Pluto).

Moores, S. (2000), *Media and Everyday Life in Modern Society* (Edinburgh: Edinburgh University Press).

Moores, S. (2001), 'The Doubling of Place: Electronic Media, Time-Space Arrangements and Social Relationships' in N. Couldry and A. McCarthy (eds.) *MediaSpace* (London: Routledge Publishing).

Morley, D. (1980), *The 'Nationwide Audience'* (London: British Film Institute).

Morley, D. (1986), *Family Television: Cultural Power and Domestic Leisure* (London: Methuen).

Morton, D. (1999), 'Birth of Cyberqueer', in J. Wolmark (ed.), *Cybersexualities: A Reader on Feminist Theory, Cyborgs and Cyberspace* (Edinburgh: Edinburgh University Press).

Moss, M. (1987), 'Telecommunications, World Cities and Urban Policy', *Urban Studies*, 24, 534–546.

Mouffe, C. (1992), *Dimensions of Radical Democracy: Pluralism, Citizenship, Community* (London: Verso).

Mouffe, C. (2005), *On the Political* (Abingdon and New York: Routledge).

Mousnier, R. (1973), *Social Hierarchies: 1450 to the Present* (London: Trinity Press).

Mukherjee, S., Beresford, B. and Sloper, P. (1999), *Unlocking Key Working: An Analysis and Evaluation of Key Worker Services for Families of Disabled Children* (Bristol: Policy Press).

Munck, R. (1990), *Latin America: The Transition to Democracy* (London: Zed).

NACLA Latin American and Empire Report (1975), 'US Runaway Shops on the Mexcan Border', vol. IX, no. 7 July.

Nadel, S.F. (1957), *The Theory of Social Structure* (London: Cohen and West).

Naisbitt, J. (1984), *Megatrends: Ten New Directions Transforming Our Lives* (New York: Warner Books).

Nakamura, L. (2000), 'Race in/for Cyberspace: Identity Tourism and Racial Passing in the Internet', in D. Bell and B.M. Kennedy (eds.), *The Cybercultures Reader* (London: Routledge).

Negroponte, N. (1995), *Being Digital* (London: Hodder & Soughton).

Negroponte, N. (1998), 'Beyond Digital', *Wired*, 6:12, 288.

Negus, K. and Pickering, M. (2004), *Creativity, Communication and Cultural Value* (London: Sage).

Nie, N.H., Hillygus, D.S. and Erbring, L. (2002), 'The Internet and Other Uses of Time', in C. Haythornwaite and B. Wellman (eds.), *The Internet and Everyday Life* (Malden, MA: Blackwell Publishing).

Noble, D.F. (1984), *Forces of Production: A Social History of Office Automation* (New York: Oxford University Press).

Norris, P. (2000), *Digital Divide: Civic Engagement, Information Poverty, and the Internet Worldwide* (New York: Cambridge University Press).

O'Donnell, K. (2006), 'Adult Education Participation in 2004–2005' (NCES 2006-077), Retrieved 15 February 2008, from http://nces.ed.gov/pubs2006/adulted/.

Office of National Statistics (ONS) Divorces in England and Wales http://www.ons.gov.uk/ons/dcp171778_246403.pdf.

Ong, A. (1984), 'Global Industries and Malay Peasants in Peninsular Malaysia', in J. Nash and M.P. Fernandez-Kelly (eds.), *Women, Men and the International Division of Labour* (New York: SUNY, Albany).

Organization for Economic Co-operation and Development (2007), 'Education at a Glance: OECD Indicators', OECD, Retrieved from http://www.oecd.org/dataoecd/36/4/40701218.pdf.

Organization for Economic Co-operation and Development (2013a), 'Measuring the Internet Economy: A Contribution to the Research Agenda', OECD Digital Economy Papers, No. 226, OECD Publishing.

Organization for Economic Co-operation and Development (2013b), 'The App Economy', OECD Digital Economy Papers, No. 230, OECD Publishing.

O'Riordan, K. and Phillips, D.J. (2007), *Queer Online: Media, Technology & Sexuality* (Bern: Peter Lang Publishing).

Orlikowski, W.J. (1992), 'The Duality of Technology: Rethinking the Concept of Technology in Organisations', *Organisational Science*, 3:3, 398–427.

Osterlund, K. and Robson, K. (2009), 'The Impact of ICT on Work-life Experiences among University Teaching Assistants', *Computers and Education*, 52, 432–437.

Outhwaite, W. (1994), *Habermas, A Critical Introduction* (Cambridge: Polity Press).

Owen, D. and Strong, T. (2004), *Max Weber: The Vocation Lectures, Science as Vocation. Politics as Vocation* (Indiana: Hackett Publishing Company).

Pahl, R.E. (ed.) (1988), *On Work: Historical and Theoretical Approaches* (Oxford: Basil Blackwell).

Papacharissi, Z. (2002), 'The Virtual Public Sphere: The Internet as a Public Sphere', *New Media and Society*, 4:1, 9–27.

Park, R.E. (1950), *Race and Culture* (Glencoe, Ill: The Free Press).

Park, R.E. (1952), *Human Communities: The City and Human Ecology* (Glencoe, Ill: The Free Press).

Parsons, T. (1949), *The Structure of Social Action* (New York: McGraw-Hill).

Parsons, T. (1951), *The Social System* (New York: Free Press).

Parsons, T. (1966), *Societies: Evolutionary and Comparative Perspectives* (New Jersey: Prentice-Hall).

Parsons, T. (1971), *The System of Modern Societies* (New Jersey: Prentice-Hall).

Pearson, R. (1988), 'Multinational Companies and Women Workers' in Pahl, R. (ed.) *On Work* (Oxford: Blackwell), pp.449–468.

Pearson, R. (1988), 'Female Workers in the First and Third Worlds: The Greening of Women's Labour', in R.E. Pahl (ed.), *On Work: Historical, Comparative and Theoretical Approaches* (Oxford: Basil Blackwell), pp.449–465.

Perkin, H.J. (1989), *The Rise of the Professional Society: England Since 1880* (London: Taylor and Francis).

Perkin, H.J. (1990), *The Rise of the Professional Society: England Since 1880* (London: Taylor and Francis).

Perrow, C. (1967), 'A Framework for the Comparative Analysis of Organisations', *American Sociological Review*, 32, 194–208.

Perrow, C. (1983), 'The Organizational Context of Human Factors Engineering', *Administrative Science Quarterly*, 28, 521–541.

Pfaffenberger, B. (1988), 'Fetishized Objects and Humanised Nature: Toward an Anthropology of Technology', *Man*, 23, 236–252.

Pfaffenberger, B. (1992), 'Technical Dramas', *Science, Technology & Human Values*, 17:3, 282–312.

Picht, P. (1993), 'Disturbed Identities: Social and Cultural Mutations in Contemporary Europe', in S. Garcia (ed.), *European Identity and the Search for Legitimacy* (London: Pinter), pp.81–94.

Pilgram, A. and Steinert, H. (2007), *Welfare from Below: Struggles against Social Exclusion in Europe. Towards a Dynamic Understanding of Participation* (Aldershot: Ashgate).

Pinch, T. and Bijker, W. (1984), 'The Social Construction of Facts and Artefacts: Or How the Sociology of Science and the Sociology of Technology might Benefit each Other', *Social Studies of Science*, 14, 399–441.

Pinch, T. and Bijker, W. (1987), 'The Social Construction of Facts and Artefacts: Or How He Sociology of Science and the Sociology of Technology might Benefit each

Other', in W. Bijker, T.P. Hughes and T. Pinch (eds.), *The Social Construction of Technology Systems* (Cambridge, MA: MIT Press), pp.399–442.

Piore, M.J. and Sabel, C. (1984), *The Second Industrial Divide: Possibilities for Prosperity* (New York: Basic Books).

Plant, S. (1995), 'The Future Looms: Weaving Women and Cybernetics', in M. Featherstone and R. Burrows (eds.), *Cyberspace/Cyberbodies/Cyberpunk* (London: Sage).

Plant, S. (1998), *Zeros+ Ones: Digital Women and the New Technoculture* (London: Fourth Estate).

Porat, M.U. (1977), *The Information Economy: Definition and Measurement*, vol. 1 (Washington, DC: Department of Commerce/Office of Telecommunications).

Porter, D. (1997), *Internet Culture* (New York: Routledge).

Poster, M. (1990), *The Mode of Information: Post-structuralism and Social Context* (Cambridge: Polity Press).

Poster, M. (2006), 'Culture and New Media: A Historical View', in L. Lievrouw and S. Livingstone (eds.), *The Handbook of New Media (student edition)* (London: Sage), pp.134–140.

Poulantzas, N. (1973), *Political Power and Social Classes* (London: New Left Books).

Powell, W.W. (1987), 'Review Essay: Explaining Technological Change', *American Journal of Sociology*, 93:1, 185–197.

Prieto, M. and Rojo, C. (1987), *No se quien nos ira a a poyar: el voto de la ecuatoriana en mayo de 1984* (Quito: CEPLAES).

Prior, D., Stewart, J. and Walsh, K. (1995), *Citizenship: Rights, Community & Participation* (London: Pitman Publishing).

Pullen, K. (2000), 'I-love-Xena.com: Creating Online Fan Communities', in D. Gauntlett (ed.), *Web.Studies: Rewiring Media Studies for the Digital Age* (London: Arnold).

Putnam, R. (2000), *Bowling Alone: The Collapse and Revival of American Community* (New York: Simon and Schuster).

Radcliffe-Brown, A.R. (1952), *Structure and Function in Primitive Society* (London: Cohen and West).

Radcliffe, S.A. and Westwood, S. (eds.) (1995), *ViVa, Women and Popular Protest in Latin America* (London: Routledge).

Radway, J. (1987), *Reading the Romance: Women, Patriarchy and Popular Culture* (London: Verso).

Ragnedda, M. and Muschert, G.W. (2013), *The Digital Divide: The Internet and Social Inequality in International Perspective* (London: Routledge).

Ravikant, N. and Rifkin, A. (2010), 'Why Twitter is Massively Undervalued Compared to Facebook', *Techcrunch*, 16 October 2010.

Rawls, A.W. (1989), 'Reply to the Interaction Order and the Micro-Macro Distinction', *Sociological Theory*, 10:1, 129–132.

Rawls, J. (1999), *A Theory of Justice* (Oxford: Oxford University Press).

Reich, R. (1997), 'The Menace to Prosperity', *Financial Times*, 3 March.

Rheingold, H. (1993), *The Virtual Community: Homesteading on the Electronic Frontier* (Cambridge, MA: Addison-Wesley).

Rheingold, H. (1995), 'Which Part is Virtual? Which Part is Community?' Retrieved August 2008, from http://www.well.com/user/hlr/tomorrow/vcreal.html.

Richardson, D. and Robinson, V. (2008), *Introducing Gender and Women's Studies* (London: Palgrave Macmillan).

Richardson, R. and Belt, V. (2001), 'Saved by the Bell? Call Centres and Economic Development', *Less Favoured Regions: Economic and Industrial Democracy*, 22:1, 67–98.

Richardson, R. and Gillespie, A. (2003), 'The Call of the Wild: Call Centers and Economic Development in Rural Areas', *Growth and Change*, 39:3, 87–108.

Ritter, M. (2014), 'Deviant Behavior in Computer-Mediated Communication: Development and Validation of a Measure of Cybersexual Harassment', *Journal of Computer-mediated Communication*, 19:2, 197–214.

Ritzer, G. (1993), *The McDonaldization of Society* (Thousand Oaks: SAGE Publications).

Ritzer, G. and Jurgenson, N. (2010), 'Production, Consumption, Prosumption: The Nature of Capitalism in the Age of Digital Prosumerism', *Journal of Consumer Culture*, 10:1, 13–36.

Roberts, D. (ed.) (2011), *Reading the Riots: Investigating England's Summer of Disorder* (London: Guardian Shorts).

Roberts, K. (ed.) (2006), *Leisure in Contemporary Society* (Wallingford: CABI).

Robins, K. (1999), 'Against Virtual Community: For a Politics of Distance', *Angelaki: Journal of the Theoretical Humanities*, 4, 163–170.

Robins, K. and Webster, F. (1999), *Times of the Technoculture: From the Information Society to Virtual Life* (London: Routledge).

Robinson, J.P., Krestbaum, M., Neustadtl, A. and Alvarez, A.S. (2002), 'The Internet and Other Uses of Time', in B. Wellman and C. Haythornthwaite (eds.), *The Internet in Everyday Life* (Malden: Blackwell Publishing), pp.244–262.

Roche, M. (1992), *Rethinking Citizenship, Welfare, Ideology and Change in Modern Society* (Cambridge: Polity Press).

Roche, M. (2000), *Mega-Events & Modernity: Olympics and Expos in the Growth of Global Culture* (London: Routledge).

Roche, M. (2007), 'Cultural Europeanisation and the "Cosmopolitan Condition": EU Regulation and European Sport', in C. Rumford (ed.), *Europe and Cosmopolitanism* (Liverpool: Liverpool University Press), Chapter 8, pp.126–141.

Roche, M. (2010), *Exploring the Sociology of Europe* (London: Sage).

Roethlisberger, F.J. and Dickson, W.J. (1939), *Management and the Worker* (Cambridge: Harvard University Press).

Rogers, E.V. (1962), *Diffusion of Innovations* (New York: Free Press).

Rogers, E.M. (1995), *Diffusion of Innovations* 4th edition (New York: Free Press).

Room, G. (1995), *Beyond the Threshold: The Measurement and Analysis of Social Exclusion* (Bristol: Policy Press).

Rosaldo, R., Lavie, S. and Narayan, K. (1993), 'Introduction: Creativity in Anthropology', in S. Lavie, K. Narayan and R. Rosaldon (eds.), *Creativity/Anthropology* (Ithaca: Cornell University Press).

Ross, A. (1989), *No Respect: Intellectuals and Popular Culture* (New York: Routledge).

Rushkoff, D. (1997), *Children of Chaos: Surviving the End of the World as We Know It* (London: Harper Collins).

Sabel, C.F. (1982), *Work and Politics* (New York: Cambridge University Press).

Sacks, H., Schegloff, E.A. and Jefferson, G. (1974), 'A Simplest Systematics for the Organisation of Turn-taking in Conversation', *Language*, 50, 696–735.

Samual, S. (ed.) (1977), *Miners, Quarrymen and Saltworkers* (London: Routledge & Kegan Paul).

Sarkar, M.B., Butler, B. and Steinfield, C. (1995), 'Intermediaries and Cybermediaries: Sarkar, Butler and Steinfield', *Journal of Computer-Mediated Communication*, Retrieved from http://onlinelibrary.wiley.com/doi/10.1111/j.1083-6101.1995.tb00167.x/full1:0.

Sassen, S. (2002), 'The Repositioning of Citizenship: Emergent Subjects and Spaces for Politics', *Berkeley Journal of Sociology*, 46, 4–25.

Scannell, P., Schelesginger, P. and Sparks, C. (1992), *Culture and Power: A Media, Culture and Society Reader* (London: Sage).

Schechner, R. (1976), 'Towards the Poetics of Performance', *Alcheringa*, 2:2, 46–86.

Schechner, R. (1977), *Essays on Performance Theory, 1970–1976* (New York: Drama Book Specialists).

Schechner, R. (1987), 'Preface', in V. Turner (ed.), *The Anthropology of Performance* (New York: PAJ Publications).

Schechner, R. and Appel, W. (1990), *By Means of Performance* (Cambridge: Cambridge University Press).

Schmookler, J. (1959), 'Technological Progress and the Modern American Corporation', in E.S. Mason (ed.), *The Corporation in Modern Society* (Cambridge, MA: Harvard University Press), pp.141–165.

Schumpeter, J. (1939), *Business Cycles: A Theoretical Historical and Statistical Analysis of the Capitalist Process* (New York: McGraw Hill).

Schumpeter, J.A. (1934), *The Theory of Economic Development: An Inquiry into Profits, Capital, Credit, Interest and the Business Cycle* 46. Cambridge, MA: Harvard University Press.

Schutz, A. (1962), *The Problem of Social Reality* (The Hague: Nijhoff).

Schutz, A. (1971), *Collected Papers*, vols. 1 and 2 (The Hague: Nijhoff).

Schütz, A. and Luckmann, T. (1974), *The Structures of the Life-World* (London: Heinemann Educational Books).

Sciulli, D. (2002), 'The Architecture of Markets: An Economic Sociology of Twenty-First Century Capitalist Societies (review)', *Social Forces*, 81:2, 665–667.

Scott, W.R. (1981), *Organisations: Rational, Natural, and Open Systems* (Englewood Cliffs, NJ: Prentice-Hall).

Sedgewick, E. (1990), *Epistemology of the Closet* (Berkeley: University of California Press).

Senker, P. (2000), 'A Dynamic Perspective on Technology, Economic Inequality and Development', in Wyatt, et al. (eds.), *Technology and In/equality: Questioning the Information Society* (London: Routledge), pp.197–218.

Sennett, R. (1998), *The Corrosion of Character: The Personal Consequences of Work in the New Capitalism* (New York: W W Norton).

Sennett, R. (2001), 'Street and Office: Two Sources of Identity', in W. Hutton and A. Giddens (eds.), *On the Edge: Living with Global Capitalism* (London: Vintage).

Sennett, R. (2006), *The Culture of New Capitalism* (New Haven: Yale University Press).

Sennett, R. (2008), *The Craftsman* (New Haven: Yale University Press).

Shaiken, H. (1985), *Work Transformed: Automation and Labor in the Computer Age* (New York: Holt, Rinehart and Winston).

Shields, R. (ed.) (1996), *Cultures of the Internet: Virtual Spaces, Real Histories, Living Bodies* (London: Sage).

Shills, E. (1975), *Centre and Periphery: Essays in Macrosociology* (Chicago: Chicago University Press).

Shils, E. (ed.) (1991), *Remembering the University of Chicago, Teachers, Scientists and Scholars* (Chicago: University of Chicago Press). Shipman, B. and Smart, C. (2007), ' "It's Made a Huge Difference': Recognition, Rights and the Personal Significance of Civil Partnership', *Sociological Research Online*, 12:1, Retrieved from http://www.socresonline.org.uk/12/1/shipman.html.

Silverstone, R. (1990), 'Television and Everyday Life: Towards an Anthropology of the Television Audience', in M. Ferguson (ed.), *Public Communication: The New Imperatives* (London: Sage), pp.173–189.

Silverstone, R. (1994), *Television and Everyday Life* (London: Routledge).

Silverstone, R. (ed.) (2005a), *Media Technology and Everyday Life in Europe* (Aldershot: Ashgate).

Silverstone, R. (2005b), 'The Sociology of Mediation and Communication', in C. Calhoun, C. Rojek and B.S. Turner (eds.), *The Sage Handbook of Sociology* (London: Sage), pp.188–207.

Silverstone, R. (2006), *Media and Morality: On the Rise of the Mediapolis* (Polity: Cambridge).

Silverstone, R. and Hirsch, E. (1994), *Consuming Technologies: Media and Information in Domestic Spaces* (London: Routledge).

Silverstone, R., Morley, D., Dahlberg, A. and Livingstone, S. (1989), 'Families, Technologies and Consumption: The Household and Information and Communication Technologies', CRICT discussion paper, Brunel University.

Simmel, G. (1950), *The Sociology of Georg Simmel* (New York: Free Press).

Simmel, G. (1955), *Conflict & The Web of Group Affiliations* (New York: Free Press).

Skeels, M.M. and Grudin, J. (2009), 'When Social Networks Cross Boundaries: A Case Study of Workplace Use of Facebook and Linkedin', Proceedings of the ACM International Conference on Supporting Group Work, pp.95–104.

Skocpol, T. (1979), 'France, Russia, China: A Structural Analysis of Social Revolutions', *Comparative Studies in Society and History*, 18:2, 104–129.

Skocpol, T., Evans, P. and Rueschemeyer, D. (1985), *Bringing the State Back In* (Cambridge: Cambridge University Press).

Slater, D. (1998), 'Trading Sexpics on IRC: Embodiment and Authenticity on the Internet', *Body and Society*, 4, 91–117.

Slevin, J. (2000), *The Internet and Society* (Cambridge: Polity Press).

Smart, C., Davies, K., Heaphy, B. and Mason, J. (2012), 'Difficult Friendships and Ontological Insecurity', *The Sociological Review*, 60:1, 91–109.

Smelser, N.J. (1959), *Social Change in the Industrial Revolution* (London: Routledge & Kegan Paul).

Smith, D. (1988), *The Everyday World as Problematic: A Feminist Sociology* (Milton Keynes: Open University Press).

Smith, D. and Wright, S. (ed.) (1999), *Whose Europe? The Turn Towards Democracy* (Oxford: Blackwell).

Smith, M.A. and Kollock, P. (2000), *Communities in Cyberspace* (London: Routledge).

Spencer, H. (1873), *The Study of Sociology* (New York: Appleton and Company).

Squires, J. (2000), 'Fabulous Feminist Futures and the Lure of CyberCulture', in D. Bell and B.M. Kennedy (eds.), *The Cybercultures Reader* (London: Routledge), pp.360–373.

Standing, G. (1981), *Unemployment and Female Labour: A Study of Labour Supply in Kingston, Jamaica* (New York: MacMillan).

Stanislavski, K. (1946), *An Actor Prepares* (Harmondsworth: Penguin).

Starks, M. (2007), *Switching to Digital Television: UK Public Policy and the Market* (Bristol: Intellect).

Stein, A. and Plummer, K. (1994), 'I Can't Even Think Straight: Queer Theory and the Missing Revolution in Sociology', *Sociological Theory*, 12:2, 178–187.

Steinert, H. (2003), *Culture Industry* (Cambridge: Basil Blackwell).

Steinert, H. and Pilgram, A. (2007), *Welfare Policy from Below: Struggles Against Social Exclusion in Europe* (Aldershot: Ashgate).

Steuer, J. (1992), 'Defining Virtual Reality: Dimensions Determining Telepresence', *Journal of Communications*, 42:4, 73–93.

Stoll, C. (1995), ' "The Internet? Bah!" Hype Alert: Why Cyberspace isn't, and will Never be, Nirvana', *NEWSWEEK Magazine*, 27 February issue.

Stonier, T. (1983), *The Wealth of Information: A Profile of the Post-Industrial Economy* (Thames: Methuen).

Strinati, D. (1995), *An Introduction to Theories of Popular Culture* (London: Routledge).

Stryker, S. (1980), *Symbolic Interactionism: A Social Structural Version* (Menlo Park, CA: Benjamin/Cummings).

Sveinsdottir, T., Wessels, B., Smallwood, R., Linde, P., Kala, V., Tsoukala, V. and Sondervan, J. (2013), *Policy RECommendations for Open Access to Research Data in Europe: Stakeholder Values and Ecosystems* (Brussels: European Commission).

Synnott, A. (1993), *The Body Social: Symbolism, Self and Society* (London: Routledge).

Tannen, D. (1995), *Talking from 9 to 5* (London: Virago).

Taylor, F.W. (1905), *Shop Management* (New York: Harper & Brothers).

Taylor, F.W. (1911), *The Principles of Scientific Management* (New York: Harper & Brothers). (Free book hosted online by Eldritch Press).

Taylor, I., Evans, K. and Fraser, P. (1996), *The Tale of Two Cities: Global Change, Local Feeling and Everyday Life in the North of England* (London: Routledge).

Taylor, M.C. (1999), *About Religion: Economies of Faith in Virtual Culture* (London: University of Chicago Press).

Taylor, P. and Bain, P. (2005), ' "India calling to the far away towns" the Call Centre Labour Process and Globalization', *Work Employment & Society*, 19:2, 261–282.

Terkel, S. (1977), *Working: People Talk About What They Do All Day and How They Feel About What They Do* (Harmondsworth: Penguin).

Thompson, J. (1985), *The Nature of Work* (2nd ed.) (London: Macmillan).

Thompson, J. (1989a), *The Nature of Work* (London: Macmillan).

Thompson, J. (1989b), 'Theory of Structuration', in D. Held and J. Thompson (eds.), *Social Theory and Modern Societies, Anthony Giddens and his Critics* (Cambridge: Cambridge University Press), pp.56–76.

Thompson, J. (1995), *The Media and Modernity. A Social Theory of the Media* (Cambridge: Polity Press).

Toennies, F. (1957), *Community and Society* (Michigan: Michigan State University Press).

Toffler, A. (1980), *The Third Wave* (London: Bantam Books).

Tomlinson, A. (ed.) (1990), *Consumption, Identity & Style: Marketing, Meanings, and the Packaging of Pleasure* (London: Routledge).

Toulmin, S. (1992), *Cosmopolis: The Hidden Agenda of Modernity* (Chicago: Chicago University Press).

Touraine, A. (1971), *The Post-industrial Society: Tomorrows Social History: Classes, Conflicts and Culture in the Programmed Society* (New York: Random House).

Touraine, A. (1981), *The Voice and the Eye: An Analysis of Social Movements* (Cambridge: Cambridge University Press).

Tovar, T. (1986), 'Barriors, ciudad, democracia y politica', in E. Ballon (ed.), *Movmientos Sociales y Democracia. Fundacion de un Nuevo Orden* (Lima: DESCO).

Toynbee, J. (2000), *Making Popular Music* (London: Arnold).

Trist, E.L., Higgin, G.W., Murray, H. and Pollock, A.B. (1963), *Organisational Choice* (London: Tavistock).

Tucker, K. (1998), *Anthony Giddens and Modern Social Theory* (London: Sage).

Turkle, S. (1984), *The Second Self: Computers and the Human Spirit* (New York: Simon & Schuster).

Turkle, S. (1995), *Life on the Screen: Identity in the Age of the Internet* (London: Phoenix).

Turner, B. (2007), 'Enclave Society: Towards a Sociology of the Immobility Regime', *European Journal of Social Theory*, 10:2, 287–303.

Turner, B.S. (1988), *Status* (Milton Keynes: Open University Press).

Turner, B.S. (1990), 'Outline of a Theory of Citizenship', *Sociology*, 24:2, 189–214.

Turner, B.S. (1993), *Citizenship and Social Theory* (London: Sage Publications).

Turner, G. (2003), *British Cultural Studies: An Introduction* (New York: Routledge).

Turner, G. (2009), *Ordinary People and the Media: The Demotic Turn* (London: Sage).

Turner, V. (1974), *Dramas, Fields and Metaphors* (Ithaca, NY: Cornell University Press).

Turner, V. (1982), *From Ritual to Theatre* (New York: PAJ Publications).

Turner, V. (1987), *The Anthropology of Performance* (New York: PAJ Publications).

Uhlig, R.P., Farber, D.J. and Bair, J.H. (1979), *The Office of the Future: Communication and Computers* (North Holland: Amsterdam).

UNDP (1999), *Human Development Report 1999* (Oxford, New York: UNDP).

Urry, J. (2000), *Sociology beyond Societies: Mobilities for the Twenty-First Century* (London: Routledge).

Van Dijk, J. (2010), 'Review of Manuel Castells (2009), Communication Power. Oxford, New York: Oxford University Press', *Communications, The European Journal of Communication*, http://www.utwente.nl/gw/mco/bestanden/CastellsCommunicationPowerReview.pdf.

Vargas, V. (1990), *The Women's Movement in Peru: Rebellion in Action*, WPH12 (The Hague: Institute of Social Studies).

Veblen, T. (1953), [1899]. *The Theory of the Leisure Class: An Economic Study of Institutions, the Mentor Edition* (New York: The Macmillan Company).

Velben, T. (1975), *The Theory of the Leisure Class* (London: MacMillan Publishers).

Verhulst, S. (2005), 'Analysis into the Social Implication of Mediation by Emerging Technologies', Draft position paper for the MIT-OII Joint Workshop, *New Approaches to Research on the Social Implications of Emerging Technologies*, Oxford Internet Institute, University of Oxford, 12–16 April 2005, Retrieved from http://www.oii.ox.ac.uk.

Vickers, G. (1965), *The Art of Judgement: A Study of Policy Making* (London: Methuen).

Virilio, P. (1995), 'Red Alert in Cyberspace!' *Radical Philosophy*, 74, 2–4.

Virilio, P. (1997), *Open Sky* (London: Verso).

Virilio, P. (2000), *The Information Bomb* (London: Verso).

Wagner, G.G., Pischner, R. and Haisken-DeNew, J.P. (2002), 'The Changing Digital Divide in Germany', in C. Haythornswaite and B. Wellamn (eds.), *The Internet and Everyday Life* (Malden, MA: Blackwell Publishing).

Wajcman, J. (1991), *Feminism Confronts Technology* (Uni Park, PA: State university Press).

Wakeford, N. (1999), 'Gender and the Landscape of Computing in an Internet Café', in M. Crang, P. Crang and J. May (eds.), *Virtual Geographies: Bodies, Space and Relations* (London: Routledge).

Wakeford, N. (2000), 'Networking Women and Girls with Information/Communication Technology: Surfing Tales of the World Wide Web', in D. Bell and B. Kennedy (eds.), *The Cybercultures Reader* (London: Routledge), pp.350–359.

Wallerstein, I. (1974), *The Modern World-System, vol. I: Capitalist Agriculture and the Origins of the European World-Economy in the Sixteenth Century* (New York: Academic Press).

Ward, K. (2003), *An Ethnographic Study of Domestic Internet Consumption in a Coastal Town*, EMTEL2 (Dublin: Deliverable).

Ward, K. (2005), 'The Bald Guy Just Ate an Orange: Domestication, Work and Home', in T. Berker, M. Hartmann, Y. Punie, and K. Ward (eds) *Domestication of Media and Technologies* (Maidenhead: Open University Press), pp.145–163.

Warner, W.L. and Lunt, P.S. (1941), *The Social Life of a Modern Community* (New Haven, Conn: Yale University Press).

Warwick, D. and Littlejohn, G. (1992), *Coal, Capital and Culture: A Sociological Analysis of Mining Communities in West Yorkshire* (London: Routledge).

Watson, J. (1997), *A Dictionary of Communication and Media Studies*, 4th Edition (London: Arnold).

Weber, M. (1922), *Economy and Society: An Outline of Interpretive Sociology* (New York: Bedminster Press).

Weber, M. (1930), *The Protestant Ethic and the Spirit of Capitalism* (London: Allan & Unwin).

Weber, M. (1949), *The Methodology of the Social Sciences*, E. Shils and H. Finch (eds.) (Glencoe: Free Press).

Weber, M. (1949), ' "Objectivity" in Social Science and Social Policy', in E.A. Shils and H.A. Finch (eds), *The Methodology of the Social Sciences* (New York: The Free Press), pp.50–112.

Weber, M. (1998, [1948]), *From Max Weber: Essays in Sociology* (London: Routledge).

Webster, F. (1995), *Theories of the Information Society* (London: Routledge).

Webster, J. (2001), 'Women's Access to ICT-Related Work' in W.H. Dutton (ed.), *Society on the Line: Information Politics in the Digital Age* (Oxford: Oxford University Press), pp.167–168.

Webster, F. (ed.) (2003), *The Information Society Reader* (London: Routledge).

Weiler, J.H.H. (1997), 'To be a European Citizen – Eros and Civilisation', *Journal of European Public Policy*, 4, 495–519.

Wellman, B. and Gulia, M. (2001), 'Virtual Communities as Communities: Net Surfers don't Ride Alone', in M. Smith and P. Kollock (eds.), *Communities in Cyberspace* (London: Routledge).

Wellman, B. and Haythornthwaite, C. (eds.) (2002), *The Internet in Everyday Life* (Malden: Blackwell Publishing).

Wessels, B. (2000), 'Telematics in the East End of London: New Media as a Cultural Form', *New Media and Society*, 2:4, 427–444.

Wessels, B. (2007), *Inside the Digital Revolution: Policing and Changing Communication with the Public* (Aldershot: Ashgate).

Wessels, B. (2008), 'Exploring the Notion of the Europeanization of Public Spheres and Civil Society in Fostering a Culture of Dialogue Through the Concept of Proper Distance', *Sociology: Thought and Action* (Sociologija. Mintis ir veiksmas), 3:23, 28–46.

Wessels, B. (2009), 'The Public Sphere and the European Information Society', in J. Harrison and B. Wessels (eds.), *Mediating Europe: New Media, Mass Communication, and the European Public Sphere* (Oxford: Berghan Publishers), pp.167–189.

Wessels, B. (2010), *Understanding the Internet: A Socio-cultural Perspective* (Basingstoke: Palgrave MacMillan).

Wessels, B. (2012a), 'Exploring Human Agency and Digital Systems: Services, Personalisation and Participation', *Information, Communication and Society*, first published on 14 August 2012 as doi:10.1080/1369118X.2012.715666.

Wessels, B. (2012b), 'Identification and the Practices of Identity and Privacy in Everyday Digital Communication', *New Media and Society*, first published on 23 July 2012 as doi:10.1177/1461444812450679.

Wessels, B. (2013), 'The Reproduction and Reconfiguration of Inequality: Differentiation and Class, Status and Power in the Dynamics of Digital Divides', in M. Ragnedda and G. Muschert (eds.) *The Digital Divide: The Internet and Social Inequality in International Perspective* (London: Routledge), pp.1–18.

Wessels, B., Anderson, R., Durrant, A. and Ellis, J. (2013), 'Mediating Genocide: Cultural Understanding through Digital and Print Media Stories in Global Communication', *The International Journal of Media and Cultural Politics*, 7: 2, 193–209.

Wessels, B. and Bagnall, V. (2002), *Information and Joining Up Services: The Case of an Information Guide for Parents of Disabled Children* (Bristol: Policy Press).

Wessels, B., Finn, R., Smallwood, R. and Wyatt, S. (in press 2014), 'Issues in the Development of Open Access to Research Data', *Prometheus: Critical Studies in Innovations.*

Wessels, B., Walsh, S. and Adam, E. (2008), 'Mediating Voices: Community Participation in the Design of E-Enabled Community Care Services', *The Information Society*, 24:1, 30–39.

Westwood, S. (2002), *Power and the Social* (London: Routledge).

White, L. Jr. (1978), *Medical Technology and Social Change* (New York: Oxford University Press).

Whyte, W.F. (1943), *Street Corner Society: The Social Structure of an Italian Slum* (Chicago: Chicago University Press).

Wilkinson, B. (1983), *The Shopfloor Politics of New Technology* (London: Heineman).

Williams, C.C. (2004), *Cash-in-Hand Work: The Underground Sector and the Hidden Economy of Favours* (Basingstoke: Palgrave MacMillan).

Williams, F. (1993), 'Gender, Race and Class in British Welfare Policy', in A. Cochrane and J. Clarke (eds.), *Comparing Welfare States: Britain in International Context* (London: Sage).

Williams, F. (1994), 'Social Relations, Welfare and the Post-Fordist Debate', in R. Burrows and B. Loader (eds.), *Towards a Post-Fordist Welfare State?* (London: Routledge).

Williams, P. (1938), *South Italian Folkways in Europe and America* (New Haven: Yale University Press).

Williams, R. (1958), *Culture and Society* (London: Chatto & Windus).

Williams, R. (1965), *Long Revolution* (Harmondsworth: Penguin).

Williams, R. (1974), *Television: Technology and Cultural Form* (London: Fontana).

Williams, R. (1981), *Culture* (London: Fontana).

Williams, R. and Edge, D. (1992), 'Social Shaping Reviewed: Research Concepts and Findings in the UK', Edinburgh PICT Working Paper No. 41.

Williams, R., Stewart, J. and Slack, R. (2005), *Social Learning in Technological Innovation: Experimenting with Information and Communication Technologies* (Cheltenham: Edward Elgar).

Willis, P. (1978), *Profane Culture* (London: Routledge and Kegan Paul).

Winner, L. (1985), 'Do Artefacts have Politics?' in D. MacKenzie and J. Wajcman (eds.), *The Social Shaping of Technology* (Milton Keynes: Open University Press), pp.26–38.

Wittengenstein, L. (1958), *Philosophical Investigations* (Oxford: Blackwell).

Wolf, M.J. (1999), *The Entertainment Economy* (London: Penguin).

Woodfield, R. (2000), *Women: Work and Computing* (Cambridge: Cambridge University Press).

Woolgar, S. (1985), ' "Why Not a Sociology of Machines?" The Case of Sociology and Artificial Intelligence', *Sociology*, 19, 557–572.

Woolgar, S. (1988), *Knowledge and Reflexivity: New Frontiers in the Sociology of Knowledge* (London: Sage).

Woolgar, S. (1991), 'The Turn to Technology in Social Studies of Science', *Science, Technology and Human Values*, 16:1, 20–50.

Woolgar, S. (1996), 'Science and Technology Studies and the Renewal of Social Theory', in S. Turner (ed.), *Social Theory and Sociology: The Classics and Beyond* (Oxford: Blackwell).

Woolgar, S. (2001), 'Virtual Witnessing in a Virtual Age: A Prospectus for Social Studies of E-Science', in C. Hine (ed.), *New Infrastructures for Knowledge Production* (Hershey, PA: Idea Group).

Wright, S. (ed.) (1994), *Anthropology of Organisations* (London: Routledge).

Wyatt, S., Henwood, F., Miller, N. and Senker, P. (eds.) (2000), *Technology and In/equality: Questioning the Information Society* (London: Routledge).

Wynne, B. (1988), 'Unruly Technology: Practical Rules, Impractical Discourses and Public Understanding', *Social Studies of Science*, 18, 147–167.

Young, J. (2000), *The Exclusive Society* (London: Sage).

Young, P.H. (1994), *Electronic Communication Technology*, 3rd Edition (Englewood Cliffs: Prentice Hall).

Zook, M.A. (2001a), 'Internet Metrics: Using Hosts and Domain Counts to Map the Internet Globally', *Telecommunications Policy*, 24:(6/7).

Zook, M.A. (2001b), 'The Web of Production: The Economic Geography of Commercial Internet Content Production in the United States', *Environment and Planning A*, 32, 411–426.

Zuboff, S. (1988), *In the Age of the Smart Machine* (New York: Basic Books) in Smith, D. *The Everyday World as Problematic: A Feminist Sociology* (Milton Keynes: Open University Press).

Index

9780230361058